Android™ 3
SDK Programming
FOR
DUMMIES®

by Rajiv Ramnath, PhD
with Roger Crawfis, PhD, and Paolo Sivilotti, PhD

WILEY

John Wiley & Sons, Inc.

Android™ 3 SDK Programming For Dummies®

Published by
John Wiley & Sons, Inc.
111 River Street
Hoboken, NJ 07030-5774
www.wiley.com

Copyright © 2011 by John Wiley & Sons, Inc., Hoboken, New Jersey

Published by John Wiley & Sons, Inc., Hoboken, New Jersey

Published simultaneously in Canada

WILEY

About the Authors

Dr. Rajiv Ramnath is Director of Practice at the Collaborative for Enterprise Transformation and Innovation (CETI), Associate Director for the Institute of Sensing Systems, and Associate Professor of Practice in the Department of Computer Science and Engineering at The Ohio State University. He was formerly Vice President and Chief Technology Officer at Concentus Technology Corp., in Columbus, Ohio, and led product-development and government-funded R&D – notably through the National Information Infrastructure Integration Protocols program funded by Vice President Gore's ATP initiative. He is now engaged in developing industry-facing programs of applied R&D, classroom and professional education (he has won two teaching awards while at OSU), and technology transfer. His expertise ranges from wireless sensor networking and pervasive computing to business-IT-alignment, enterprise architecture, software engineering, e-Government, collaborative environments and work-management systems. He teaches software engineering at OSU and is heavily involved in industry-relevant and inter-disciplinary curriculum development initiatives. Dr. Ramnath received his Doctorate and Masters' degrees in Computer Science from OSU and his Bachelors degree in Electrical Engineering from the Indian Institute of Technology, New Delhi. Rajiv is also a member of the Association of Computing Machinery. You can contact him at ramnath@acm.org.

Roger Crawfis is an Associate Professor at The Ohio State University in the Department of Computer Science and Engineering, an Adjunct Professor in the Biomedical Engineering Department, and an Adjunct Professor in the Advanced Computing Center for Art and Design (ACCAD). Roger received a BS degree in computer science, as well as a BS degree in Applied Mathematics from Purdue University in 1984. He received his MS and PhD in Computer Science from the University of California, Davis in 1989 and 1995, respectively. From 1984 to 1996, he was a researcher at the Lawrence Livermore National Laboratories, where he led the research efforts in scientific visualization. His research interests lie in the areas of computer graphics, high-performance computing and rendering, game technologies, scientific visualization and medical imaging. He serves or has previously served on the Editorial Board for the IEEE Transactions on Visualization and Computer Graphics, the IEEE Visualization conference series, the Eurographics/ACM visualization conference series and many smaller workshops. Roger has authored nearly 100 scientific publications, and is actively involved in the Scientific Visualization community. He is a member of the IEEE Computer Society and ACM SIGGRAPH.

Paolo Sivilotti is an Associate Professor in the Department of Computer Science and Engineering at The Ohio State University. He received his Ph.D. and M.S. degrees in Computer Science from Caltech (1997, 1993), and a B.Sc.H. in Biochemistry and Computing Science from Queen's University (1991). His research interests lie at the intersection of distributed systems and software engineering, with a focus on techniques for the creation of high-confidence distributed software. His work has been recognized with three Best Paper awards at international conferences. He has also earned his department's Outstanding Teaching award three times.

Dedication

This book is dedicated to my wife, Priya, and son, Arman.

– Rajiv Ramnath

To my grandchildren who keep me young enough to pursue these undertakings.

– Roger Crawfis

To my wife and children, for their support and inspiration.

– Paolo Sivilotti

Authors' Acknowledgments

We would like to sincerely thank our project editor Blair Pottenger and our acquisitions editor Kyle Looper. Your efforts helped keep the book on track and finally published.

Our technical editor and former graduate student Krista Dombroviak also gets our sincere thanks. It couldn't have been easy "grading" the work of your former professors, and doing such a careful, thoughtful job — while in the midst of planning your wedding! We think editing is in your blood; maybe a new career in editorship waits?

We would like to thank CETI graduate student Zoya Ali for all the help she gave us in preparing examples, and doing all kinds of background research for the book. Thank you, Zoya!

Thank you also to the other graduate and undergraduate students at CETI — in particular, Tom Lynch, Mike Herold, Chris Dean and Alex Stevens — who reviewed parts of the book essentially by using it as reference material for their coursework and projects.

We thank Sprint and Motorola for so kindly making a range of devices available for us to test on. Several of the insights in the book on testing came from experience gained by working on these devices.

Last but not least, here's a shout out to all the mostly anonymous folks on the Web who ask and answer questions in the Android forums. We have found so much useful information and tips to solve problems that we would otherwise have to research and discover on our own. We can't thank you enough! All of us are resolved to give back by contributing actively to these forums.

Finally, and simply put, we couldn't have written this book without all of you. Thank you all so much!

Publisher's Acknowledgments

We're proud of this book; please send us your comments at http://dummies.custhelp.com. For other comments, please contact our Customer Care Department within the U.S. at 877-762-2974, outside the U.S. at 317-572-3993, or fax 317-572-4002.

Some of the people who helped bring this book to market include the following:

Acquisitions, Editorial, and Vertical Websites

Project Editor: Blair J. Pottenger

Acquisitions Editor: Kyle Looper

Copy Editors: Becky Whitney, Teresa Artman

Technical Editor: Krista Dombroviak

Editorial Manager: Kevin Kirschner

Vertical Websites Project Manager: Laura Moss-Hollister

Vertical Websites Project Manager: Jenny Swisher

Supervising Producer: Rich Graves

Vertical Websites Associate Producers: Josh Frank, Marilyn Hummel, Douglas Kuhn, and Shawn Patrick

Editorial Assistant: Amanda Graham

Sr. Editorial Assistant: Cherie Case

Cover Photo: ©istockphoto.com / yewkeo; ©istockphoto.com / Viktoriya Sukhanova

Cartoons: Rich Tennant (www.the5thwave.com)

Composition Services

Project Coordinator: Nikki Gee

Layout and Graphics: Sennett Vaughan Johnson, Lavonne Roberts, Corrie Socolovitch

Proofreaders: Laura Bowman, Melissa Cossell

Indexer: Sharon Shock

Publishing and Editorial for Technology Dummies

Richard Swadley, Vice President and Executive Group Publisher

Andy Cummings, Vice President and Publisher

Mary Bednarek, Executive Acquisitions Director

Mary C. Corder, Editorial Director

Publishing for Consumer Dummies

Kathy Nebenhaus, Vice President and Executive Publisher

Composition Services

Debbie Stailey, Director of Composition Services

Contents at a Glance

Table of Contents

Part II: Building the Core of an Android Application ... 101

Introduction

*T*he Android operating system now powers 32 percent of the smartphones in the United States. Android has not only a plurality of users but also a well-designed Java-based SDK to make developing apps straightforward and fun. With that, welcome to *Android 3 SDK Programming For Dummies!*

About This Book

This book explains the workings of the latest version of the Android SDK (version 3.1 when this book was printed). The book is aimed at the following audiences of software developers:

- **You have experience in developing other kinds of Java applications but not those for a mobile device.** If this is you, don't worry — this book serves as a mobile applications primer and discusses resource conservation, network disconnection, location changes, and hardware-software interaction, for example.

- **You have mobile application development experience and are looking to develop an Android application equivalent to an app on another platform (such as the iPhone).** You will be able to quickly understand the Android programming model (which is similar to, but also different from, the iOS and BlackBerry models) and then navigate to the chapters in the book that you're most interested in.

- **You have Android experience and are looking to upgrade a program written for an earlier version of Android.** You can easily identify the changed or new capabilities in the various versions of the Android SDK. If you're looking to identify what additional application functions or user experiences can be provided in a new release, this book helps you in that area as well.

This book explains to you how to build exciting, engaging Android apps. You can find out how to make *high-quality* apps that are fit for the enterprise or the consumer market because they perform well, are bug-free, and behave well even under stressful situations (such as when network failure occurs or a device runs out of power). We include a chapter that describes how to make the app available on the Android Market (see Chapter 13) and by way of other avenues so that you can make your app available to the masses.

High quality cannot be achieved without proper design. We therefore devote a chapter to the proper design of object-oriented Android applications built on the Android framework (see Chapters 7, 8, and 9). We also include a chapter that tells you how to make the best use of the Android SDK within the Eclipse integrated development environment, or IDE (see Chapter 12), with a heavy emphasis on the unit-testing framework provided by the SDK and integrated into Eclipse.

To put the explanations of the SDK in context, we provide, and use, a complete working example built around a Tic-Tac-Toe game application.

No *For Dummies* book would be complete without "The Part of Tens," so we close this book with two of these chapters (Chapters 14 and 15): The first lists Android resources, and the second lists what we believe are ten of the top Android applications now on the market.

Throughout this book, we use our own extensive development experience to distill the extensive Android documentation available on the web into a form that's necessary in order to understand the SDK. However, this book certainly isn't a replacement for the SDK documentation. We try, as much as possible, therefore, to cover the essential areas and then point you to the web for additional details.

Conventions Used in This Book

This book guides you through a discussion of the Android SDK and shows you how to build high-quality applications by using it. The conventions we use in the book are described in this list:

- ✓ **Code examples** appear in monofont so that they stand out better. The code you see looks like this:

```
public void onClick(View v){…}
```

The source code for the Tic-Tac-Toe example is on this book's companion website, at `www.dummies.com/go/android3sdkprogramming`. From time to time, we provide updates to the code and post other material that you might find useful.

- ✓ **URLs** appear in monofont, like this:

```
http://en.wikipedia.org/wiki/Tictactoe
```

- ✓ **Sidebars** provide you with background information about certain topics. This information can be helpful, but you don't have to read it to be able to understand the topic.

   ✔ **Chapters that delve into the specific capabilities of the SDK are organized into two broad parts (each consisting of several sections):**

- The "how-to" section describes various capabilities and provides examples.

- The section titled "Understanding the SDK Components Used in This Chapter" describes in greater detail key classes from the SDK and provides links to detailed information about these classes available in the Android documentation on the web.

Foolish Assumptions

The common denominator for anyone reading this book is an interest in developing high-quality apps for Android. One thing you'll already need to have is a good knowledge of Java — because we don't explain how to use it. If you don't know how to use Java, we recommend the introductory *Java For Dummies,* 5th Edition, by Barry Burd, and *Java All-in-One For Dummies,* 3rd Edition, by Doug Lowe. We also assume that you have used at least one IDE to develop software, and, ideally, Eclipse. Though we cover some basic Eclipse information (see Chapter 12), we focus on how to use the Android-specific capabilities within Eclipse (available via the add-on ADT Plug-in For Eclipse).

How This Book Is Organized

This book is divided into several parts, to help you conveniently find the information you need.

Part 1: Getting the Android SDK to Work

This part of the book talks about getting set up to develop programs using the Android SDK. Chapter 1 is an overview of the unique needs and capabilities of mobile applications *and* the Android framework — its components and its application model. Chapter 2 gets you started using the Eclipse IDE and its Android extensions via the Tic-Tac-Toe sample application. Chapter 3 also uses the Tic-Tac-Toe sample application to introduce you to the components of the Android Application Model; if you read only one chapter in this book, this chapter is the one we suggest.

Part II: Building the Core of an Android Application

Part II builds on Part I by showing you the elements you need in order to design and build the core of your application. Chapter 4 tells you how to choose the correct SDK level, Chapters 5 and 6 address user interface components in depth, and Chapter 7 shows you how to properly design an Android application using object-oriented design techniques and how to fit the basic design into the Android framework.

Part III: Making Your Applications Fit for the Enterprise

Though Part II talks about building the right application, Part III tells you all about *building the app right.* Chapter 8 helps you make your app fast and responsive (which, by the way, aren't the same qualities, as you will see), and Chapter 9 talks about security. Without speed, responsiveness, and security, your app won't be successful when it's released, however cool its features might be.

Part IV: Enhancing the Capabilities of Your Android Application

Part IV is all about which SDK components may be used to add advanced capabilities to your app. Thus, Chapter 10 covers integrating the web and location services into your app. Chapter 11 covers using audio, video, and (most importantly) sensors.

Part V: Effectively Developing, Testing, and Publishing Apps

In Part V, we discuss Eclipse again (in Chapter 12) to cover in more detail the Android add-ons to Eclipse. In particular, we describe the unit testing and performance optimization capabilities that Eclipse on Android gives you. Chapter 13 focuses on the endgame: After you develop your app, you presumably want to make it commercially available.

Part VI: The Part of Tens

No *For Dummies* book is complete without "The Part of Tens." Chapter 14 covers the top ten developer resources on the web, and Chapter 15 describes the best of the Android applications, not so much to advertise them as to give you examples of how these cool apps (and they *are* cool) leverage the Android SDK.

Icons Used in This Book

Little pictures in the margin of tech books help you find certain types of information such as tips or warnings quickly. Here are the ones you should look for in this book:

Tips are like little advice columns that provide advice about the current topic or other great things you can do to push your Android 3 SDK programming experience to the next level.

Remember icons signal either a pertinent fact that relates to what you're reading at the time (but is also mentioned elsewhere in the book) or a reiteration of a particularly important piece of information that's, well, worth repeating.

Warning icons alert you to potential pitfalls, so don't ignore them.

This icon marks information that goes beyond the basics.

Where to Go from Here

You can read *Android 3 SDK Programming For Dummies* in either of two ways:

- ✔ Read the chapters in sequential order, from cover to cover. If this book is your first real exposure to Android SDK terminology, concepts, and technology, this method is probably the way to go.

- ✔ Read selected chapters or sections of particular interest to you in any order you choose. The chapters have been written to stand on their own as much as possible.

Part I

Getting the Android SDK to Work

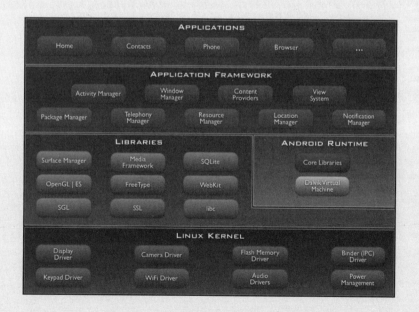

In this part . . .

This part of the book gets you ready to start developing programs using the Android SDK. Chapter 1 is an overview of the unique needs and capabilities of mobile applications, as well as an overview of the Android framework (its components and its application model). Chapter 2 gets you started on the Eclipse IDE and its Android extensions via the Tic-Tac-Toe sample application. Chapter 3 also uses the Tic-Tac-Toe sample application, but this time to introduce you to the components of the Android Application Model.

Chapter 1

Taking a Quick Look at Mobile Applications on Android

*M*obile devices are everywhere. For cellphones alone, the current ownership level in the United States has more than quadrupled from approximately one phone per every four people in 1998 to (as of 2011) a little less than one phone per person, with 35 percent of these phones being smartphones (http://edition.cnn.com/2011/TECH/mobile/07/11/pew.smart phone.report.gahran/), such as the Apple iPhone and the BlackBerry — and, of course, Android devices, which can run powerful applications that can truly make a difference in how people live, work, and play. Many folks already use smartphones just as they used to use computers: They create and edit documents; interact with others via e-mail, telephone, and chat; play highly entertaining games; and shop and manage money. Even schools, which used to ban cellphones in the classroom, are considering delivering educational material to students via smartphones. In other words, because the smartphone is ubiquitous and becoming increasingly robust, you might say that it's now our primary computing and communication device.

The smartphone is more than simply a computing and communication device, however. Because this mobile device goes everywhere with you, letting you be constantly connected so you can work and interact with others, at all times, and because it can remember with whom you talk, where you've been, and how much you spend, it has intimate knowledge of you. Mobile applications can therefore take advantage of this intimate relationship between the device and its users to provide personalized, circumstance-specific, highly targeted services, and services that users will love.

Writing Apps for a Mobile Platform

We assume that you've probably written applications for other platforms, such as desktop or laptop computers or the web. A lot of this experience will carry over to writing applications for mobile devices — including cellphones, tablets, and PDAs. However, writing applications for mobile devices is different because you're venturing into a whole new world that requires you to consider the potential problems we describe in the following list.

Yes, you face challenges, but keep in mind that mobile platforms such as Android are the next great frontier of opportunity for application developers. We (and this book) will help you master specific techniques for dealing with these issues, and we will help you master them:

Don't let the following list of troublesome issues intimidate you:

✔ **Tiny keyboards:** Smartphone and PDA keyboards make data entry *very* difficult. Data entry is no easy task, and *touchscreen* virtual keyboards, which you press with your thumbs, are prone to data entry errors and require using smart spell checking.

What to do? Of course, sometimes data entry is most of what an application requests (think Twitter or e-mail apps), but if it isn't, try to limit data entry by prefilling commonly used default values, providing pull-down lists the user can select from, and so on.

✔ **Limited "real estate":** The display on today's smartphones varies considerably, particularly on Android phones, which come in many shapes and sizes. The largest area you can work with is around 5 inches, diagonally.

What to do? Working with small displays obviously creates challenges as well as opportunities for developers. A well-designed application allows users to move intuitively in the program (without getting confused by a maze of screens) and to use controls (buttons, for example) that are large enough to press confidently but that are placed in a way to help avoid inadvertent clicks.

✔ **A profusion of devices:** Any Android application you come up with should be able to run on a range of devices with varied capabilities: that is, on every device that runs the appropriate version of the Android platform. Figure 1-1 shows a few of the form factors that mobile devices come in.

What to do? Applications should function well on smaller Android displays and on the largest ones (refer to the preceding bullet). Applications should also work — and work well — on devices with touchscreens, those with only hardware buttons, and so on.

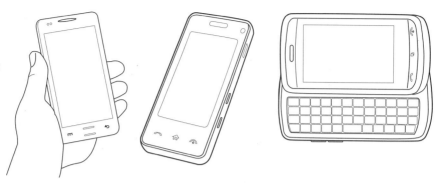

Figure 1-1:
The vari-
ous shapes
and sizes
of Android
phones.

✔ **Limited storage:** Even though mobile devices are powerful computers, they can store only about one-tenth of the information that PCs can, in both memory and persistent storage (flash or disk).

What to do? Don't try to store large quantities of images, music, or (especially) video, lest a device run out of space pretty darn quick!

✔ **Unreliable networks:** It's a fact of life: Mobile devices periodically lose network connectivity. And even when a device has a stable connection, the amount of data that can be sent or received varies based on the strength of the connection.

What to do? Buffer incoming data when the network connectivity is good. Save outgoing data locally. Receive and transmit data on a separate background thread.

✔ **Device unavailability:** A mobile device is turned on and off depending on its user's circumstance (for example, boarding a plane). Or, the device might suffer damage (by being dropped) or slowly degrade in terms of computing speed, and even shut down, as battery life is consumed.

What to do? Your application must deal with all these situations, for example, by periodically "check-pointing" its state and by having low-power modes of operation (for example, a video-playing app might switch to only playing audio when the battery is low).

✔ **A range of use environments:** Mobile devices, understandably, are used in many varied locations: rooms with low ambient lighting or sports stadiums with high levels of background noise, for example.

What to do? Your applications must be able to adapt to these types of situations. For example, your app may lower the brightness of the screen by detecting when the ambient light is low, or it may increase its audio volume when background noise is high.

Seeing What Android Has to Offer

Many types of smartphones and mobile devices abound in today's market: iPhone, BlackBerry, the new WebOS devices from Palm, and Android-based phones, of course.

So what makes the Android platform so popular, especially considering that it's a relative newcomer to this market? To begin with, Android is an open source, Linux- and Java-based, software framework for mobile and portable devices that was created by a group of industry players (the Open Handset Alliance), with one notable member — Google.

This means that there are several benefits for you to develop on the Android platform, as follows:

- ✔ **Wide acceptance:** Android has "legs" — it's inside millions of devices from a range of vendors and is also a major platform for application developers. Thus, your app has a ready-made market.

- ✔ **Openness:** The Android platform is a truly *open* platform in that all capabilities of the device are available to you. In fact, you can replace existing capabilities on a phone (such as e-mail) with your own applications. In other words, your app can become the "go-to" app for millions of users.

- ✔ **No cost:** That's right — the Android platform is *free*. You can provide applications on it without paying for the right to do so, or for the development platform.

- ✔ **Built-in, reusable capabilities:** Android has lots of existing capabilities and services you can reuse. It has built-in support for rich graphics, location finding, and data handling that you can use in your application. In other words, you don't have to code from scratch all the capabilities of your application.

- ✔ **Java:** Android applications are written in Java, one of the most widely used modern programming languages. You're probably already familiar with Java and have access to all its capabilities, so you can get started with developing applications today!

- ✔ **Framework-based guidance for developers:** Because Android is a framework — not just a toolkit composed of a set of libraries — it imposes a structure on applications by using an application model (defined in the later section "Doing the Sample Application Thing). And in return for this imposition, you receive a lot of benefit. For example, you get to follow a systematic path in designing a robust application, which frees you to focus on providing rich capability rather than on figuring out the application structure and high-level design, or on nonfunctional tasks, such as managing your application's life cycle. (You know what we mean — the starting-it-up stuff and the restoring-its-state-after-shutdown stuff, for example).

Doing the Sample Application Thing

It's time now to describe how framework-based guidance helps you build cool applications more easily. As we mention in the earlier section "Seeing What Android Has to Offer," Android provides this guidance by imposing an application model that constrains and guides how you have to build your application — and, in return, gives it capabilities that you don't have to program from scratch. We will describe the application model through the lens of a simple game application: Tic-Tac-Toe.

Let's start by describing Tic-Tac-Toe. Our Tic-Tac-Toe game works just like the simple two-player game everyone knows: Each player claims a symbol — usually an O or an X — and attempts to alternately place the symbol in empty locations in a 3 x 3 grid, so as to place three of the same symbol adjacent to each other in a straight line, either in a row or column or across a diagonal. Figure 1-2 shows a sample sequence of plays.

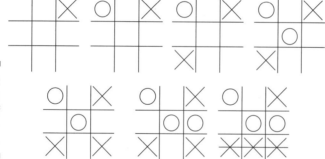

Figure 1-2: A sample sequence of plays in Tic-Tac-Toe.

For simplicity's sake, our Tic-Tac-Toe application allows only one player to play against the device.

We want the application to offer the following game-related functionality:

- Allow the user to create a profile, consisting of a playing name, who goes first in the game — the user or the computer (Chapter 3).
- Allow the user to start and play the game: That is, present the Tic-Tac-Toe board, allow the user to alternate moves with the computer, and display the resulting updates to the board (Chapter 3).
- Identify when the game has progressed to a draw, a victory for the user, or a victory for the computer and display the results (Chapter 3).
- Allow the user to exit the game at any time (Chapter 3).
- Record and save the results of a completed game, such as whether it was a loss or a win (Chapter 3).

All these functionalities are obviously needed in order to play the game. But we aren't done yet. If the application is intended for the Android Market, it needs to be robust: safe, secure, and maintainable, for example. Thus, we show you how to give the app these additional benefits:

✔ Make the user's game data private by creating player accounts (Chapters 3 and 9).

✔ Simplify debugging the game by having the program log its execution to a file (Chapter 12).

✔ Make the game crash resistant so that it can begin where it left off after a forced shutdown (Chapter 3).

Finally, because we're also using this game as a means for illustrating how to leverage Android's capabilities, we give the game even more features so that it:

✔ Invokes external services, such as location services (Chapter 10)

✔ Lets the user send the results of a game by e-mail to an address book contact (Chapter 11).

✔ Allows the user to play music from a library in the background and record music as well (Chapter 11).

It's robust, *n'est-ce pas?*

Understanding the Android System Architecture and the Android Application Model

In this section, we show you how an Android device is put together (also known as its system architecture), how an Android application runs on the Android system, and how the system architecture relates to the Android Application Model.

The system architecture of an Android device (shown in Figure 1-3) is composed of the following components, each layered on the other, in the order below:

✔ **Linux kernel:** Every Android device runs the Linux operating system (OS), also known as the Linux "kernel." The Linux kernel acts as an abstraction and management layer for the hardware. In other words, it presents the different Android devices in a standard way so that folks like you can develop an application just once and be able to run it on all Android devices. The kernel also provides the basic system services such as security, memory management, process management, networking, and drivers for devices (such as the touchscreen, keyboard, and so on).

✔ **Libraries:** These are "native," device-specific C/C++ libraries that are used by the operating system as well as the various components of Android. These libraries are of two kinds: (a) C and C++ libraries that are considered to standard components of Linux (such as `libc`, socket-based networking, and so on), and (b) libraries that provide Android-relevant capability (such as a lightweight database known as SQLite and OpenGL-based graphics).

✔ **Android runtime:** These are both native applications and Java libraries that enable the development of Java applications for Android.

✔ **Application framework:** This is a set of standard Java classes that you will use to develop your app.

✔ **Applications:** These are the apps themselves. These include apps that come with every Android device (such as e-mail, the browser, and so on) and apps that developers (such as you) write.

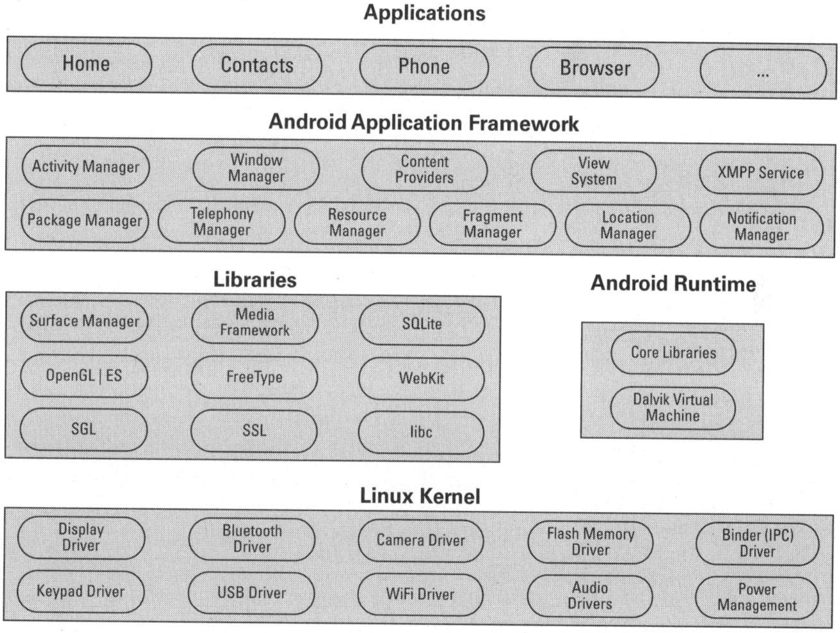

Applications

| Home | Contacts | Phone | Browser | ... |

Android Application Framework

| Activity Manager | Window Manager | Content Providers | View System | XMPP Service |
| Package Manager | Telephony Manager | Resource Manager | Fragment Manager | Location Manager | Notification Manager |

Libraries

Surface Manager	Media Framework	SQLite
OpenGL	ES	FreeType	WebKit
SGL	SSL	libc

Android Runtime

| Core Libraries |
| Dalvik Virtual Machine |

Linux Kernel

| Display Driver | Bluetooth Driver | Camera Driver | Flash Memory Driver | Binder (IPC) Driver |
| Keypad Driver | USB Driver | WiFi Driver | Audio Drivers | Power Management |

Figure 1-3:
The Android system architecture.

Understanding the hardware aspects of an Android device

Before we describe the software components, it is important for you to understand what the device itself is. Essentially, every mobile device is a computer, composed of a set of hardware components: processor, memory, input/output (I/O) devices (such as a keyboard, touchpad, and screen), and storage (disks and flash, for example). Android devices are hardware devices that, like most mobile devices — except, say, the iPhone, whose hardware configuration is controlled completely by Apple — come in a multitude of shapes and sizes and consist of many different kinds of components. For example, one Android device might come supplied with a touchscreen and no keyboard, and another might come supplied with a pullout keyboard and a separate, numeric keypad.

Working with the Linux operating system

Folks do a lot of work to write an application program, even if all they have to work with is the hardware. As you might imagine, the problem is worse for mobile devices because so many different kinds of them exist. Think about your application having to run in a similar manner and make all its capability available on all these diverse devices. Hence, Android makes use of a piece of software known as the *operating system* (OS), which provides a device-independent interface to the hardware through what are known as drivers (we don't get into drivers in this book, other than to mention that several of the important drivers are listed in Figure 1-3). The OS also provides a standard interface to computing capabilities (such as starting and stopping programs) that the application developer and the program can use.

Thus, operating systems make writing and running applications easier, and they're especially helpful — in fact, essential — on mobile devices. On Android, the OS is the *Linux Kernel,* an open source (hence, free!), industrial-strength product that has achieved wide acceptance.

Unless you really and truly want to, you will never see Linux, nor will your program. However, you must recognize that it's there — Android does certain things in certain ways because it runs on Linux. For example, on Linux, every running program is assigned a process. Thus, when an Android program is started, a Linux process becomes active. This process takes over an area of the screen on the device and allows the user to interact with the application. If another application is started, it pushes the first application to the background. At this point, the process assigned to the first application may be (arbitrarily) terminated by the operating system to save device resources. Before this happens, the application is notified by the Android runtime to save its state.

Note that the Linux operating system we're talking about is the OS that manages the device on which your apps run. This is different from the operating system that manages the personal computer on which you develop apps (such as Windows, the MacOS, and, actually, Linux as well).

Taking advantage of native libraries

Layered on Linux are native C and C++ libraries compiled for the specific hardware of the device. Many of these libraries are the ones that come standard with Linux — such as libraries to manipulate strings or perform mathematical operations — although some have been rewritten specifically for use on mobile devices. Also, some libraries are specifically available on Android devices. The Android folks wrote these libraries because they wanted to provide higher-level, and hence more easily programmable, interfaces to certain kinds of functionality. Also, because they wanted this functionality to run fast, they implemented the libraries *natively* for better performance — they wrote the libraries in C or C++ and then compiled them into machine code that runs directly on the hardware. If these libraries had been written in Java, their code would be interpreted by a program known as a Java virtual machine and would run quite a bit slower. The native libraries that are provided are described in this list:

- **libc:** The standard C library
- **SSL:** The Secure Socket Library for secure, encrypted communications
- **SGL:** The library in which Android's 2D graphics capability is built
- **OpenGL/ES:** 2D and 3D graphics that follow a programming model known as OpenGL
- **Surface Manager:** A window manager that manages the display
- **WebKit:** An open source web browser engine that powers the built-in Android browser (and an Android framework component known as `WebView`)
- **FreeType:** A library for rendering fonts
- **Media Framework:** For playing and recording video and music (provided as software components known as codecs)
- **SQLite:** A database that can be used for persistent storage by an application

Note that the capabilities of these native libraries are provided by way of Java, so you don't have to know C or C++ to use them. In fact, as with the Linux operating system, you might not even realize that these libraries exist. But, once in a while, you see certain ways of doing things that exist because certain functionality is implemented in C or C++, and not in Java.

The Android Runtime

This piece of the system architecture, another software program, is a Java virtual machine that lets you write and run Android programs in Java rather than in C or C++. Android uses a special, optimized implementation of a JVM known as the Dalvik Virtual Machine. It's supported by the core Java libraries that let you, for example, manipulate strings and make I/O and mathematical calculations in Java. Taken together, these components make up the Java Runtime Engine on Android.

The Android Application Framework

Using only the Dalvik Virtual Machine, you can write Java programs for Android. But the Android folks didn't stop there: To help you out, they added a set of components written in Java, known collectively as the Android Application Framework (or simply the Android framework). These major components of the Android framework are described in the following list:

- **Activity Manager:** A container for all Android applications that have been written in Java. It manages the "life cycle" of all Android applications. That is, it handles the start-up and shutdown aspects of an Android application and the other, in-between, states as well. (We cover these states later, in Chapter 3.)

- **Fragment Manager:** A fragment represents a portion of the user interface of an activity. You can combine multiple fragments in a single activity to build multi-part user interfaces as well as reuse fragments in multiple activities (see Chapter 3 for more on fragments). The Fragment Manager manages fragments and also provides a programming interface to fragments.

- **Content Providers:** Encapsulate data that needs to be shared *between* applications. The Contacts application on an Android device is a content provider. Content providers are further discussed in Chapter 3.

- **Resource Manager:** Provides access to the resources used by your program — such as literal strings that can be displayed in several different languages or bitmaps representing pictures that your application might use as backgrounds.

- **Location Manager:** Provides location information about the device, such as its GPS coordinates.

- **Notification Manager:** Allows your application to present events to the user (usually while he is busy doing something else) so that he can take action on it.

Just for completeness, we describe the other components as well. However, you are unlikely to directly use these framework components in your program.

- ✔ The Window Manager and the View System together manage the user interface (UI). The Window Manager manages the physical rendering and display of the UI across applications. The View System provides the UI components (widgets) to build the UI, manages the hierarchy of views, and manages the handling of user events.

- ✔ The Package Manager holds information about the applications loaded on the system (such as the device features it needs).

- ✔ The Telephony Manager provides information regarding the telephony services on the device and some types of subscriber information, and also can be set up to provide notification of telephony state changes.

- ✔ The XMPP Manager requires some explanation. The Extensible Messaging and Presence Protocol (XMPP) is an open XML technology for instant messaging (IM) and online presence detection. Android apparently used a variation of this to provide remote debugging capability, but the platform doesn't appear to support this.

Having this system architecture allows the Android designers to provide the final layer — a set of built-in, base Java packages, Java classes, and interfaces, known as the *Android Application Model*. When you write your Android program, you (must) start by inheriting from these base classes and/or writing your own classes that implement the interfaces in the Android Application Model. By doing so, you're building your Android application in a certain way — a way that will make your application robust and make developing it easier.

Understanding the Android Application Model

In this section, we take a more in-depth look at the Android Application Model. We start by looking at its components: applications, tasks, services, activities, intents, views, app widgets, fragments, menus (and the action bar), content providers, resources, shared preferences, and context. There are also add-on support capabilities, specifically, capabilities to write files on internal and external storage, and a lightweight database called SQLite. We describe these components and capabilities in the following sections and explain what you use them for.

Applications

You may already be intuitively familiar with the concept of an *application:* a program that interacts with the user to perform a set of related tasks. An Android application or *app* is an application that is intended to be the primary focus of the user (and, as a consequence, take over the entire screen of the device). The Tic-Tac-Toe game in the example earlier in this chapter is an application.

A standard application — the Home application — is the initial application you see when the Android device starts up. The screen it displays is known as the Home screen. All other applications are started from the Home application, with each application running in its own process, in its own Java virtual machine.

App widgets

App Widgets are miniature application *views* that can be embedded in other applications and receive periodic updates. When the App Widget is embedded in the Home application, it is also known as a Home screen widget. Note that you may see the term *widget* used to describe any UI component (such as a pull-down list or radio button). Do not confuse these (generic) widgets with App Widgets.

Services

Services are programs that run in the background but don't interact with the user. Services can be used to do something continuously in the background (such as play music) while other things are taking place in the foreground (such as editing a document). Using our Tic-Tac-Toe app, we show you a music player service that plays music in the background (see Chapter 11).

Activities

An *activity* represents one cohesive step within an Android application along with its UI. An application can have multiple activities. Sample activities in the Tic-Tac-Toe example, earlier in this chapter, are the user entering the application, setting preferences, playing the game itself, and turning on and off background music.

The Android Application Model prescribes that each cohesive step be implemented by an activity. A step implemented by an activity is treated specially by the Android framework in that built-in mechanisms are provided in order to save and restore its state, including the state of its UI, such as mouse position and highlighted fields. Also, Android maintains a navigation history of all activities that are currently active. Switching from one activity to another adds a new entry to the navigation history. Thus, a user can move to an earlier activity by pressing the Back key on his Android device.

Views

An application presents information to the user in several different ways, using several different screens. Each application screen presented to a user is a *view*. Thus, a view is a basic building block for UI components. It occupies a rectangular area on the screen and is responsible for drawing and event handling. A view can contain other views, in which case it's known as a *view group*. In this chapter's Tic-Tac-Toe example, the start-up screen, the screen for collecting and displaying the user profile, and the game-playing screen are all views.

Fragments

Starting with the release of Android 3.0, the Android SDK introduced a new paradigm and a set of components — both called *fragments* — for building complex user interfaces. The main reason for introducing fragments was to take advantage of the larger screens in tablets. Fragments enable the separation of the UI of an activity from the activity. A fragment has its own life cycle and receives its own input events, and you can add or remove fragments while the activity is running. In Tic-Tac-Toe we use fragments to combine the login and the account creation functionality into one multi-pane screen (see Chapter 3).

Menus and the Action Bar

Every Android phone sports a Menu button — either a physical button or a button labeled Menu on the user interface. This Menu button can be tied into functionality that needs to be always available while the activity is in progress (for example, in Tic-Tac-Toe, you can exit a game at any time through a Menu selection). Because an application-specific menu is a standard part of every app's UI, we consider the menu to be part of the Android Application Model (rather than just another UI component, like a drop-down list or radio button).

Starting from Android 3.0 (once again to take advantage of tablets), menu items can also be displayed on an Action Bar that is a standard part of the user interface of any activity. You can also add *context menus,* which pop up whenever a user presses and holds an item onscreen.

Shared preferences

The Android framework provides you with various ways to *persistently* store application data: That is, the data is preserved even if the application dies. For small bits of primitive application data (such as integers, strings, Booleans, floats, and longs) used to maintain the application "configuration" (such as the name of the user, the language selected, the level of a game, the names of the icons to be used for game pieces, and so on), the Android framework provides you with a simple, built-in capability to persistently save these data as name-value pairs. The components that provide this capability are collectively known as Shared Preferences. For larger pieces of data (such as a document created by the app), additional mechanisms are provided, which we describe below.

Files on internal and external storage

You can save files directly on the Linux file system. Files can be saved on the internal storage of an Android device or on its external storage. Internal storage is always on the permanent storage available on the device. External storage can be the permanent storage on the device as well as removable storage such as on a regular and micro-SD card or a USB drive. By default, files written to internal storage are private to your application and cannot be read or written by other applications or the user. Files on external storage can be accessed by any application, are visible to the user, and can be manually removed, renamed, or moved.

Content providers

Your application might need to create data that will be used by another application (and vice versa). Within the Android Application Model, content providers manage data that needs to be accessible to, and shared by, all applications. In the Tic-Tac-Toe game example in this chapter, we show you how to gain access to the content provider of the Contacts in order to register a user (see Chapter 3).

Resources

A *resource* is a text string or bitmap value that's needed by your application. Rather than define and use the string directly in the program, you can choose to declare it as a resource.

When you do so, a program accesses the string indirectly, through the name of the resource, which is mapped to its actual value in a separate resource file. This indirection lets you have different resource mapping files with different values for the resources so that, for example, you can have the program display labels in different languages without having to change and recompile the program code. Thus, your program can use a resource, but its actual value might be different at the different times when the program runs.

Resources are useful for internationalizing an application. For example, a user in Germany sees all labels, prompts, and error messages in German, but a user in the United States can be shown these elements in English — all without the program having to change. Resource examples in the Tic-Tac-Toe game are the bitmap image used for the game background, the messages posted by the game, the labels on entry fields, and the names of the menus and menu items.

Intents and intent filters

An intent is an abstract description of an operation to be performed. Its main use is to launch one activity from another. The requesting activity sends out the intent to Android whenever it needs the capability. The Android system then finds the appropriate activity to respond to it.

Activities that want to provide services to other objects define intent filters. For example, the Tic-Tac-Toe splash screen, which is the starting activity in the app, declares an intent filter specifying that it's the activity that will respond when Tic-Tac-Toe is "launched" from the Home screen.

Android is supplied with a set of predefined, built-in intents, such as sending e-mail. Whenever a user clicks the Send Email icon in Tic-Tac-Toe, for example, the "send e-mail" intent is broadcast. An application with an activity that has an intent filter corresponding to this intent, such as the (built-in) e-mail program on Android, is launched in response to the sending of this intent. We show this in Chapter 11.

Tasks

A *task* is a group of activities, arranged in a stack. When one activity starts another, the second activity is pushed on top of the task stack and then starts running. When the Back button is pressed, Android returns the user to the previous activity in the stack (which can be the activity that started the current one, but not necessarily so, as you shall see).

In most cases, a task is composed of activities from the same application, though this doesn't have to be the case in Android. In fact, an activity can launch an activity in another application, if it needs that capability and doesn't want to implement it itself. Android makes it appear to the user that both activities are part of the same application — though they aren't. Incidentally, note that a task is an entity managed by Android; though you can never directly refer to it in your program, you can control its behavior.

Context

A *context object,* managed by Android, provides access to global information about the environment in which an application runs. In Java terms, the implementation of this abstract class is provided by the Android system. It allows access to application-specific resources and classes as well as to operations, such as launching activities and broadcasting and receiving intents.

Designing Android Applications

Now that you have been introduced to the Android Application Model and the Android framework, we quickly walk you through how an Android application may be designed — at a high level. As with most rewarding endeavors, designing a good Android app involves planning ahead and defining all major components before trying to build them. Android helps by prescribing the major parts of your application and ensuring that if you define your parts in this manner, they all work together well. In other words, when you're designing an Android application, think about it in terms of the components of the Android Application Model. In other words, follow the steps laid out below:

1. Decide whether you're building an application or a service that runs independently.

2. Identify the separate steps that the application needs to implement, and design each one as an activity. Consequently, identify which state needs to be initialized as well as saved for each activity (in addition to the UI state).

3. Identify the screens for each activity that then become views. Incidentally, an activity (if it's complex) can have multiple views.

4. Identify the persistent data that your application must maintain. The data can be stored as shared preferences, if the data can consist of a few bits of name-value pairs, or in files — either on the device or on removable storage, such as an SD or MicroSD card.

5. Identify the sources and repositories of data that you want to share across applications. They will be the content providers.

6. Identify any displayable information, such as status and error messages, menu items, labels on entry fields, and bitmaps. These will become resources.

7. If you would like to incorporate functionality that has been conveniently provided by another application into your app, you'll need to define and send out appropriate intents.

8. Conversely, if you would like to provide functionality in your app that other apps can invoke, you have to define appropriate intent filters for your activities.

9. If you want to provide the user with a standard menu or an activity-specific menu of capabilities, perhaps to allow the behavior of your application to be modified while it's running, define one or more menus.

After you write your high-level design, you're ready for detailed design and implementation. We show you how to do that through our Tic-Tac-Toe example application as well. To begin with, in Chapter 2, we show you how Tic-Tac-Toe is compiled, installed, and run. Then, in Chapter 3, we show you how the Android framework was used in the game. Finally, in Chapter 7, we show you how the game may be designed using well-established object-oriented principles and then layered on the Android Application Model. After all this, you'll be ready to tackle building your own app.

Chapter 2

Setting Up an Android Development Environment

In This Chapter

▶ Setting up your development environment

▶ Importing and building the sample application

▶ Running the application on an Android emulator

▶ Installing and running the application on an Android device

*A*n Android application is developed and tested on a computer running Windows, Mac OS X, or Linux and then installed on an Android device for further testing, or for real-world use. This chapter walks you through the tools you need to have on your computer and helps you start using them. We use our sample Tic-Tac-Toe application in this chapter as well.

Android applications are mostly developed in Java. (If you're a glutton for punishment — as some of us freely admit that we are — you can develop Android applications in C or C++ instead, but we don't cover that topic in this book.) Also, if you're a Java purist, you can just use a text editor and the command line interface (CLI) to do your development.

Nowadays, however, most folks like to make their lives a little easier (or at least that's the story the software tool developers want developers to believe), so they use an integrated development environment (IDE) for their Java development. The most widely accepted IDE in the Java developer community is Eclipse. Also, the Open Handset Alliance (in particular, Google) has provided a set of tools that can be integrated into Eclipse that significantly helps with Java development for Android. These tools include the Android SDK Starter Package, the Android SDK Components, and the Eclipse plug-in for Android.

In this chapter, we show you how to install these tools in the order you need to do so. Because installing add-ons to Eclipse is often tricky, we also show you how to verify whether you have installed them correctly. Then we show you how to import and run the source code of the Tic-Tac-Toe application. If you're ready, "Read on, MacDuff!"

Setting Up Java

Your first task in setting up Java is to verify whether you have Version 1.5 or higher of the Java Development Kit (JDK). To do this, you work from the command line interface inside a cmd (Windows), Terminal (Mac), or shell (Linux) window. In order to bring up such a window interface, do as follows:

- **Windows:** Choose Start⇨Run. In the dialog box that opens, enter **cmd** as the name of the program you want to run.

- **Mac OS X:** Open the Terminal application by double-clicking its icon (you can find the Terminal application in the path Applications/Utilities on your hard drive).

- **Linux:** A window running a Linux shell is usually already on your screen because that's how Linux users primarily interact with their computers.

In this window, enter **javac -version** at the command prompt. *Note:* You enter **javac** (not **java**, which invokes the Java runtime) to invoke the Java compiler. If you see a message similar to the following, you're good to go:

```
javac version "1.6.0_22"
```

If your Java version starts with 1.5, that's also fine. However, if you have an earlier version, you don't have the correct JDK installed on your machine. If you get an error message, that probably means one of two things. It could mean that the JDK is installed but not in your system's *path,* which are the directories in which the system looks to find programs. It could also mean that the JDK isn't even installed (this is most likely to happen with only Windows and Linux; Macs come pre-installed with Java, and you only have to update the installation).

If the JDK is not on your path, you need to add it as described here: http://www.java.com/en/download/help/path.xml. Again, this problem is unlikely to occur on a Mac because Macs come pre-installed with Java. However, if the problem does occur, follow the instructions for Linux on the link provided.

If the JDK is old, or not installed, you have to download the JDK. Go to www.oracle.com/technetwork/java/javase/downloads/index.html and follow the instructions there. You might be asked to set up an account or log in, but this step is optional.

Be sure to select Development Kit during the installation process because only the Java Runtime Environment (JRE) is installed (by default) and it isn't enough.

After you successfully install the JDK, add to your `PATH` environment variable the `bin` subdirectory of the directory in which the Java software has been installed. Incidentally, and especially if you've installed Java in the past, note that after Oracle's purchase of Sun Microsystems, part of the download site and process changed — and might also change later. This information was current only at the time this book was written.

On Mac OS X, Java and the JDK are preinstalled by Apple, so you shouldn't have to do anything. If the version is too old or you want to upgrade to the latest version, choose Software Update from the Apple menu and begin the Java upgrade from there.

After you handle the necessary installations, try the verification step again to make sure that everything is up to snuff.

Setting Up Eclipse

As we say in the introduction to this chapter, the most widely accepted IDE in the Android developer community is Eclipse. You can download Eclipse from

```
http://eclipse.org/downloads
```

Select for your platform the latest version of the Eclipse IDE for Java Developers. (At the time this book was written, the latest version was Helios.) Then complete the download of the package. It's in ZIP format, so extract the files into a suitably named directory. After you extract the files, you see something like what is shown in Figure 2-1.

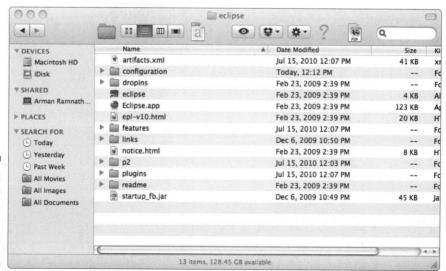

Figure 2-1: Executables in the Eclipse Install directory.

To verify that Eclipse has been installed correctly, simply navigate to the installed directory, locate the `Eclipse.exe` program, and double-click to run it. If the program starts up, give it a location in which to store its workspaces and then open the Eclipse Workbench. If the Resource perspective (see Figure 2-2) opens, you're ready to work with Eclipse.

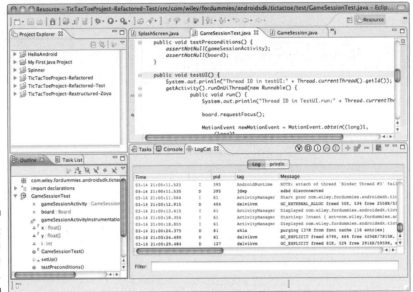

Figure 2-2:
The Eclipse
Resource
perspective.

While you're at it, create a shortcut (an *alias* on the Mac) for Eclipse on your desktop so that you don't have to navigate to its location every time you need to start it up.

Setting Up Android Development Components

We now show you how to install the Eclipse components needed for Android development. These components are discussed in-depth in the following sections.

Android SDK Starter Package and the Android SDK Components

Follow these steps to download and install the Android SDK Starter Package and the Android SDK Components:

1. **Download the Android SDK Starter Package from** `http://developer.android.com/sdk/index.html`.

2. **Like the Eclipse package, the starter package is a ZIP file, so go ahead and extract it into a directory.**

   Make a note of the directory path because you will need it later.

3. **If you're on Windows, look for the program named** `SDK Manager.exe` **in the installation directory and run this program. On Mac and Linux, look for the program named** `android` **in the** `tools` **directory (see Figure 2-3) and run this program. If you're doing this for the first time, you see a list of packages (see Figure 2-4).**

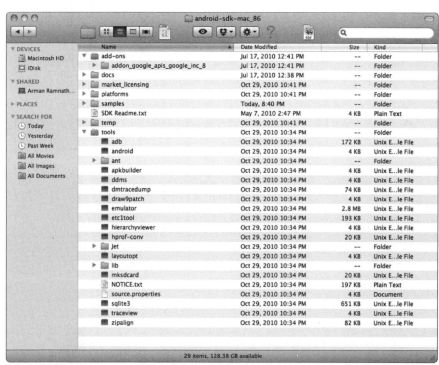

Figure 2-3:
Android
SDK
directory
(Macintosh).

4. Select Accept All.

The SDK components are installed. Note that this installation may take a while, so be patient.

You can also selectively get and install packages by selecting only the packages you really want (see Figure 2-4).

Figure 2-4:
Android
SDK
Components.

This part of the process has no separate verification step, so just hang in there for now!

Eclipse plug-in for Android

Google provides an Eclipse component (known as a *plug-in*) for Android development. This Android Development Tools (ADT) plug-in adds powerful extensions that help you create and debug Android applications easily.

Specifically, the ADT plug-in:

✔ Gives you access to other Android development tools from inside the Eclipse IDE

For example, ADT lets you take screen shots, manage port forwarding for remote debugging, set breakpoints, and view threads and process information directly from Eclipse.

✔ Provides the New Project Wizard, which helps you quickly create and set up all the basic files you need for a new Android application

✔ Automates and simplifies the process of building your Android application

✔ Provides an Android code editor that helps you write valid XML code for the various configuration files needed by your Android application

✔ Lets you export your project into a signed installable (known as an *APK,* for Android PaCKage), which can be distributed to users.

You can read more about the ADT plug-in at `http://developer.android.com/guide/developing/eclipse-adt.html`.

Here's how to install the ADT:

1. **Start Eclipse.**

2. **(Optional) If you're prompted to provide a workspace directory, identify a directory where you want Eclipse to place all your code (or pick the default).**

3. **Choose Help⇨Install New Software.**

4. **In the Work With entry field, type `https://dl-ssl.google.com/android/eclipse` and then click Add.**

5. **In the Add Repository dialog box that opens, name the site (Android Development Tools, for example) and then click OK. You see `Developer Tools` listed in the pane beneath it, as shown in Figure 2-5.**

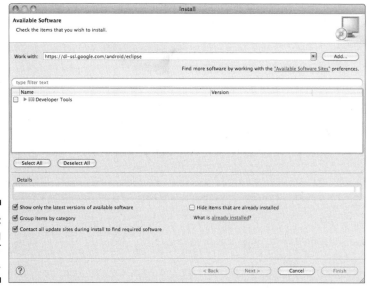

Figure 2-5:
Installing
the ADT
plug-in.

 6. **Select all the tools and proceed with the installation by clicking Next.**

    The installation continues. It takes some time, so be patient.

 7. **When you're asked whether you want to restart Eclipse, do it.**

To easily verify that everything has been installed correctly, run a sample program on an emulator from a template that ADT provides. The next section shows you how.

Verifying the Development Environment

In this section we show you how to verify that the development environment has been installed correctly by creating and starting an emulator and then running a sample program on it.

Creating an emulator

The first part of verifying the development environment is to create an emulator that serves as a (virtual) device on which the test application will run. Follow these steps:

 1. **From the Eclipse menus, choose Window⇨Android SDK and AVD Manager.** *Note:* **You might have to set the path to the Android SDK directory (Figure 2-2).**

 2. **Select Virtual Devices and then click the New button.**

 3. **In the dialog box that opens (see Figure 2-6), enter a name for the virtual device. The name must consist of alphabetic characters (a–z, A–Z), numbers (0–9), the underscore (_), the hyphen (-), and the period (.).**

 4. **Set the target to an Android version. In our example, we have set it to Android 3.1 – API Level 12. You may leave the other parameters (such as the SD card size, skin, and so on) alone.**

 5. **Click the Create AVD button.**

    The device is created and you see the Virtual Devices screen again.

 6. **From the list of devices, select the device you just created and click Start.**

    The device starts running. Stay patient; starting a new device takes time.

Figure 2-6:
Creating an
emulator.

Creating and running a sample program

ADT has a simple program example you can use to ensure that your development environment is set up correctly.

1. **From the Eclipse menu, choose File⇨New⇨Project.**

2. **From the New Project screen, open Android and select Android Project.**

3. **Enter a project name and then select an Android version (we have used Android 3.1) as the build target.**

4. **Enter a name for the application (any string is allowed, we used Hello Android), the package (you must follow the Java rules for naming packages, we used `com.wiley.androidfordummies. HelloAndroid`), and the main activity (we used `HelloActivity`).**

   You must follow the Java rules for naming classes.

5. **Click Finish.**

   An Android project is created (see Figure 2-7).

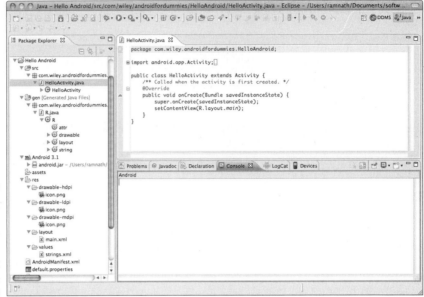

Figure 2-7:
Eclipse proj-
ect for the
Hello World
Android test
program.

6. Right-click the project you just created and choose Run As⇨Android Application.

Be patient (again). After a while, you see a screen similar to the one shown in Figure 2-8, with the name you gave your main activity in place of the displayed string "Hello World HelloActivity." *Note:* If you get an error (for example, something like "Unable to open class file …\R.java: No such file or directory," try restarting Eclipse).

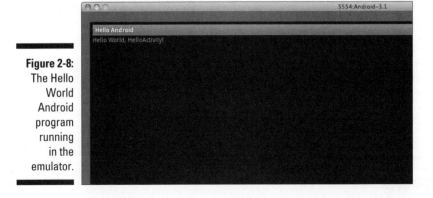

Figure 2-8:
The Hello
World
Android
program
running
in the
emulator.

If you completed all the steps in this section, your installation was successful.

Understanding the files in the sample project

Before we discuss our Tic-Tac-Toe example, we want to walk you through the purpose of the various files created in the hierarchy of the sample project (refer to Figure 2-7):

1. The name of the project — in this case, HelloAndroid — is the top level in the project hierarchy.

2. The `src` directory is where all the application source code — the code you will write — is located. For the simple HelloAndroid application, the ADT plug-in generated the code for you. You can see that this code is inside the package you specified for this application.

3. We step out of order here, for just a moment, to say that the `res` directory contains resources used by the sample program. These resources include an XML file that specifies the layout of its screen (`main.xml`) and string constants (`strings.xml`) used by the program. Also, in the various `drawable` directories (`drawable-hdpi`, `drawable-mdpi`, and `drawable-ldpi`) are icons used by the program for Android devices with high (`hdpi`), medium (`mdpi`), and low (`ldpi`) density screens, respectively.

4. When an application runs, the Android framework doesn't use XML files directly from the `res` folder. Instead, it generates code in the form of a resource (`R`) class, in which these values are embedded. This class is placed in the `gen` directory, which is the place for source code generated by the ADT plug-in specific to your application.

5. Under `Android 2.2` are the Android support libraries (covered in Chapter 1), in the form of JAR files.

6. The critically important `AndroidManifest.xml` file describes the single externally visible component of the sample application — its main activity. If this application had additional services or activities, they would be described here.

7. The `default.properties` file is another auto-generated file. You will see that it contains an entry for the target Android version you specified.

Importing, Running, and Debugging Tic-Tac-Toe

So far, we've walked you through setting up your development environment. That was the complicated part. The rest, as they say, is downhill from here!

Running on an emulator

The next steps are to install and run the sample Tic-Tac-Toe application, both on the emulator and then on an actual Android device. To do this, first copy the Tic-Tac-Toe project from this book's companion website (`www.dummies.com/go/android3sdkprogramming`) into a suitable directory. Then follow these steps:

1. **From the Eclipse menu, choose File⇨Import.**

2. **Open the General tree and select Existing Projects into Workspace.**

3. **Set the `Root` directory (see Figure 2-9) by browsing to the location where you saved the Tic-Tac-Toe project.**

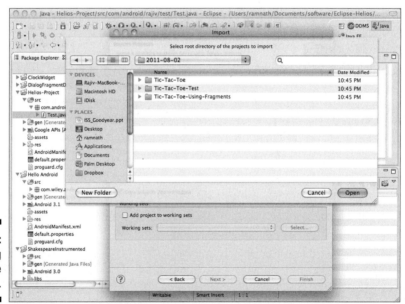

Figure 2-9:
Importing
Tic-Tac-Toe
into Eclipse.

4. **Select the Copy Projects into Workspace check box (refer to Figure 2-9).**

5. **Click Finish.**

   The Tic-Tac-Toe project is imported into your Eclipse workspace.

6. **Right-click the newly imported project and choose Android Tools⇨Fix Project Properties.**

   This step cleans up configuration information in your project so it can run in the Eclipse environment it is in.

7. Run Tic-Tac-Toe, just as you ran the template program.

Voilà! Tic-Tac-Toe appears on the emulator (see Figure 2-10). Knock yourself out playing the game!

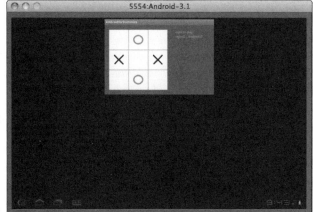

Figure 2-10:
Playing Tic-
Tac-Toe
on the
emulator.

Setting up debugging and running on an Android device

Testing and debugging on a physical device are straightforward tasks although they require a few more configuration steps. You start by declaring your application as "debuggable" in its manifest:

1. In Eclipse, view the manifest.

2. On the Applications tab, set the Debuggable field to `true`.

Alternatively, if you prefer to edit the XML directly, add `android:debuggable="true"` as an attribute to the `<application>` element in the `AndroidManifest.xml` file.

3. Turn on USB debugging from the Home screen of your device by pressing the Menu button, choosing Applications⇨Development, and then selecting the USB Debugging check box.

4. Set up your system to detect the device:

- *Mac OS X:* Don't do anything.

- *Windows:* Install the `adb` USB driver for the Android debugger.

We don't go into the details because the Windows USB driver documentation at `http://developer.android.com/sdk/win-usb.html` is quite clear.

• *Linux:* Add a rules file that contains a USB configuration for every type of device you use for development.

You can verify that your device is connected by running the command `adb devices` from your `SDK tools/` directory. If your device is properly connected, you see your device name listed.

After declaring your application as debuggable, you install and run the program, running or debugging as usual from Eclipse. You see the Device Chooser dialog box (see Figure 2-11), which lists available emulators and connected devices. Select the device on which you want to install and run the application, and you will see the Tic-Tac-Toe splash screen appear (see Figure 2-12). That's it!

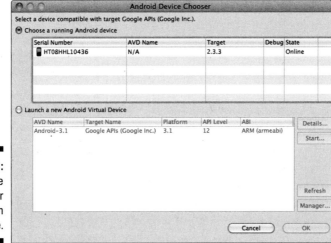

Figure 2-11:
Device
Chooser
dialog box in
Eclipse.

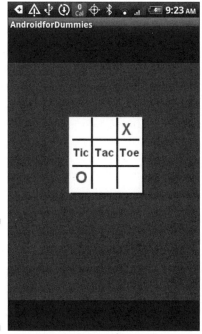

Figure 2-12:
Tic-Tac-
Toe splash
screen on
an HTC EVO
device.

Chapter 3

Making Apps Using the Android SDK

In This Chapter

▶ Implementing a basic Android application

▶ Understanding the Android Application Model

▶ Creating a sample Tic-Tac-Toe application

*I*f you read only one chapter in this book, this chapter is the one we suggest. We use the Tic-Tac-Toe sample application to illustrate the various components of the Android SDK and the Android Application Model. If you read this chapter in its entirety, you should have a working knowledge of all Android SDK components and capabilities. The main concept, however, is the Android Application Model: It gives you a sense of how other built-in components (such as activities, views, menus, preferences, intents, and intent filters) and capabilities (such as files and SQLite) work together within this model.

One quick note before we get into this chapter. To fully understand what is presented here, you must be familiar with the system architecture of an Android device and an Android application and the application model that Android applications must conform to, and you must know how to install the development tools, create a project for the application, recognize the various code and configuration files in the project, import code into the project, and, finally, build and run an application. We have covered these elements in Chapters 1 and 2, so either read them before reading this chapter, or refer back to them as needed.

 Also, the code examples in this chapter are from two Eclipse projects, namely, Tic-Tac-Toe and Tic-Tac-Toe-Using-Fragments (which you can download from the website for this book: www.dummies.com/go/android3sdk programming). In order to follow along with the examples, you may want to import and open these projects and browse their structure, the various source code, and other types of files as we present and discuss them (see Chapter 2 for how to import projects). We show you where to look for its files in the next section, "Walking Through the Eclipse Project for Tic-Tac-Toe."

Walking Through the Eclipse Project for Tic-Tac-Toe

If you haven't already imported the code for the tic-tac-toe game, select the Downloads tab at www.dummies.com/go/android3sdkprogramming and download it. There are two projects that are of relevance to this chapter — Tic-Tac-Toe and Tic-Tac-Toe-Using-Fragments. Import both projects. Now open Tic-Tac-Toe. After you do this, you will see the elements shown in Figure 3-1.

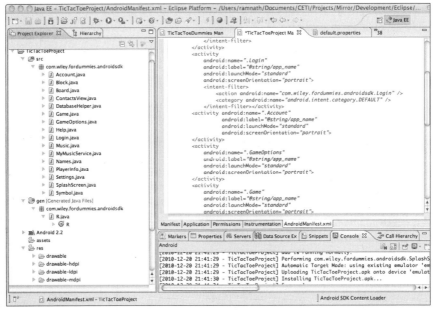

Figure 3-1:
The Tic-
Tac-Toe
project in
Eclipse.

This list describes the project elements shown in Figure 3-1:

- **The src tree:** src stands for *source*. Expand this tree to see all developer-written source code (.java) files for the Tic-Tac-Toe project.

- **The gen tree:** gen stands for *gen*erated. You see one file containing Java code (R.java, generated by the Android Development Tools, or ADT, plug-in for Eclipse) consisting of references to all resources defined in the program.

- **The *Android SDK level* tree:** This tree contains the libraries that make up the Android SDK (as Java .jar files). The label on this tree is the version of the Android SDK you're building against. Our project is building against the 3.0 version of the SDK with the Google API add-ons for maps; hence this tree is labeled Google APIs [Android 3.0].

✔ **The `assets` tree:** The `assets` tree is used to hold application-specific types of resources for use by the application. (_Resources_ are simply files containing data needed by your apps.) You most likely don't need to use this tree because most of the standard resource types you need (such as icons, strings, and menus) are placed in the `res` tree, described in the following bullet. You haven't used any assets in Tic-Tac-Toe.

✔ **The `res` tree:** `res` stands for _resources_. This tree contains the resources used by the Tic-Tac-Toe app. The `res` tree has additional sub-trees, as follows:

  • `layout`: Contains files that specify the layouts of various screens in Tic-Tac-Toe.

  • `drawable`: Holds icons used by the program, such as for Android devices with high- (`hdpi`), medium- (`mdpi`), and low- (`ldpi`) density screens, respectively.

  • `menu`: Indicates the layout and values of the program menus.

  • `values`: Holds several files, such as `strings.xml` and `colors.xml`, where the values for all constants (such as strings and colors) are defined. The `R.java` file in the `gen` subtree is generated from the information stored in this `res` tree.

✔ **The `AndroidManifest.xml` file:** We refer to this important configuration file several times in this chapter. For now, suffice it to say that it contains configuration information about the Tic-Tac-Toe application and all its externally visible components, such as its activities and services.

✔ **The `default.properties` file:** This auto-generated file stores all project settings.

Read on for details about developing the Tic-Tac-Toe application.

Developing the Tic-Tac-Toe Application

Our Tic-Tac-Toe example plays just like regular tic-tac-toe on paper, but is limited to a human playing the computer.

In addition to showing you how to implement game-playing functionality by using the Android SDK, we use our tic-tac-toe game to illustrate the full range of Android capabilities. Because we designed this game to have features in addition to simple game play, it can also

✔ **Remain resilient to program termination:** If your device crashes or is terminated by Android, for example, resources can be conserved.

✔ **Separate your score from other people who use the device:** It can implement a user ID plus a password-based account using a SQLite database.

✔ **Play background music:** The music can soothe you so that you don't become too agitated by losing or too excited by winning.

✔ **Let you look up your friends' contact information in your address book:** Then you can send them e-mail or call them to gloat about your victories.

Understanding the Different Types of Android Programs

The primary kind of Android program that you will write is an application (or *app*). An app is intended to be the primary focus of the user. As a consequence, an app takes over and uses most of the entire screen of the device.

The initial program that starts up when an Android device is turned on is also an app — known as the *Home* app. All other applications (or apps) are *launched* (started) from the Home application. The Home application's user interface (UI) is known as the Home screen. Just like the UI for any app, the Home screen takes over most of the screen real estate on the device. Whenever an app is launched from the Home screen, the launched app's UI will take over the Home screen.

Services are programs that run in the background and need no UI of their own. You use services for activities such as playing music and automatically keeping track of user locations. To illustrate services within the context of Tic-Tac-Toe, we created an add-on — a music playback service named `MyPlaybackService`.

A third kind of Android program is an App Widget. We don't cover App Widgets in the book, but only mention them here for completeness. App Widgets are (seemingly) constantly running programs embedded in the user interface of an app and used to display changing information from the app, such as the time, the weather, or the user's location. You can think of an App Widget as a small, view-only user interface coupled to a service. When the App Widget is embedded in the Home application, it is also known as a *Home screen widget*.

Understanding Activities

After you understand the different types of Android programs, your next step in the application development process is to design and implement the activities in the application. As we explain in Chapter 1, an Android *activity* represents a cohesive step in an Android application and its corresponding user interface. In other words, activities are the building blocks of an Android application.

Figure 3-2 shows a selected portion of the activity flow through the Tic-Tac-Toe application.

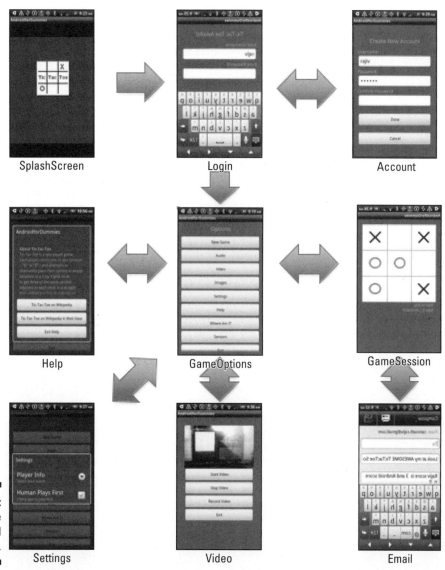

Figure 3-2:
Tic-Tac-Toe activity and screen flow.

SplashScreen   Login   Account

Help   GameOptions   GameSession

Settings   Video   Email

Below is a description of the Tic-Tac-Toe activities themselves:

✔ SplashScreen: The first activity that runs in Tic-Tac-Toe. It first displays a picture, but then — when the user taps anywhere on the splash screen — it launches the next activity, which is Login, and disappears.

✔ Login: Allows the user to log in and then launches the GameOptions activity and exits. If the user has no account, Login lets her create one by launching the Account activity. The user then notices two behaviors:

  • If the user proceeds to creating a new account (or decides not to create an account and taps the Cancel button), the user returns to this login page.

  • However, after the user successfully logs in, he can't return to the login page unless he restarts Tic-Tac-Toe. This behavior is logical, of course, but it also serves to illustrate how the Android Activity Manager manages activities. We touch on managing activities in the "Managing the Activity Life Cycle" section later in this chapter.

✔ Account: Allows the user to create an account (required in order to play the game). To create an account, the user must provide a username and password, and the password must be entered correctly in both the Password and Confirm Password fields.

✔ GameOptions: The entry point into game-related actions. From here the user can launch the following (sub) activities (presented in the order in which they appear in the GameOptions user interface):

  • GameSession: Encapsulates and manages Tic-Tac-Toe game play. This activity is launched when the user starts a new game.

  • Audio: Allows the user to play and record audio. (This activity invokes the built-in audio recorder on the device.)

  • Video: Allows the user to play and record video. (This activity invokes the built-in video recorder.)

  • Images: Allows the user to view images. (This activity invokes the built-in camera.)

  • Settings: Allows the user to specify a "playing" name and decide whether to play first (or let the computer play first). If no playing name is set, it defaults to the username of the account.

  • Help: Provides information about how to play the game.

  • WhereAmI: Allows the user to show points of interest or his own location on a map.

  • Sensors: Shows how the built-in sensors on the device work (such as the accelerometer and the light sensor).

Specifying activities in the AndroidManifest.xml file

Every activity must have an entry in the `AndroidManifest.xml` file. Listing 3-1 shows a snippet of this file with the most useful entries for three activities in Tic-Tac-Toe: `SplashScreen`, `Login`, and `Account`.

Listing 3-1:   Declaring Activities in the Manifest File

```
<activity android:name=".SplashScreen"
    android:label="@string/app_name"
    android:launchMode="standard"
    android:screenOrientation="portrait">
    <intent-filter>
        <action android:name="android.intent.action.MAIN"/>
        <category android:name="android.intent.category.LAUNCHER"/>
    </intent-filter>
</activity>

<activity android:name=".Login"
    android:label="@string/app_name"
    android:launchMode="standard"
    android:screenOrientation="portrait"
    android:permission=
        "com.wiley.fordummies.androidsdk.tictactoe.LAUNCHACTIVITY">
    <intent-filter>
        <action
            android:name="com.wiley.fordummies.androidsdk.tictactoe.Login">
        <category android:name="android.intent.category.DEFAULT" />
    </intent-filter>
</activity>

<activity android:name=".Account"
    android:label="@string/app_name"
    android:launchMode="standard"
    android:screenOrientation="portrait">
</activity>
```

As you can see, each activity is specified in an `<activity>` . . . `</activity>` XML block (or *element*). Every activity element defines a set of attributes: in this case, its name, launch mode, and screen orientation. (*Note:* These are the main attributes, but many others exist.) The `name` attribute is the same as the name of the Java class that implements it. The launch mode (see the later section "Managing the Activity Life Cycle") can be `standard`, `singleTop`, `singleTask`, or `singleInstance`.

The `SplashScreen` and `Login` activities have an `<intent-filter>` element, which describes the invocation messages that the activity will respond to and handle. These invocation messages may originate from within the containing Tic-Tac-Toe application or another application, including the Home application. We explain this concept in the "Starting activities using intents and intent filters" section, later in this chapter.

Implementing activities

Every activity in an application is implemented by a Java class. This Java class must extend the `Activity` base class of the Android framework. To illustrate, look at the declaration of the `Login` and `Game` classes:

```
public class Login extends Activity implements OnClickListener{
    ...
    ...
}
public class GameSession extends Activity {
    ...
    ...
}
```

Note that `Login`, in addition to being a subclass of `Activity`, implements `OnClickListener` while `GameSession` does not. The reason is that `Login` implements its own user interface, whereas `Game` delegates the *interactive* component of its user interface (the Tic-Tac-Toe board) to the `Board` class. So now, let us show you how the user interface of an activity is implemented.

Implementing an Activity's User Interface

Activities within Android applications interact with users by displaying information and accepting input by way of a user interface. In Android, the UI is implemented by using objects of the `View` and `ViewGroup` classes. These and their related classes and subclasses are defined in the `android.view` package.

The Android SDK provides an extensive, built-in collection of UI components, also known as *widgets* (not to be confused with Home screen widgets) — such as scrollable windows, entry fields, buttons of various types, check boxes, and pull-down lists — that can be composed into a view. You can see, later in this chapter, a couple of examples of using these UI components, and you can find more detail about implementing UIs in Chapter 5.

Laying out a view

The Android SDK provides a way to specify the layout of a view without any programming by means of an XML file known as a layout file. Each entry in the layout file specifies either an aspect (such as the width and height) or a component (such as a button) of the user interface. The layout file for the Login activity is shown in Listing 3-2. It is named login.xml and resides in the layout sub-tree of the Tic-Tac-Toe project, within the res tree. ***Note:*** We matched the names of activities and other view classes with the names of their layout files. You don't have to match them, but doing so helps to clarify the correspondence between the activity class and its layout file.

Listing 3-2: Layout File for the login Activity

```
<?xml version="1.0" encoding="utf-8"?>
<ScrollView xmlns:android="http://schemas.android.com/apk/res/android"
    android:background="@color/background"
    android:orientation="horizontal"
    android:layout_width="match_parent"
    android:layout_height="match_parent"
    android:padding="20dip">
  <LinearLayout android:orientation="vertical
        android:layout_width="match_parent"
        android:layout_height="match_parent">
      <TextView android:text="@string/login_title"
          android:layout_height="wrap_content"
          android:layout_width="wrap_content"
          android:layout_gravity="center"
          android:layout_marginBottom="15dip"
          android:textSize="20.5sp"/>
      <TextView
          android:text="Enter Username"
          android:layout_height="wrap_content"
          android:layout_width="wrap_content"
          android:layout_gravity="left"
          android:textSize="15.5sp"/>
              <EditText
          android:id="@+id/username_text"
          android:singleLine="true"
          android:layout_width="match_parent"
          android:layout_height="wrap_content"/>
      <TextView
          android:text="Enter Password"
          android:layout_height="wrap_content"
          android:layout_width="wrap_content"
          android:layout_gravity="left"
```

(continued)

Listing 3-2 *(continued)*

```
                android:textSize="15.5sp"/>
            <EditText
                android:id="@+id/password_text"
                android:singleLine="true"
                android:layout_width="match_parent"
                android:layout_height="wrap_content"/>
            <Button
                android:id="@+id/login_button"
                android:text="Login"
                android:layout_marginTop="20dip"
                android:layout_width="match_parent"
                android:layout_height="wrap_content"/>
            <Button
                android:id="@+id/cancel_button"
                android:text="Exit"
                android:layout_width="match_parent"
                android:layout_height="wrap_content"/>
            <Button
                android:id="@+id/new_user_button"
                android:text="New User"
                android:layout_marginTop="10dip"
                android:layout_width="match_parent"
                android:layout_height="wrap_content"/>
    </LinearLayout>
</ScrollView>
```

You can see that the layout file consists of the elements described below:

✔ An outermost `ScrollView` element: Indicates that the highest-level (or root) window in this view is a scrollable window. This outermost window is a container — it contains other user interface elements.

✔ A `LinearLayout` element: This is nested inside the `ScrollView`, and it is also a container that indicates that its component elements are to be displayed in the order they are placed in the container. Nested inside the `LinearLayout` element are the following elements:

   • `TextView`: This element corresponds to and describes the title "Tic-Tac-Toe Awaits!" (which is defined in `res/values/strings.xml`).

   • `TextView`: This element corresponds to and describes the string `Enter Username` (which is defined in `res/values/strings.xml`).

   • `EditText`: This element is a specification of the entry field where the user would enter a username.

   • `TextView`: This element is a specification of the string `Enter Password`. Note that we have put the string directly in the layout file (just to show you that values of literals do not have to be in a separate file).

- EditText: This element is a specification of the entry field where the user would type in a password.

- Button: This element is a specification of the Login button.

- Button: This element is a specification of the Exit button used to exit the login screen (and, therefore, the game).

- Button: This element is a specification of the New User button used to enroll a new user.

The screen components that are specified in the layout file are shown in Figure 3-3.

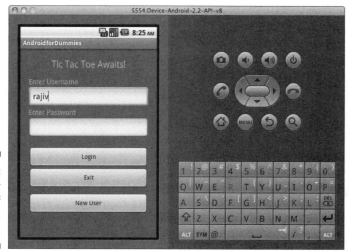

Figure 3-3: The user interface of the Login activity.

The Android SDK has many more types of views than ScrollView (such as HorizontalScrollView), more layouts in addition to LinearLayout (including AbsoluteLayout, FrameLayout, and RelativeLayout), and more widgets in addition to TextView, EditText, and Button. Note the nested nature of the layout. Essentially, two base classes define views: the ViewGroup base class for UI elements that can contain other elements and the View base class for terminal UI components. The suitable composition of container classes that extend ViewGroup (such as LinearLayout) and elementary widgets that have View as their base class allow views to be nested to any appropriate level.

The layout files for the activities in an application are translated into Java code that resides within the resource R class in the res subtree in the project. This translation reduces the overhead of generating the view from its XML specification every time.

In the following section, we show you how to implement the functionality behind a view.

Implementing the user interface logic by using event listeners

An event listener is an object that is registered with a user interface and which responds to user events such as mouse clicks. In the Android SDK, an activity can act like an event listener object for events in its view. The following code segment, extracted from the Login class, shows how this is done:

```
public class Login extends Activity implements OnClickListener{
    ...
    private EditText userNameEditableField;
    private EditText passwordEditableField;

    @Override
    public void onCreate(Bundle savedInstanceState) {
        super.onCreate(savedInstanceState);
        setContentView(R.layout.login);
        userNameEditableField=(EditText)findViewById(R.id.username_text);
        passwordEditableField=(EditText)findViewById(R.id.password_text);
        View btnLogin=(Button)findViewById(R.id.login_button);
        btnLogin.setOnClickListener(this);
        View btnCancel=(Button)findViewById(R.id.cancel_button);
        btnCancel.setOnClickListener(this);
        View btnNewUser=(Button)findViewById(R.id.new_user_button);
        btnNewUser.setOnClickListener(this);
    }
    ...
}
```

The Login activity extends the Activity base class (as any activity should), and also implements the OnClickListener interface. This interface implements an activity that intends to interact with the user. Note the onCreate(Bundle) method of the Login activity. The Android framework calls this method when the activity is created. (For more on the activity life cycle, see the "Managing the Activity Life Cycle" section, later in this chapter.) In this onCreate(Bundle) method, the call to setContentView(R.layout.login) creates and initializes the user interface for Login.

After the view for the activity is created, variables such as userNameEditableField and btnCancel are initialized to refer to the various widgets in the view (such as the field just below the Enter Username string in which the username is entered, and the Cancel button). Note how the reference to the widget is found by passing the resource that corresponds the id of the widget (such as R.id.cancel_button) to the findViewById(...) method. Finally, the Login activity (that is, this) is set as a listener on every button element the user interacts with (such as Login, Cancel, and NewUser). Whenever the user clicks on one of these buttons, the button object calls a standard method, named onClick, on each listener object (for example, on the Login activity object).

The onClick method for the user interface of the Login activity is shown here:

```
public void onClick(View v) {
    switch (v.getId()) {
    case R.id.login_button:
        checkLogin();
        break;
    case R.id.cancel_button:
        finish();
        break;
    case R.id.new_user_button:
        startActivity(new Intent(this, Account.class));
        break;
    }
}
```

The logic of the onClick(...) method is simple. The following list describes what happens when the user taps the buttons:

- ✔ **Login:** Calls checkLogin(...), which verifies the username and password and then launches the GameOptions activity
- ✔ **Cancel:** Simply finishes the current activity
- ✔ **New User:** Launches the Account activity to let the user create a new account

The pattern for handling other types of events is similar. These events can qualify as a touch (physically touching a touchscreen or clicking the mouse button on the emulator) or a key being pressed. You simply implement the onTouch(View) or the onKey(View) listener method in the activity and register it with the appropriate view by using setOnTouchListener and setOnKeyListener, respectively.

Implementing the user interface by implementing your own View class

The View base class can directly handle events. Therefore, you can also implement UI functionality by implementing your own View class, extending View (or one of its subclasses, such as Activity) and overriding one or more existing callback methods of the View to listen for specific events that occur within it.

To illustrate this concept, here's an example from the GameSession activity and the Board view in Tic-Tac-Toe. We start with the GameSession class, which is declared simply as a subclass of Activity, like this:

```
public class GameSession extends Activity {
...
}
```

Note that GameSession implements no other interface, such as onClick-Listener. Take a look at its layout file (named gamesession.xml in the res/layout directory) in Listing 3-3.

Listing 3-3:   Layout of the GameSession Activity with Board As an Embedded View

```
<?xml version="1.0" encoding="utf-8"?>
<LinearLayout
            xmlns:android="http://schemas.android.com/apk/res/android"
            android:layout_width="match_parent"
            android:layout_height="match_parent"
            android:orientation="vertical"
            android:background="#676767"
            android:gravity="center_horizontal"
            android:padding="20dip">
    <com.wiley.fordummies.androidsdk.tictactoe.Board
        android:id="@+id/board"
        android:layout_width="match_parent"
        android:layout_height="280dip"
    />
    <TextView
        android:id="@+id/gameInfo"
        android:layout_width="match_parent"
        android:layout_height="wrap_content"
        android:text="Loading..."
        android:gravity="center_vertical"
        android:paddingLeft="10dip"
    />
    <TextView
        android:id="@+id/scoreboard"
        android:layout_width="match_parent"
        android:layout_height="wrap_content"
        android:gravity="center_vertical"
        android:paddingLeft="10dip"
    />
</LinearLayout>
```

This layout file can be considered to have three components: a LinearLayout ViewGroup containing a view element referring to a class named Board, a TextView field titled game info, and another TextView field titled scoreboard. The Board class referred to in the view element is a subclass of View and is declared as follows:

```
public class Board extends View {
...
}
```

Board has been specialized from its parent View class by overriding the ontouchEvent(MotionEvent) method inherited from View and by giving this method an implementation that's specific to the Tic-Tac-Toe app. This method is shown in Listing 3-4.

Listing 3-4: The onTouchEvent Callback in Board View

```
public boolean onTouchEvent(MotionEvent event) {
    if( !this.enabled ) {
        System.out.println("Board.onTouchEvent: Board not enabled");
        return false;
    }
    int posX = 0;
    int posY = 0;
    int action = event.getAction();
    switch (action){
        case MotionEvent.ACTION_DOWN:
            float x = event.getX();
            float y = event.getY();
            System.out.println("coordinates: " + x + "," + y);
            if( x > width && x < width * 2 ) posX = 1;
            if( x > width * 2 && x < width * 3 ) posX = 2;

            if( y > height && y < height * 2 ) posY = 1;
            if( y > height * 2 && y < height * 3 ) posY = 2;

            gameSession.humanTakesATurn(posX, posY);
            break;
    }
    return super.onTouchEvent(event);
}
```

This onTouchEvent(...) callback receives the *x,y* coordinate positions of every touch, converts those *x,y* positions into the coordinates (0, 1, or 2) of the Tic-Tac-Toe square, and then calls the humanTakesATurn(...) method of the GameSession object with these coordinates. The Board view is created by the GameSession activity in its onCreate(...) method. This method also passes its GameSession activity to Board, which then enables Board to invoke humanTakesATurn(...) on GameSession.

Handling user interactions in the activity itself

Because an `Activity` is also a `View`, it can itself implement some of its own UI functionality. The requirement to do so arises if the activity must deal with user interaction *outside* the boundaries of any UI components in its view, such as in grayed-out areas near the edges. An example is in the `SplashScreen` activity in the Tic-Tac-Toe app, where any touch, no matter where it happens on the screen, is a signal from the user to interrupt the splash screen and continue. Take a look now at the code for the `SplashScreen` activity shown in Listing 3-5:

Listing 3-5:   The `SplashScreen` Activity

```
public class SplashScreen extends Activity {
    protected boolean active=true;
    protected int splashTime=5000;
    protected int timeIncrement=100;
    protected int sleepTime=100;

    /** Called when the activity is first created. */
    @Override
    public void onCreate(Bundle savedInstanceState) {
        super.onCreate(savedInstanceState);
        setContentView(R.layout.splash);

        // thread for displaying the SplashScreen
        Thread splashThread=new Thread() {
            @Override
            public void run() {
                try {
                    int elapsedTime=0;
                    while(active && (elapsedTime < splashTime)) {
                        sleep(sleepTime);
                        if(active) elapsedTime=elapsedTime + timeIncrement;
                    }
                } catch(InterruptedException e) {
                    // do nothing
                } finally {
                    finish();
                    startActivity(new Intent(
                        "com.wiley.fordummies.androidsdk.tictactoe.Login"));
                }
            }
        };
        splashThread.start();
    }
```

```
    @Override
    public boolean onTouchEvent(MotionEvent event) {
        if (event.getAction()==MotionEvent.ACTION_DOWN) {
            active=false;
        }
        return true;
    }
}
```

When the `SplashScreen` activity is created, a new thread is launched. The thread sleeps for `splashTime` milliseconds while periodically awaking to check an `active` flag to see whether it needs to quit. At the same time, the original application thread (which, of course, was never authorized to knock off work) is still running. This main thread makes the activity active and then waits in an event loop for the user to interact with the splash screen. When the user interacts with it (specifically, by touching the screen before the timer runs out), an `onTouch` event is generated. This event is trapped by the `onTouchEvent(MotionEvent)` method in the `Activity` class, which in turn sets the (`active`) splash screen flag to `false`. This, in turn, terminates the timer and causes the splash screen activity to finish and start the next activity, which is `Login`.

Initiating actions from menus and the Action Bar

You can use menus and, starting in Android 3.0, the Action Bar to provide functionality similar to a sidebar that a user can access while using the primary capabilities of the app. Think of a capability as allowing the user to exit a game or find help at any time while playing the game. In this section, we discuss menus first and then the Action Bar.

Programming Options menus

Every Android device has a button labeled *Menu* that can be used to open an application menu known as an Options menu. A menu (activated by the Menu button) is considered a standard part of the user interface of an activity. Applications (and their activities) should make good use of menus because they're interface components that are always available when an activity is running, regardless of what it is doing. Finally, note that you can have different menus for different activities.

To implement menus, you must follow these three steps:

1. Define the onCreateOptionsMenu() or onCreateContextMenu() callback method (or both) in the class that implements your activity.

2. Declare the menu items, which you can do in XML. At the appropriate time, Android automatically calls this method to create the menu.

3. Implement the methods onOptionsItemSelected() and onContext ItemSelected() in your activity.

That's it. Menus handle their own events, so you don't need to implement event handlers. Note that a menu is linked to the activity it belongs to in the onCreateOptionsMenu(...) method. (See Listing 3-6, later in this section.)

Tic-Tac-Toe implements menus in the activities GameSession and Game Options. Here's the layout file (named menu.xml) for the menu in the GameOptions activity:

```
<?xml version="1.0" encoding="utf-8"?>
<menu xmlns:android="http://schemas.android.com/apk/res/android">
    <item android:title="Settings"
        android:id="@+id/menu_settings"
        android:icon="@android:drawable/ic_menu_preferences"
    />
    <item android:title="Help"
        android:id="@+id/menu_help"
        android:icon="@android:drawable/ic_menu_info_details"
    />
    <item android:title="Exit"
        android:id="@+id/menu_exit"
        android:icon="@android:drawable/ic_menu_close_clear_cancel"
    />
    <item android:title="Contacts
        android:id="@+id/menu_contacts"
        android:icon="@android:drawable/ic_menu_view"
    />
</menu>
```

This layout file defines four obvious items: Settings, Help, Exit, and Contacts. Their identifiers are menu_settings, menu_help, menu_exit, and menu_contacts, respectively. The following icons for these items are standard in the Android SDK:

```
@android:drawable/ic_menu_info_details

@android:drawable/ic_menu_preferences

@android:drawable/ic_menu_close_clear_cancel

@android:drawable/ic_menu_view
```

The layout file is compiled into resources specified in the R class in the gen subtree of the Android project. You can see references to the R class in the code shown in Listing 3-6, which shows the menu-relevant code from the GameOptions activity.

a menu item that contains a sub-menu. For more on Context menus and sub-menus, see `http://developer.android.com/guide/topics/ui/menus.html`.

Using the Action Bar

Starting in Android 3.0, users have access to contextual options, navigation, widgets, and other types of content on the *Action Bar,* which is displayed at the top of the screen and is always visible when an application is running.

For the code examples in this section, refer to the Eclipse project `Tic-Tac-Toe-Using-Fragments`.

The coding for Action Bar items is *exactly* the same as for menus. All you do is implement the `onCreateOptionsMenu(Menu)` and `onOptionsItemSelected(MenuItem)` methods in exactly the same way as you do for menus. The difference is that you can then make a menu item appear on the Action Bar (rather than on the menu) by declaring the menu item with the additional attribute `android:showAsAction` with the value `"ifRoom"`, `"never"`, `"withText"`, or `"always"`. You can also combine these directives. In the example below, the Help menu from `menu.xml` has been declared as a menu to be shown on the Action Bar. The result of doing this is shown in Figure 3-4 where you can see the Help menu on the Action Bar, and the result of selecting it.

```
<item
    android:title="Help"
    android:id="@+id/menu_help"
    android:icon-"@android:drawable/ic_menu_info_details"
    android:showAsAction="always|withText"
/>
```

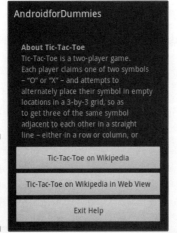

Figure 3-4:
Putting
menu items
on the
Action Bar.

Setting application preferences

Most mobile applications have different modes of working, depending on user preferences. For example, a route-finding application might ask users to set their home locations, on the assumption that most user-requested routes begin from home. Also, games have preferences such as character icons and game levels. Because preferences are common features in mobile applications, Android provides you with built-in ways to set and read them as name-value pairs.

We illustrate this capability by using an example from Tic-Tac-Toe. Take a look at the `Settings` activity, which is an example of an activity that sets preferences. The `Settings` activity is started when a user taps the `Settings` menu item in the `GameOptions` activity. We show its implementation in Listing 3-7.

Listing 3-7:   An Implementation of `Settings`, a `PreferenceActivity`

```
package com.wiley.fordummies.androidsdk.tictactoe;
import android.content.Context;
import android.os.Bundle;
import android.preference.PreferenceActivity;
import android.preference.PreferenceManager;

public class Settings extends PreferenceActivity {
    private final static String OPT_NAME="name";
    private final static String OPT_NAME_DEF="Player";
    private final static String OPT_PLAY_FIRST="human_starts";
    private final static boolean OPT_PLAY_FIRST_DEF=true;

    @Override
    protected void onCreate(Bundle savedInstanceState){
        super.onCreate(savedInstanceState);
        addPreferencesFromResource(R.layout.settings);
    }
    public static String getName(Context context) {
        return PreferenceManager.getDefaultSharedPreferences(context)
                .getString(OPT_NAME, OPT_NAME_DEF);
    }
    public static boolean doesHumanPlayFirst(Context context) {
        return PreferenceManager.getDefaultSharedPreferences(context)
            .getBoolean(OPT_PLAY_FIRST, OPT_PLAY_FIRST_DEF);
    }
}
```

You can see that the `onCreate(...)` method is building the user interface for this activity in this line:

```
addPreferencesFromResource(R.layout.settings)
```

The user interface for this activity is then specified in an XML file named `settings.xml`, like this:

```
<?xml version="1.0" encoding="utf-8"?>
<PreferenceScreen xmlns:android=http://schemas.android.com/apk/res/android
    android:title="Settings"
    android:background="@color/background">
    <EditTextPreference android:key="name"
        android:title="Player Info"
        android:summary="Select your name"
        android:defaultValue="Player 1"/>
    <CheckBoxPreference android:key="human_starts"
        android:title="Human Plays First"
        android:summary="Check box to play first"
        android:defaultValue="true"  />
</PreferenceScreen>
```

Note the difference between the names of the XML elements in this file and the names of other kinds of activities in layout files: They all end with `Preference`. Every element specifies four attributes of the preference:

- ✔ **The name-value pair that defines the preference**
- ✔ **The form in which the preference is displayed**
- ✔ **A helpful description of the preference**
- ✔ **The default value of the preference**

In the preceding XML file, therefore, the first preference is the name of the human player, which is a string to be displayed as an editable text field, with a default value of `Player 1`. The second preference is a Boolean value that specifies whether the human or the machine plays first. Whoever plays first uses the X symbol, and the human plays first, by default.

Back to the code itself — the first thing to notice about this code is (drum roll, please) that there's *no code to save preferences!* This process is handled automatically by the Android framework, by making `Settings` a subclass of the `PreferenceActivity` class, which implements all necessary callbacks to store the values.

However, the `Settings` activity still needs to make available methods to *read* preferences. In the Tic-Tac-Toe app, `Settings` does this by providing two static methods (see Listing 3-7):

✔ `getName(..)`: Gets the name of the player

✔ `doesHumanPlayFirst(..)`: Returns `true` if the player starts first and `false` if the machine is supposed to play first

These methods use two methods of the `PreferenceManager` class to get the preference values, namely `getString(...)` and `getBoolean(...)`. The first parameter to these methods is the name of the preference. It should be the same as the value of the `android:key` attribute for the corresponding element in the `settings.xml` file. The second parameter to these methods (such as the Boolean variable `OPT_PLAY_FIRST_DEF`) is the default value to return if the key doesn't exist.

Building Rich User Interfaces for Larger Screens Using Fragments

Until Android 3.0, an activity and its user interface were coupled together. In the release of Android 3.0, the Android SDK introduced a new paradigm and a set of components, or *fragments,* for building user interfaces. The main reason for introducing fragments is to take advantage of the larger screens on Android tablets.

In this section, we explain what fragments are and show you a couple of examples. One quick thing; for the code examples in this section, refer to the Eclipse project `Tic-Tac-Toe-Using-Fragments`.

Understanding fragments

Fragments enable the separation of the user interface of an activity from the activity itself. A fragment has its own life cycle and receives its own input events. You can add or remove fragments while the activity is running, which lets you design a more complicated (and, possibly, better) interface, with its own flow. Of course, the user interface has to tie into the activity, but it ties into it in limited and well-defined ways that allow you to design both items separately. (The notion of separating the user interface life cycle and the business logic of the application isn't new. If you have done web development using Enterprise Java — specifically, using Java Server Faces — you should be quite familiar with this concept.)

Think of a fragment as representing a part of the user interface of an activity. You can use multiple fragments to build a user interface consisting of multiple stand-alone parts (known as a multi-pane user interface). You can also reuse a fragment in more than one activity.

Fragment capability is supplied by a new set of components related to the user interface — namely, `Fragment`, its subclasses (`DialogFragment`, `ListFragment`, `PreferenceFragment`, and `WebViewFragment`), and its related classes (`FragmentActivity`, `FragmentManager`, and `FragmentTransaction`). Fragment-based functionality isn't in only the 3.0 and later versions of the Android SDK. Along with Android 3.0, Google also released the Android Compatibility Library (ACL), which lets you develop fragment-based user interfaces using SDK versions 1.6 through 2.3.3. Figure 3-5 shows how to add the ACL (and other, additional libraries) into the build path of your project. (We describe this process in more detail in Chapter 2.)

Figure 3-5:
The Tic-
Tac-Toe
project with
the ACL
in its build
path.

Let us now show you an example of how to use fragments from (what else?) the Tic-Tac-Toe app (once again, refer to the Eclipse project named `Tic-Tac-Toe-Using-Fragments` with regard to all the code examples in this section). The example first demonstrates the use of a fragment in creating a multi-pane interface for larger screens by showing you how to combine into a single activity the `Login` and `New Account` functionality, when the application is used in Landscape mode (such as on a tablet). However, when the application is in Portrait mode (on a smaller device, for example), the login and account creation are split across two activities. Figure 3-6 shows the user interface for the two modes.

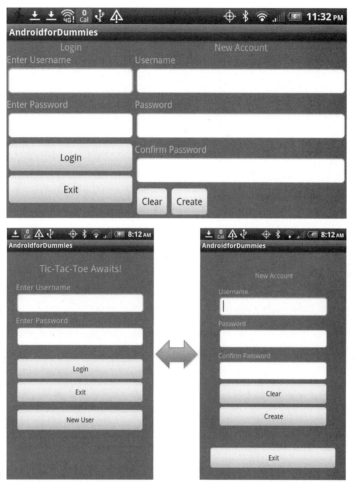

Figure 3-6:
The user
interface in
Landscape
and Portrait
modes, for
logging in
and creat-
ing a new
account.

By looking at these screens, you can clearly see how the Tic-Tac-Toe app provides login and new account-creation capabilities in different ways in the two
orientations. In the next example, we show you how it's done in a way that
reuses the fragment. This example also illustrates a couple of other concepts:
how a fragment can be incorporated into the user interface declaratively (via
layout files) or programmatically (via coding). We also touch on how the life
cycle of the fragment and the activity interact.

You start, though, by looking at the `AndroidManifest.xml` file. To create
different looks and implementations for Portrait and Landscape modes, you
must first set the `android:screenOrientation` attribute for the activity
to be either `unspecified` or `sensor`. You set the specification of the login
activity this way:

```
<activity
    android:name=".Login"
    android:label="@string/app_name"
    android:launchMode="standard"
    android:screenOrientation="unspecified"
    …
>
```

Embedding fragments in activity layouts

To understand the details of how to use fragments, you first have to incorporate the fragment in the layout of the activity. To see how it's done, look in res/layout-land/login.xml for the landscape layout of the Login activity, shown in Listing 3-8.

 The listings in this section are rather long, so we removed several entries that aren't relevant to this discussion. Of course, the entire chunk of code is available in the source code provided.

Listing 3-8:   Landscape Layout File for the Login Activity

```
<?xml version="1.0" encoding="utf-8"?>
<LinearLayout
    xmlns:android="http://schemas.android.com/apk/res/android"
    …
    android:orientation="horizontal"
    android:layout_width="match_parent"
    android:layout_height="match_parent"
    android:textSize="15.5sp">
    <ScrollView
    xmlns:android="http://schemas.android.com/apk/res/android"
    …
    android:orientation="vertical"
    android:layout_width="200dip"
    android:layout_height="300dip">
    <LinearLayout
        android:orientation="vertical"
        android:layout_width="match_parent"
        android:layout_height="match_parent">
        <TextView
            android:text="Login"
            …/>
            <TextView
                android:text="@string/enter_username"
                …/>
            <EditText
```

```
                    android:id="@+id/username_text"
                    .../>
            <TextView
                    android:text="Enter Password"
                    .../>
            <EditText
                    android:id="@+id/password_text"
                    .../>
            <Button
                    android:id="@+id/login_button"
                    android:text="Login"
                    .../>
            <Button
                    android:id="@+id/cancel_button"
                    android:text="Exit"
                    .../>
        </LinearLayout>
    </ScrollView>
    <fragment class="com.wiley.fordummies.androidsdk.tictactoe.AccountFragment"
            android:id="@+id/titles" android:layout_weight="1"
            android:layout_width="0px"
            android:layout_height="match_parent"
            android:background="#00550033"/>
</LinearLayout>
```

Note the use of the `fragment` element in the layout file; note specifically how
the `class` attribute has been initialized to the name of a fragment class. (We
describe this class itself in the following section.) While you're looking at
layout files, look at the one for the login activity while in Portrait mode (see
Listing 3-9). You see that the first part of the file is quite similar to the previous one, except that the `fragment` element for adding a new user is missing
(because a separate `Account` activity handles creating a new user) and a
`New User` button is added (that launches the `Account` activity).

Listing 3-9: Portrait Layout File for the `Login` Activity

```
<?xml version="1.0" encoding="utf-8"?>
<ScrollView
    xmlns:android="http://schemas.android.com/apk/res/android"

    ...
    android:orientation="vertical"
    android:layout_width="match_parent"
    android:layout_height="match_parent"
    android:textSize="15.5sp"
    ...>
    <LinearLayout
        android:orientation="vertical"
```

(continued)

Listing 3-6: Handling Menus in the GameOptions Activity

```
public class GameOptions extends Activity implements    OnClickListener{
...
public boolean onCreateOptionsMenu(Menu menu) {
    super.onCreateOptionsMenu(menu);
    MenuInflater inflater=getMenuInflater();
    inflater.inflate(R.menu.menu, menu);
    return true;
}

public boolean onOptionsItemSelected(MenuItem item) {
    switch (item.getItemId()) {
    case R.id.menu_settings:
        startActivity(new Intent(this, Settings.class)); return true;
    case R.id.menu_help:
        startActivity(new Intent(this, Help.class));
        return true;
    case R.id.menu_exit:
        quitApplication();
        return true;
    case R.id.menu_contacts:
        startActivity(new Intent(this, ContactsView.class));
        return true;
    }
    return false;
}
...
}
```

In this chunk of code, the onCreateOptionsMenu(Menu) method creates the menu. You don't have to specifically call this method in any of your code: The Android runtime automatically calls it at the appropriate time, passes in the correct menu object to be created, and sets up the current activity as a listener on the menu. MenuInflater inflater=getMenuInflater() is a (factory) method that's called to get an object that can initialize this menu object with its items specified in the menu.xml file, which in turn is done by using inflater.inflate(R.menu.menu, menu).

When the user taps the menu and selects an item, onOptionsItem Selected(MenuItem) is called and the selected item is passed to it. In this method, the switch statement directs execution to launching either the Settings, the Help, or the Contacts activity — or, if Exit has been selected, the code that terminates the Tic-Tac-Toe app (see the method quitApplication(..)).

In addition to menus launched using the Menu button (known as *Options menus*), you can add Context menus that open whenever the user selects an item by pressing and holding the mouse button or trackball (or by holding down a finger on a device with a touchscreen). You can also add sub-menus to menus that appear as a floating list of menu items when the user touches

```
        android:layout_width="match_parent"
        android:layout_height="match_parent">
    <TextView
        android:text="@string/login_title"
        …/>
    <TextView
        android:text="@string/enter_username"
        …/>
    <EditText
        android:id="@+id/username_text"
        …/>
    <TextView
        android:text="Enter Password"
        …/>
    <EditText
        …/>
    <Button
        android:id="@+id/login_button"
        android:text="Login"
        …/>
    <Button
        android:id="@+id/cancel_button"
        android:text="Exit"
        …/>
    <Button
        android:id="@+id/new_user_button"
        android:text="New User"
        …/>
    </LinearLayout>
</ScrollView>
```

Look at the layout of `AccountFragment` in Landscape mode (shown in Listing 3-10) and Portrait mode (shown in Listing 3-11).

Listing 3-10:   Landscape Layout File for `AccountFragment`

```
<?xml version="1.0" encoding="utf-8"?>
<LinearLayout
    xmlns:android="http://schemas.android.com/apk/res/android"
    …
    android:orientation="vertical"
    android:layout_width="match_parent"
    android:layout_height="match_parent"
    android:textSize="15.5sp">
    <LinearLayout
        android:orientation="vertical"
        …
        <TextView
            android:text="New Account"
            …/>
```

```
        <TextView
            android:text="Username"
            .../>
        <EditText
            android:id="@+id/username"
            .../>
        <TextView
            android:text="Password"
            .../>
        <EditText
            android:id="@+id/password"
            .../>
        <TextView
            android:text="Confirm Password"
            .../>
        <EditText
            android:id="@+id/password_confirm"
            .../>.
        <LinearLayout
            android:orientation="horizontal"
            ...>
            <Button
                android:id="@+id/cancel_button"
                android:text="Clear"
                .../>
            <Button
                android:id="@+id/done_button"
                android:text="Create"
                .../>
        </LinearLayout>
    </LinearLayout>
</LinearLayout>
```

Listing 3-11:   Portrait Layout File for `AccountFragment`

```
<?xml version="1.0" encoding="utf-8"?>
<LinearLayout
    xmlns:android="http://schemas.android.com/apk/res/android"
    android:background="@color/background"
    android:orientation="horizontal"
    android:layout_width="match_parent"
    android:layout_height="match_parent"
    android:padding="20dip">
    <LinearLayout
        android:orientation="vertical"
        ...>
        <TextView
            android:text="New Account"
            .../>
        <TextView
            android:text="Username"
```

(continued)

```
                ../>
            <EditText
                android:id="@+id/username"
                ../>
            <TextView
                android:text="Password"
                ../>
            <EditText
                android:id="@+id/password"
                android:password="true"
                ../>
            <TextView
                android:text="Confirm Password"
                ../>
            <EditText
                android:id="@+id/password_confirm"
                ../>
            <LinearLayout
                android:orientation="vertical"
                ..>
                <Button
                    android:id="@+id/cancel_button"
                    android:text="Clear"
                    ../>
                <Button
                    android:id="@+id/done_button"
                    android:text="Create"
                    ../>
            </LinearLayout>
        </LinearLayout>
    </LinearLayout>
```

When you contrast Listing 3-10 and Listing 3-11 (which shows the portrait layout file), you see that the UI components are exactly the same. The only difference is that the Clear and Create buttons are one below the other in the portrait layout, and next to each other in the landscape layout (because vertical space is at a premium in Landscape mode).

Finally, we show you the portrait layout file for the Account activity (Listing 3-12). Again, note that this activity is the one that handles the addition of new users whenever the application is run in *Portrait* mode. This activity is not used when the device is in Landscape mode.

Listing 3-12: Portrait Layout File for the Account Activity

```
<?xml version="1.0" encoding="utf-8"?>
<LinearLayout
    xmlns:android="http://schemas.android.com/apk/res/android"
    android:background="@color/background"
```

```
        android:orientation="vertical"
        android:layout_width="match_parent"
        android:layout_height="match_parent"
        android:padding="20dip">
    <FrameLayout
        android:id="@+id/accountdetails"
        android:layout_weight="2"
        android:layout_width="match_parent"
        android:layout_height="match_parent" />
    <Button
        android:id="@+id/exit_button"
        android:text="Exit"
        android:layout_marginTop="20dip"
        android:layout_width="match_parent"
        android:layout_height="wrap_content"/>
</LinearLayout>
```

Note that no mention is made of the fragment in the layout file. However, the FrameLayout element accountdetails defines a placeholder for it that the Account activity programmatically fills with AccountFragment. You can see how it's done in the following section.

Implementing fragments

To look at how to implement fragments, start with the code for Account Fragment, shown in Listing 3-13.

Listing 3-13:   Implementation of AccountFragment

```
public class AccountFragment extends Fragment implements OnClickListener{
    private EditText etUsername;
    private EditText etPassword;
    private EditText etConfirm;
    …
    public View onCreateView(LayoutInflater inflater, ViewGroup container,
                        Bundle savedInstanceState) {
        // Inflate the layout for this fragment
        View v =  inflater.inflate(R.layout.accountfragment, container, false);
        etUsername= (EditText)v.findViewById(R.id.username);
        etPassword= (EditText)v.findViewById(R.id.password);
        etConfirm = (EditText)v.findViewById(R.id.password_confirm);
        View btnAdd= (Button)v.findViewById(R.id.done_button);
        btnAdd.setOnClickListener(this);
        View btnCancel= (Button)v.findViewById(R.id.cancel_button);
        btnCancel.setOnClickListener(this);
        return v;
```

(continued)

```
        }

    private void CreateAccount(){
        …
    }

    public void onClick(View v) {
        switch (v.getId()) {
            case R.id.done_button:
                CreateAccount();
                break;
            case R.id.cancel_button:
                etUsername.setText("");
                etPassword.setText("");
                etConfirm.setText("");
                break;
        }
    }
}
```

AccountFragment looks much like an activity. One difference is that it has (obviously) an onCreateView(…) method rather than an onCreate(…) method, which an activity might have. The reason that this onCreateView(…) method might look like a life cycle method is that it *is* one. It's the method that's called after the fragment has been created. Other differences in this method are described in this list:

✔ To get a reference to the view of the fragment, the layout file for the fragment has to be inflated by using the following helper method from the inflater class (earlier in this chapter, we showed the use of a similar inflater method for menus):

```
View v =  inflater.inflate(R.layout.accountfragment, container, false);
```

✔ The view in the preceding line must be used in order to get handles to the components of the view, as shown in the following example:

```
etUsername= (EditText)v.findViewById(R.id.username);
```

✔ The view has to be returned by the method. This view, in fact, is handed back to the enclosing activity to be made part of the activity's view hierarchy.

Incorporating fragments into activity behavior

In this section, we describe the code additions or modifications that are needed in the activities in order to use fragments. In the Login activity, there's just one code change due to the fact that fragments are being used. In the onCreate method, a test if (btnNewUser!=null) has been added, which tests whether the New User button exists. This test is needed because in the layout file for Login in landscape mode this button does not exist. Of course, do note that Login now extends FragmentActivity, rather than the Activity base class.

```
public void onCreate(Bundle savedInstanceState) {
    ...
    android.view.View btnLogin=(Button)findViewById(R.id.login_button);
    btnLogin.setOnClickListener(this);
    android.view.View btnCancel=(Button)findViewById(R.id.cancel_button);
    btnCancel.setOnClickListener(this);
    android.view.View btnNewUser=(Button)findViewById(R.id.new_user_button);
    if (btnNewUser!=null) btnNewUser.setOnClickListener(this);
}
```

When the layout of the activity is inflated into the activity's view (when the activity is created), the inflator reads the class name in the fragment entry and creates an instance of the fragment. Then, by calling onCreateView(...) on the fragment instance, the inflator inflates its view as well. This view is returned by onCreateView(...) and hooked into the activity's view. The Android framework does all this under the hood and — voila! — your activity, its view, and its fragments are ready for service.

We also show you how to implement the Account activity where an AccountFragment isn't declaratively incorporated into the activity, but is instead incorporated by using code. Take a look at the code for the Account activity:

```
package com.wiley.fordummies.androidsdk.tictactoe;
import com.wiley.fordummies.androidsdk.tictactoe.R;
...
//Fragment specific imports
//For Android 3.0 and above comment out the lines below
import android.support.v4.app.FragmentManager;
import android.support.v4.app.FragmentTransaction;
import android.support.v4.app.FragmentActivity;

// For Android 3.0 and above uncomment the lines below
// import android.app.FragmentManager;
// import android.app.FragmentTransaction;
// import android.app.FragmentActivity;

public class Account extends FragmentActivity implements OnClickListener{
    public void onCreate(Bundle savedInstanceState) {
        super.onCreate(savedInstanceState);
        setContentView(R.layout.account);
        // Install the Account fragment
        // For Android 3.0 and above comment out the line below

        AccountFragment accountFragment = new AccountFragment();
```

```
        FragmentManager fragmentManager = getSupportFragmentManager();
        // For Android 3.0 and above uncomment the line below
        // FragmentManager fragmentManager = getFragmentManager();
        FragmentTransaction fragmentTransaction =
                                    fragmentManager.beginTransaction();
        fragmentTransaction.add(R.id.accountdetails, accountFragment);
        fragmentTransaction.commit();

        // Initialize the Exit button
        View buttonExit= (Button)findViewById(R.id.exit_button);
        buttonExit.setOnClickListener(this);
    }
    public void onClick(View v) {
        switch (v.getId()) {
        case R.id.exit_button:
            finish();
            break;
        }
    }
}
```

In this code example, start by noting the package imports needed for using
fragments. We include two sets of imports: one for SDK versions earlier than
3.0 and the other for building apps against Android 3.0 or higher.

Now look at the code itself: Notice how the Account activity inherits from
FragmentActivity. (By the way, we missed this crucial step and spent half
a day trying to figure out why our code simply wouldn't work.) Then note
how a new fragment is created that is similar to any standard Java object.

Then the good stuff happens: A fragment manager is provided by the get
FragmentManager() method, and then the newly created fragment is added
to the FrameLayout component, named accountdetails, of the Account
activity's view. (If this component is unfamiliar to you, see the section
"Embedding fragments in activity layouts," earlier in this chapter.) Finally,
note how the fragment is added within a transaction enclosed by fragment
Manager.beginTransaction() and fragmentManager.commit() calls.

That's it — you're ready to work with fragments!

Managing the Activity Life Cycle

An activity is taken through several stages by the Android runtime from the
time the activity is created to the time it is killed. These stages make up the
activity's life cycle. As the activity goes through each stage, a set of standard
methods is invoked. These methods are known (naturally) as the *life cycle
methods* of the activity. You can insert application-specific functionality by
overriding these methods and providing your own implementation for them.

For example, you can save the current state of an activity to a file or database before it is destroyed. Then when a new instance of the activity is started, this new instance can read back the persistent state, so that the activity appears to start where it left off.

To begin with, an activity is launched by either the Home application or another activity. As shown in Figure 3-7, an activity is then in one of these four states:

- ✔ Created: The activity was just created.
- ✔ Active: The activity is running and visible to users.
- ✔ Paused: The activity isn't running temporarily, because another activity has been brought to the foreground and is still visible. In this state, all member variables and locations in its execution code are maintained.
- ✔ Stopped: The activity has been obscured by another activity. Its member variables and other elements are still being maintained, but it's vulnerable to being destroyed by the Android runtime, if resources on the device are running low.

Within this overall life cycle are several transitions. The first is the transition of the activity to being Created (from the Zen state of not existing). The subsequent transitions are from Created to Active, from Active to Paused, from Paused back to Active, from Paused to Stopped, from Stopped back to Active, and from Stopped to no longer existing.

At every transition, the Android framework calls one of these methods on the activity:

- ✔ onCreate(Bundle savedInstanceState): Called immediately after the activity is created. You should set up the activity within this method — for example, create its views and reinitialize its state from the Bundle object (described in the section "Saving the transient state of activities") that's passed to it by the Android runtime.
- ✔ onStart(): Called just before the activity becomes visible to the user. At this stage, you might load current data into the activity. Immediately after onStart() is completed, the method named onRestoreInstanceState(Bundle savedInstanceState) is called, so you can restore any instance state needed.
- ✔ onResume(): Called just before the activity starts interacting with the user. At this point, the activity is in the Active state. onResume() is always called after onStart() (refer to Figure 3-7). Thus, you can choose either onStart() or onResume() in which to implement any processing needed before the object becomes visible — such as retrieving fresh data.

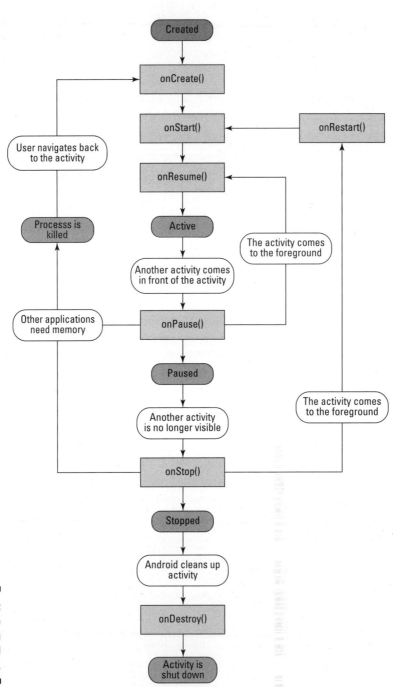

Figure 3-7:
The life cycle of an Android activity.

✔ onPause(): Called when Android decides to hide this activity, most often because it wants to start another one. This method is used to save any persistent data and gracefully return resources, such as threads and open files. onPause() should quickly do whatever it does because it's holding back the next activity from becoming active. Note that the process running an activity may be closed by Android in order to save memory and power. Thus, this method is the last of the methods guaranteed to be called by the Android runtime, and is thus often your last chance to save *persistent activity state* or clean up resources (such as open files).

✔ onStop(): Called when the activity is no longer visible to the user. This method will be called either because the activity is being destroyed or because a new activity has been started that is completely covering the original activity. This method might *not* be called if the process associated with the activity has already been destroyed by Android.

Incidentally, you might be wondering why both onPause() and onStop() are needed. The difference between the two is actually quite subtle. When one activity is launched over another, the newly launched activity may not cover the first activity completely. To see an example of this in Tic-Tac-Toe, launch the Help activity from the GameOptions activity. You will see that the Help UI doesn't quite cover the Game Options UI. In this case, onPause() will be called, but onStop() will not be. If the newly launched activity completely covers the current activity, then onStop() will also be called.

✔ onRestart(): Called just before the activity is started again from the Stopped state. If, by any chance, the process for the activity might have been destroyed, and its state lost, you need to restore the activity state in this method.

✔ onDestroy(): Called before the activity is destroyed. This method, which is the final call the activity receives, is called on two occasions:

- *If* finish() *is called on the activity:* For example, see the on Create method in the SplashScreen activity. You can see that finish is called on the SplashScreen activity itself after control is transferred to the Login activity.

- *If the system is temporarily destroying this instance of the activity to save space.*

You can distinguish between these scenarios by a call to the is Finishing() method. This method will return true for the first case or false in the second case.

Default implementations of these methods are provided in the Activity base class. Of course, you would need to override these default methods as necessary to customize the behavior activity. You will see that you must always override the onCreate() method. (We've always had to, anyway.)

Coordinating activities

When one activity starts another, the initiating activity pauses and can stop. The state transitions — and, therefore, the calls to the life cycle methods of the two activities — might need to be coordinated. Thus, the Android framework clearly defines the order of the life cycle methods:

1. The current activity's `onPause()` method is called.

2. The starting activity's `onCreate()`, `onStart()`, and `onResume()` methods are called in sequence.

3. If the starting activity is no longer visible onscreen, its `onStop()` method is called.

Starting activities using intents and intent filters

Activities (within an application) are initiated by way of messages, known as *intents*. An intent contains an `Intent` object that specifies a desired action and is sent to the Android framework by a requesting activity. This `Intent` object is matched against a set of intent filters (registered with the Android framework by every activity that can be called by another). All activities that have intent filters matching the intent are activated and passed the intent object. These activities can examine and extract information from the intent and perform their function. The intent object can be retrieved by calling `getIntent(...)`. If an existing activity is intended to handle a new intent, the `Intent` object will be passed to the activity by way of an `onNew Intent()` call.

The following list describes the four fields used for matching that can be set within an intent:

- **The name of the component (optional):** A field that explicitly specifies the target activity by using its fully qualified name (the package name plus the class name).

- **The action to be performed:** A string constant. The Android framework specifies a set of standard actions; the most common are shown in Table 3-1. If you "roll your own" string, make sure that it's guaranteed to be unique, by prefixing the package name to the string.

✔ **The data to be sent to the activated object:** The Uniform Resource Identifier (URI) of the data to be acted on and the MIME type of that data. (MIME is short for Multipurpose Internet Mail Extensions, a specification for describing how non-ASCII content — such as an image file — has been formatted).

✔ **The category of the object to be activated:** Essentially, additional information about this object, consisting of a string.

The common standard intents in Android are shown in Table 3-2. For a complete list of intent actions and categories, see `http://developer.android.com/reference/android/content/Intent.html`.

Table 3-1	**Standard Intents, Targets, and Actions**	
Intent Action	*Target Component*	*Action*
`ACTION_CALL`	Activity	Initiate a phone call.
`ACTION_EDIT`	Activity	Display data for the user to edit.
`ACTION_MAIN`	Activity	Start up as the initial activity of a task, with no data input and no returned output.
`ACTION_SYNC`	Activity	Synchronize data on a server with data on the mobile device.
`ACTION_BATTERY_LOW`	Broadcast receiver	Indicate that the battery is low.
`ACTION_HEADSET_PLUG`	Broadcast receiver	Plug in a headset, or unplug it.
`ACTION_SCREEN_ON`	Broadcast receiver	Turn on the screen.
`ACTION_TIMEZONE_ CHANGED`	Broadcast receiver	Change the time zone setting.

Table 3-2	Standard Intent Categories in Android
Category	*Meaning*
CATEGORY_BROWSABLE	The target activity can be safely invoked by the browser to display data referenced by a link — for example, an image or an e-mail message, for example.
CATEGORY_GADGET	The activity can be embedded inside another activity that hosts gadgets.
CATEGORY_HOME	The activity displays the Home screen, the first screen the user sees when the device is turned on or when the HOME key is pressed.
CATEGORY_LAUNCHER	The activity can be the initial activity of a task and is listed in the top-level application launcher.
CATEGORY_PREFERENCE	The target activity is a preference panel.

In the AndroidManifest.xml in the Tic-Tac-Toe application, you see that the SplashScreen activity (the initial activity in the Tic-Tac-Toe application) defines an intent filter with the action android.intent.action. MAIN and the category android.intent.category.LAUNCHER. Used together, these entries indicate that this activity is the first (or main) activity of the Tic-Tac-Toe application, and that it's launched from the Home application. The Login activity, on the other hand, is defining an intent filter with the string value "com.wiley.fordummies.androidsdk.tictactoe. Login". This activity then responds to any invocation message containing this string. An intent is typically sent by a call to android.app.Activity. startActivity(Intent). Thus, the SplashScreen activity launches the Login activity by using the following call:

```
startActivity(new Intent("com.wiley.fordummies.androidsdk.Login"));
```

The Account activity has no intent filter because this activity is invoked by a direct reference (specifically, by the Login activity). This is shown in the following call (from the onClick method of the Login activity):

```
startActivity(new Intent(this, Account.class));
```

Because all remaining activities within Tic-Tac-Toe are invoked using this direct strategy, these activities don't need intent filters and you don't need to define the filters in the AndroidManifest.xml file.

Saving the transient state of activities

Android tries to save the transient state of activities by shutting down applications that it believes aren't being used, such as applications that have been pushed into the background because the user has started up new ones. For example, a user playing Tic-Tac-Toe might be notified of an incoming e-mail message, causing him to switch to the Mail application to read the message. When the user returns to Tic-Tac-Toe, Android displays the screen that was previously open. Any data the user entered remains; in fact, the cursor even resumes blinking at the same spot.

A user who switches from the Tic-Tac-Toe application to spend time using the Mail application, for example, can still legitimately expect the game to return to the state it was in before the switch. After all, if Android shuts down Tic-Tac-Toe's process during the switch and preserves the state, why would the behavior be different simply because the user spent time using another application? In other words, the active state of all activities should be preserved when the application is shut down by Android, and then restored when the application is revisited. We're referring not to data that the application has saved to a file or database (also known as *persistent* state) but, rather, to the *transient* state, which changes as the application is used and ends when the user quits the application.

Incidentally, if the orientation of the device is changed, Android destroys and re-creates the current activity so that it can re-create its layout for the new orientation. Thus, to test whether transient state is being managed correctly, you can simply rotate the phone while the activity is still running to see if the pieces of data shown onscreen are retained after the orientation changes. This policy of destruction and re-creation upon change of orientation also means that you must ensure that the transient state is saved and restored whenever the orientation of the device changes.

To save and restore this transient state, you may simply use the built-in activities and views that the Android framework provides. Android saves the transient state of the user interface if Android kills your process, and then it restores the state when the user returns to the activity. To be precise, the base classes (`Activity` and `View`, `PreferenceActivity`, for example) implement `onSaveInstanceState()` and `onRestoreInstanceState ()` methods that handle this save and restore.

If you implement your own views, you have to handle the transient state yourself, as described in this list:

✔ To capture the state before the activity is killed, you must implement an `onSaveInstanceState(...)` method for the activity. As we mention in the earlier section "Managing the Activity Life Cycle," this method is called before `onPause(...)` is called.

✔ To extract and restore the saved state when the activity is started again, note that the saved state is passed to `onCreate(...)` and `onRestore InstanceState(...)`. Both of these methods are called after `onStart(…)`. Either method can extract the saved state and repopulate it in the activity.

The transient state is saved as name-value pairs in an object of the class `Bundle` that is passed to the re-created activity when it's restarted. To restore the activity's state, you must extract the value from the `Bundle` object and repopulate the activity's variables.

The following example is from the `WhereAmI` activity in Tic-Tac-Toe. Again, we show only the code that's relevant to state management:

```
package com.wiley.fordummies.androidsdk.tictactoe;
...
import android.os.Bundle;
...
public class WhereAmI extends MapActivity implements OnClickListener {
    ...
    private String whereAmIString=null;
    private static final String WHEREAMISTRING="WhereAmIString";

    protected void onCreate(Bundle savedInstanceState) {
        ...
    }

    public void onClick(View v) {
        switch(v.getId()){
        ...
        case R.id.button_locate_me:
            Location myLocation=null;
            myLocation = myGeoLocator.getBestCurrentLocation();
            if(myLocation == null){
                myLocationField.setText("GeoLocation not available. Retry#:"+
                                    locationQueryCount++);
            }else{
                ...
                myLocationField.setText(whereAmIString=
                        myGeoLocator.getNameFromLocation(myLocation)));
                ...
            }
            break;
        ...
```

```
            }
        }
          ...
    protected void onSaveInstanceState (Bundle outState){
        super.onSaveInstanceState(outState);
        if (whereAmIString != null) outState.putString(WHEREAMISTRING,
            whereAmIString);
    }

    protected void onRestoreInstanceState (Bundle savedInstanceState){
        super.onRestoreInstanceState(savedInstanceState);
        whereAmIString = savedInstanceState.getString(WHEREAMISTRING);
        if (whereAmIString != null) myLocationField.setText(whereAmIString);
    }
}
```

Note that a descriptive name of the current location is being found in the
`onClick(...)` method. This name is assigned to the private `String` variable
`whereAmIString`. This string is saved to the `Bundle outState` passed
in by the Android framework to the `onSaveInstanceState(...)` method.
Finally, note that the string is extracted from the bundle in `onRestore
InstanceState(...)` and is assigned to the field `myLocationField` that
displays the name of the location.

If the instance is intentionally destroyed (by the user tapping the Back key,
for example), `onSaveInstanceState(...)` is *not* called. The user cannot
return to the activity, so there's no reason to save the state.

Using tasks to manage the behavior of groups of activities

Whenever an activity is launched, Android places it inside a *task* — an
Android entity that contains and manages groups of activities and runs inside
(and corresponds to) a Linux process. A task is an implicit object because
Android manages all tasks, and you as an application programmer cannot
therefore create them (or gain access to them). However, you can control
how specific activities behave within a task.

Because the information in this section is somewhat advanced, you're unlikely
to need it in order to develop your first few Android applications. However,
we mention the topic in this book for completeness — just so you know that
this behavior exists.

An activity can be launched into a new task, such as when the Home application (also known as the *Launcher*) kicks off an application, or it can be
launched into an existing task to cohabit with other activities already in that

task. An activity can also move from one task to another *after it has been launched into one task* if it later finds a task that it likes better — or a task for which it has a greater *affinity*.

The activities in a task are arranged as a stack. If a task is active and a new activity is launched, it's typically placed on top of the stack in the same task and begins running. If the user taps the Back button, the new activity is popped off the stack (and stops running) while the previous activity in the task is brought to the top of the stack and resumes. You can clearly see this behavior when you click the Help button in the GameOptions activity: The Tic-Tac-Toe Help screen — that is, the Help activity — is launched on top of the GameOptions activity. Note that this Help activity is launched into the same task as GameOptions but placed on the top of the task stack. Note also, that because of the transparent user interface that the Help activity uses, you can see the GameOptions activity underneath it. When a user taps the Back button, the Help activity is popped off the stack and disappears, and the GameOptions activity becomes active again, as shown in Figure 3-8.

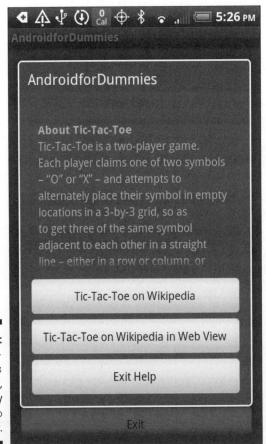

Figure 3-8:
The Game-
Options
activity,
covered by
the Help
activity.

However, an activity might not necessarily be launched in the same task as the previously running activity. To determine in which task the activity is launched, you use a combination of two sets of directives:

- ✔ **The intent that launches the activity:** The intent can, for example (and we don't go into all the options here), request that the activity be launched into a new task, be moved to the top of the stack (if an activity of that class exists), or be reset to its initial state before processing the intent; or that a new instance of the activity be launched, but not if the activity is already running on top of the stack.

- ✔ **Certain attributes of the launched activity as declared in the manifest file:** An activity can declare an *affinity* for another in the AndroidManifest.xml by using the taskaffinity attribute. If it does so, an activity will be launched into an existing task if the task has an activity for which the new activity has declared an affinity.

  An activity can also declare that it can have only one instance in any task via the launchmode attribute in the manifest file. This means that in addition to there being only one instance of the activity, it must be the *only* instance. Or an activity can declare that it can start in any task, but it must be moved to a task containing activities with which it has an affinity, if such a task were to be launched later. Finally, an activity can declare that it cannot be moved to another task once it has been launched in a particular task.

Implementing Services

You aren't likely to develop lots of services in comparison to the number of apps you develop, but every so often you need complementary functionality that is implemented as a service.

A service is intended to be run in the background, without the need for a user interaction, and hence no user interface. A service is meant to do its work behind the scenes, even as the user interacts with apps in the foreground. Thus, a service can be used to play music in the background, listen to events from the outside, or serve as an upload or download queue for print jobs, messages, or images.

Android provides two kinds of services:

- ✔ *Local:* Accessible only by a single application.

- ✔ *Remote:* Accessible by all applications on the device. (This type is also known as *AIDL-supporting, AIDL, external, RPC,* or *bound* service.)

We talk only about local services in this book, but you can find out more about remote services at

```
http://developer.android.com/guide/topics/fundamentals/services.
              html#CreatingBoundService
```

We illustrate how a local service is implemented by showing you an example of the MyPlaybackService in the Tic-Tac-Toe application, which plays music in the background. Here's the code for this service:

```java
package com.wiley.fordummies.androidsdk.tictactoe;
import com.wiley.fordummies.androidsdk.tictactoe.R;
import android.app.Service;
import android.content.Intent;
import android.media.MediaPlayer;
import android.net.Uri;
import android.os.Bundle;
import android.os.IBinder;

public class MyPlaybackService extends Service {
    MediaPlayer player;
    @Override
    public IBinder onBind(Intent intent) {
        return null;
    }
    @Override
    public void onCreate() {
        player = MediaPlayer.create(this, R.raw.sampleaudio);
        player.setLooping(true);
    }

    @Override
    public int onStartCommand(Intent intent, int flags, int startId) {
        super.onStartCommand(intent, flags, startId);
        Bundle extras = intent.getExtras();
        if(extras !=null){
            String audioFileURIString = extras.getString("URIString");
            Uri audioFileURI=Uri.parse(audioFileURIString);
            try {
                player.reset();
                player.setDataSource(this.getApplicationContext(), audioFileURI);
                player.prepare();
            catch (Exception e) {
                // TODO Auto-generated catch block
                e.printStackTrace();
            }
        }
        player.start();
        return START_STICKY;
    }
```

```
@Override
public void onDestroy() {
    player.stop();
}
}
```

The following list describes the main points in this listing (note that we cover only the service management aspects of this component — the functionality of this component with respect to playing music is covered in Chapter 11):

✔ As with activities, the Android framework calls the onCreate(...) method of the service after it has been created. This method is used to complete any setup needed for the service. In the service that's shown, this method creates a local member that is a MediaPlayer object. This object is used to play the music.

✔ When the service is started by using StartService(...) — see the following code sample — the method onStartCommand(...) of the service is called and the invocation parameters of StartService(...) are passed to the service. In this case, the URL of the audio file is passed in.

✔ When the service is terminated, onDestroy() is called so that the service can stop its activity (in this case, stop the audio player) and release any other resources.

Services versus threads

Threads, like services, work in the background. To determine when to use threads and when to use services, follow this rule of thumb: Use a thread whenever you have a single, time-bounded task that's specific to a particular component of your application (such as a method listening for a touch to terminate a splash screen). In contrast, use a service to perform multiple tasks or tasks that are relevant to (or completed alongside) multiple components of your application, such as printing text or playing music.

Threads are more lightweight than services in that they consume fewer resources. They are also more vulnerable to being destroyed along with your app, if your app is killed by the operating system (for example, to free up memory). Services, on the other hand, are less likely to be killed along with the app. Because you can specify that a service be restarted if the operating system terminates it, the service is a more secure choice for large-grain activities, such as multiple uploads or downloads.

Note that a service runs in the main thread of its hosting process. If the service wants to perform a task in the background, it should spawn its own thread in which to do its work.

Shown next are extracts from the `Audio` activity that uses `MyPlayback Service`. The user interface for this activity has two buttons, `Start` and `Stop`, that start and stop the music service, respectively. (We omitted descriptions of two other buttons, `Record` and `Exit`, because they aren't relevant to the service.) Clicking the `Start` button starts the service by invoking `startService(…)`. Clicking the `Stop` button stops the service by invoking `stopService(…)`. Note that parameters to the service are passed via an `Intent` (which we described earlier in this chapter in the section "Starting activities using intents and intent filters"):

```java
public class Audio extends Activity implements OnClickListener{
    private boolean notStarted=true;
    String audioFilePath="/mnt/sdcard/SampleAudio.mp3";
    Uri audioFileURI=null;
    ...

    @Override
    protected void onCreate(Bundle savedInstanceState) {
        ...
        Button buttonStart=(Button)findViewById(R.id.buttonAudioStart);
        buttonStart.setOnClickListener(this);
        Button buttonStop=(Button)findViewById(R.id.buttonAudioStop);
        buttonStop.setOnClickListener(this);
        ...
        audioFileURI=Uri.fromFile(new File(audioFilePath));
    }

    public void onClick(View v) {
        switch(v.getId()){
            case R.id.buttonAudioStart:
                if(notStarted){
                    Intent musicIntent=
                        new Intent(this, MyPlaybackService.class);
                    musicIntent.putExtra("URIString", audioFileURI.toString());
                    startService(musicIntent);
                    notStarted=false;
                }
                break;
            case R.id.buttonAudioStop:
            stopService(new Intent(this, MyPlaybackService.class));
            notStarted=true;
            break;
            ...
        }
    }
.}
```

Managing Persistent Application Data

Now is a good time to talk about how to manage the persistent state of Android applications and services. Note that persistent data is data that needs to be preserved between uses of the application. For Tic-Tac-Toe this includes every user's game settings and game histories and all their user accounts (usernames and passwords). The Tic-Tac-Toe example illustrates how to save each of these three types of data in one of the three different ways in which persistent data can be saved:

- ✔ Shared preferences
- ✔ Files in the Linux file system
- ✔ The lightweight database known as SQLite

Using Shared Preferences to save persistent data

The first (and easiest) way to save application data persistently is to save the data as name-value pairs, using the shared preferences capability built into the Android development framework. In the "Setting application preferences" section, earlier in this chapter, we cover most of this topic except for how the preferences are saved. (In our example, it happens automatically.) Our explanation in this section goes a little deeper and adds to the example to show how preferences can be saved.

Android saved these preferences (or, more accurately, the name-value pairs of data that we're referring to as *preferences*) as a file on the Linux file system. You can specify a filename and the Android framework will either store it there, use a preference file per activity, or use a default preference file for the whole application. This last file is managed by the Android framework, and you don't know its name (so that you cannot corrupt it inadvertently). Note in all cases that the names of the different bits of data you want to store (the name-value pair) have to be unique within a file, or else you'll overwrite data that you might want to keep.

In the following code snippet from the `Login` activity, you set the login username as the name of the human player:

```
...
private final static String OPT_NAME="name";

// Save username as the name of the player
SharedPreferences settings=PreferenceManager.
```

```
                                     getDefaultSharedPreferences(this);
SharedPreferences.Editor editor=settings.edit();
editor.putString(OPT_NAME, username);
editor.commit();
...
```

This example illustrates the following concepts:

✔ The `PreferenceManager` class in the Android framework has the static method `getDefaultSharedPreferences(Context context)`, which returns a `SharedPreferences` object that represents the default preferences file.

✔ The `settings.edit()` method call creates an `Editor` object. The object is used to add or change name-value pairs via calls to `put-String(...)` (which we just listed), `putBoolean(...)`, and `putInt-eger(...)`, for example.

✔ After the value has been set in the `Editor` object, it has to be committed by calling the `commit()` method.

To complete this example, we repeat the code (for the `getName(..)` method) from the `Settings` class that reads the player name from the Preferences area:

```
private final static String OPT_NAME="name";
private final static String OPT_NAME_DEF="Player";

...
public static String getName(Context context) {
        return PreferenceManager.getDefaultSharedPreferences(context)
                .getString(OPT_NAME, OPT_NAME_DEF);
}
```

Using files

Another way to save persistent application data is by writing it to a file. We haven't included examples of file usage in Tic-Tac-Toe because this is not Android-specific — just plain old Java coding. However we would like to point out a few things about how Android deals with files.

Files can be in either *internal* storage on the Linux file system or in *external* storage (for example, on an SD card). By default, files saved to internal storage are private to your application — other applications cannot gain access to them, and users cannot see them. When the user uninstalls your application, these files are removed.

Using external storage is similar except that you need to set `File` to a path inside the file system on the external storage device. Here's one way to do it:

```
File ScoresFile=new File(getExternalFilesDir(null), "Scores.txt");
```

Passing null to getExternalFilesDir(...) returns the root directory on the external storage device. Once you have a path to the file, writing to or reading from external storage is the same as writing to a file in internal storage.

You cannot assume that an external storage device is available. Also you must follow certain conventions in the pathnames of files if you want to share files with other applications or enable the automatic cleanup of an application's files on external storage when the application is uninstalled. We show you how to do this and more in Chapter 7, where we talk about making your applications scalable, maintainable, and reliable.

Employing SQLite

Another way of persisting application state is by using SQLite. To quote from the SQLite web page:

> *SQLite is a software library that implements a self-contained, server-less, zero-configuration, transactional SQL database engine. SQLite is the most widely deployed SQL database engine in the world.*

In a nutshell, *SQLite* is a Java package that provides a collection of methods allowing you to create a local relational database, create tables in it, and read and write from those tables. Because the SQLite library is compactly written, its code occupies little space and is efficient and fast. It is therefore a suitable means of implementing rich relational database (RDBMS) functionality on a resource-constrained device while retaining most of the capability of an RDBMS to reliably read, write, and query data.

In the Tic-Tac-Toe application, you use SQLite to manage user accounts. We use a database named TicTacToe.db, in which we create a table named Accounts. Figure 3-9 shows what the Accounts table might look like.

Figure 3-9: Records in the Accounts table of the Tic-Tac-Toe SQLite database.

Accounts

ID	Name	Password
1	Rajiv	R#24!rr
2	Paul	$55541@#
3	Roger	#44%%1@

Most of the SQLite-specific code has been encapsulated into a `Database Helper` class, inside of which is a private `inner` class named `TicTacToe OpenHelper`. To see how database operations are implemented, we show you code from this class. To begin with, here's the `private` class `TicTacToeOpenHelper`:

```
private static class TicTacToeOpenHelper extends SQLiteOpenHelper {
    TicTacToeOpenHelper(Context context) {
        super(context, DATABASE_NAME, null, DATABASE_VERSION);
    }
    @Override
    public void onCreate(SQLiteDatabase db) {
        db.execSQL("CREATE TABLE " + TABLE_NAME +
                    "(id INTEGER PRIMARY KEY, name TEXT, password TEXT)");
    }
    @Override
    public void onUpgrade(SQLiteDatabase db, int oldVersion, int newVersion) {
        Log.w("Example",
            "Upgrading database, this will drop and re-create the tables.");
        db.execSQL("DROP TABLE IF EXISTS " + TABLE_NAME);
        onCreate(db);
    }
}
```

In these bits of code from the `DatabaseHelper` class, take a look at how the database is created:

```
private static final String
    INSERT="insert into " + TABLE_NAME + "(name, password) values (?, ?)" ;
public DatabaseHelper(Context context) {
    this.context=context;
    TicTacToeOpenHelper openHelper=new TicTacToeOpenHelper(this.context);
    this.db=openHelper.getWritableDatabase();
    this.insertStmt=this.db.compileStatement(INSERT);
}
```

A record is inserted into the database this way:

```
public long insert(String name, String password) {
    this.insertStmt.bindString(1, name);
    this.insertStmt.bindString(2, password);
    return this.insertStmt.executeInsert();
}
```

The following records that correspond to a username are queried and returned as a list:

```
public List<String> selectAll(String username, String password) {
    List<String> list=new ArrayList<String>();
    Cursor cursor=
        this.db.query(TABLE_NAME,
                    new String[] { "name", "password" },
                    "name='"+ username +"' AND password= '"+
                        password+"'", null, null, null, "name desc");
    if (cursor.moveToFirst()) {
        do {
            list.add(cursor.getString(0));
            list.add(cursor.getString(1));
        } while (cursor.moveToNext());
    }
    if (cursor != null && !cursor.isClosed()) {
        cursor.close();
    }
    return list;
}
```

Finally, in the `checkLogin()` method in the `Login` activity, you test for a successful login by checking the size of the list returned in the `selectAll` method in the preceding code block:

```
private void checkLogin(){
    String username=this.userNameEditableField.getText().toString();
    String password=this.passwordEditableField.getText().toString();
    this.dh=new DatabaseHelper(this);
    List<String> names=this.dh.selectAll(username,password);
    if(names.size() >0){ // Login successful
        ...
    }
    ...
}
```

Sharing data across applications through content providers

Suppose that you win a bunch of games against the computer and you're so excited that you just want to tell *somebody*. Wouldn't it be fun if the Tic-Tac-Toe application provided you with the capability to look up a friend's contact information in your address book so that you can call and gloat?

As your applications become richer in functionality, you generally find that you need to access data that's managed by other applications. Maybe you're writing a shared calendar application that lets you enter meetings and appointments. Being able to access the address book from your phone would be extremely useful, and *much* more convenient, so that the calendar can use these same entries rather than have to store its own addresses.

You can certainly share data using files by making them readable or writable by the world (by all other applications). In this all-or-nothing strategy, however, you share either the entire file or none of it, and you share it with every other application or with no application. Also, the format of the file has to be exposed and understood by all applications that are interested in it. Finally, the sharing application cannot enforce the management of the shared data in particular ways, such as enforcing the use of transactions. In other words, this means of sharing is easy but not optimum. To standardize, and hence make convenient, data sharing across applications, the Android SDK provides an abstraction, known as a *content provider,* which provides a standard interface for querying data and modifying and adding to it.

Android also makes available several built-in content providers for contacts in your address book, for various types of media, and for a dictionary of user-specified words. We use the Tic-Tac-Toe example to show you how to use the Contacts content provider while illustrating content provider concepts.

In Tic-Tac-Toe, you create a `ContactsView` activity, which implements browsing contacts. Here's the code for the `onCreate` method of that activity:

```
public void onCreate(Bundle savedInstanceState) {
    super.onCreate(savedInstanceState);
    setContentView(R.layout.contacts);
    TextView contactView=(TextView) findViewById(R.id.contactsView);
    Cursor cursor=getContacts();
    while (cursor.moveToNext()) {
        String displayName=
            cursor.getString(cursor.getColumnIndex(
            ContactsContract.Data.DISPLAY_NAME));
            contactView.append("Name: ");
            contactView.append(displayName);
            contactView.append("\n");
    }
}
```

This method is calling a local method — `getContacts` — that's returning a data structure known as a *cursor,* which, as you might already know, is a reference to a collection of similar data elements (also known as *records*) identified via a query. Every time you request (that is, your *code* requests) a record from the cursor, it retrieves and provides a new (unprocessed) element so that you can process it.

This example illustrates a few concepts — some explicitly and some implicitly. The first, of course, is how to retrieve records by using a cursor. Implicit in the use of the cursor is that the (only) data model the content provider *exposes* (how it presents the data that it manages) is as a table with columns and that contains rows of records. ***Note:*** Internally, the content provider can store the data however it wants. Passing the constant `ContactsContract.Data.DISPLAY_NAME` to the `cursor.getColumnIndex(...)` method returns the column index corresponding to the column name that, in turn, corresponds to the display name of the contact.

Next, you have to know the type of data being retrieved. In this case, the data to be extracted is the display name of the contact, which is a string. The data is then extracted from the cursor by using getString, which takes the aforementioned index as a parameter.

The rest of the code in onCreate retrieves contact elements by using the cursor, extracting the display name of each contact, and displaying the name by appending it to the view of the ContactView activity, which is a TextView component.

Here's a look at getContacts to help you understand more about content providers and how the cursor was created in the first place:

```
private Cursor getContacts() {
    Uri uri=ContactsContract.Contacts.CONTENT_URI;
    String[] columns=new String[]{ContactsContract.Contacts._ID,
                              ContactsContract.Contacts.DISPLAY_NAME};
    String selection=ContactsContract.Contacts.IN_VISIBLE_GROUP +
                   "='"+ ("1") + "'";
    String[] selectionArgs=null;
    String sortOrder=ContactsContract.Contacts.DISPLAY_NAME+
               " COLLATE LOCALIZED ASC";
    return this.managedQuery(uri, columns, selection, selectionArgs, sortOrder);
}
```

Please note the following about the above code:

✔ The class that manages phone contacts is named ContactsContract. Contacts.

✔ A content provider often manages many different collections of data, each of which must, of course, be exposed as a table. Every collection must be identified by using a unique URI.

A *URI,* or Universal Resource Identifier, is a World Wide Web (WWW) standard for exposing a resource — such as a collection of data that is stored remotely on the web or locally on a computer. All URIs for content providers begin with the string "content://".

Constants for standard URI on your Android device have been defined in the appropriate classes. The constant ContactsContract.Contacts. CONTENT_URI has therefore been set as the URI for the contacts on your computer.

✔ After you know the URI, you have to set the columns you need in an array of strings. In the following example, you're setting two columns in the string array Columns:

• _ID: The name of a special column that contains a unique identifier for each row

• DISPLAY_NAME: The descriptive display name of each contact

✔ Next, you select the rows you need from this table by specifying a select condition that's similar to a WHERE class in a database query. To make contacts visible, you set this clause to be ContactsContract. Contacts.IN_VISIBLE_GROUP=1. Note how the query string is being formulated (by using string concatenations) in order to specify this line:

```
String selection=ContactsContract.Contacts.IN_VISIBLE_GROUP +
                   "='"+ ("1") + "'";
```

Essentially, = 1 means true.

✔ This parameter selectionArgs may be used to specify additional selection arguments. In this example we have left it as null.

✔ We have specified COLLATE LOCALIZED ASC as the sort order as the fifth and final parameter. This means that the results of the query will be sorted in ASCII order, as per the local language setting.

✔ The query is invoked by using the statement this.managed-Query(...). It returns the cursor that is used in the onCreate(..) method to extract the display names of the contacts that are populated on the view.

✔ this.managedQuery(...) is doing more than executing the query and returning the cursor. *It's putting the cursor under management of the activity.* If the activity is paused, deactivated, or reactivated, therefore, so too is the cursor.

There is one last task to complete in order for the code to work properly. Note that Tic-Tac-Toe is reading the user's address book. This is private data for which the application must be granted access. So, in the AndroidManifest.xml file, we have added the following entry to request access to the content provider:

```
<uses-permission android:name="android.permission.READ_CONTACTS"/>
```

When the Tic-Tac-Toe application is installed on the Android device, the user is prompted to allow the permission. If access is allowed, all is well and good. If not, this piece of functionality is disallowed.

The application is now ready to be run. When you enter the ContactsView activity, you see a display that looks like the one shown in Figure 3-10.

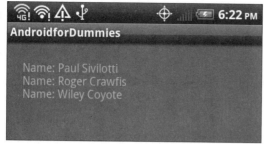

Figure 3-10:
Displaying
contacts in
the
Contacts
View
activity.

Part II
Building the Core of an Android Application

In this part . . .

This part consists of three chapters that show you what you need in order to design and build the foundation of an application. Chapter 4 helps you choose the right SDK level, and Chapters 5 and 6 cover user interface components in depth.

Chapter 7 shows you how to properly design an Android application. This chapter also covers the basics of object orientation and then introduces responsibility-driven design, an essential technique and best practice for good object-oriented software design. We then round out your design skills by showing you how to use a pattern-based approach to enhance this basic design to layer it on the Android framework.

Chapter 4

Determining the Appropriate SDK for Your Application

In This Chapter

▶ Looking at the variety of Android devices and SDKs

▶ Analyzing the differences between SDK versions

The great thing about versions is that there are so many to choose from.

Paraphrased from — Unknown

The Android Software Development Kit (SDK) is a moving target. The engineers at Google continually tweak and improve the SDK by adding new features and pushing others aside. While these new versions become available on newly purchased phones (and tablets), existing devices might not be updated to the most recent version. As a result, you have to consider a wide variety of SDKs when developing an application.

Every version of the Android SDK has been named after a dessert, in alphabetical order: Cupcake, Donut, Eclair, Froyo (short for *frozen yo*gurt), and Gingerbread. For every release, Google marks the occasion by placing a giant sculpture of the corresponding dessert on its Googleplex campus in Mountain View, California. As of February 2011, the latest major version of the SDK, version 3.0, is codenamed Honeycomb. This has been quickly followed by two incremental releases — version 3.1 and, in July 2011, version 3.2. The next major release is expected to be Android 4.0 (also known as Ice Cream Sandwich).

Along with the cool marketing name (Honeycomb, Ice Cream Sandwich, and so on) and the version, each SDK release is numbered with an always-increasing Application Programming Interface (API) level. Thus, Android SDK version 1.5 was API level 3, and the latest version 3.2 is API level 13.

Note that not all possible SDK versions and API levels are assigned to SDKs — or if they are, some versions are not released to external developers (those outside Google). For example, there was a version 2.3.1 and a version 2.3.3, but no Android SDK version 2.3.2 was ever released.

In this chapter, you discover what the most important differences are between the major versions of the Android SDK and how to select the right version for targeting your application.

As with the other chapters, we have not tried to simply re-hash everything from the Google Android site here. For all the gory details, see `http://developer.android.com/sdk/index.html`.

Exploring the Variety of Android Devices and SDKs

Android is available on a wide variety of devices. These devices have different characteristics such as screen size and screen resolution, and they can also have different versions of the Android SDK installed. The various combinations of devices and SDK versions can be a boon for consumers and a headache for application developers.

Understanding display characteristics

Screens on Android devices can be categorized into one of four general display sizes: small, normal, large, and extra large. They can also be categorized into a set of four generalized densities: low density, medium density, high-density, and extra-high-density. As of June 2011 (see Figure 4-1 and refer to `www.androidontop.com/2011/06/22/android-screen-sizes-and-densities-distribution-until-june-1/`), roughly three-quarters of the Android devices were of normal size with high-density displays (240 dots per inch). Relatively few devices have extra-high-density displays (320 dots per inch) although you can expect this number to increase. Similarly, relatively few devices used to have extra large displays (7 inches or more). With the advent of tablets, however, you can now expect this number to increase soon as well.

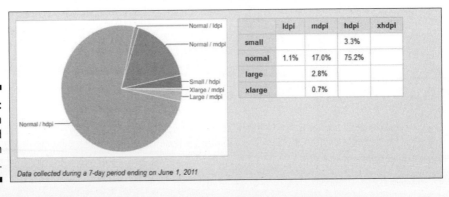

Figure 4-1: Distribution of Android screen sizes.

	ldpi	mdpi	hdpi	xhdpi
small			3.3%	
normal	1.1%	17.0%	75.2%	
large		2.8%		
xlarge		0.7%		

Data collected during a 7-day period ending on June 1, 2011

Avoid using pixels to specify positions and dimensions. For the most part, Android does the heavy lifting of making your application run on any of these platforms and display on any of these screen sizes and resolutions, but you can still benefit from following this important piece of advice.

The reason to avoid pixels as units of measurement is that the size of a measurement such as 80 pixels depends on the resolution of the screen. For example, on a medium-density display with a resolution of 160 dots per inch, every pixel is $\frac{1}{160}$ of an inch. An 80-pixel width, then, appears on the display as about half an inch, or roughly the width of your fingertip. However, on an extra-high-density display with a resolution of 320 dots per inch, the same 80-pixel width appears as only a quarter-inch, or roughly the width of a standard pencil. If the button size is specified in pixels, your application may look fine at one resolution but be annoyingly difficult to use at higher resolutions.

A better measurement unit to use is the *density independent pixel,* or *dp.* It's the same physical size — about $\frac{1}{160}$ of an inch — regardless of the resolution density of the display. In other words, for a medium-density display (160 dots per inch), a dp is equal to exactly 1 pixel. On the other hand, for an extra-high-density display (320 dots per inch), a dp is equal to 2 pixels. When you work with positions and sizes in terms of dps, your user interface will have the same physical feature size on all displays.

In addition to *dp,* other abbreviations for *density independent pixel* are sometimes used by Android developers and in the Android SDK documentation. In particular, you might see *dip* or *DIP.* Rest assured that they all mean the same thing. But just to confuse matters, *dpi* refers to a completely different concept: dots per inch.

Unfortunately, many methods in the SDK use the pixel as the unit of measurement. When calling these methods (or using their return values), you need to convert between dps and pixels. The `android.util.DisplayMetrics.density` field contains the scale factor needed for this conversion. For example, on an extra-high-density display, this field has the value 2.

The Tic-Tac-Toe example (which we tell you how to install in Chapter 3) is an example of a resolution-independent application. If you examine the `Board` class, you see two private fields: width and height. Both fields are in pixels, but they're calculated dynamically in the `onDraw(...)` method based on the size of `Canvas`. This approach guarantees that the Tic-Tac-Toe board fills the entire `Canvas`, regardless of the size or resolution of the display.

Recognizing there's more than one version of the SDK

Android devices not only have different hardware configurations, such as screen size and resolution, but can also have different software configurations. That is, several different versions of the Android SDK itself exist. Since the initial release of the Android SDK, it has undergone many revisions. On one hand, this quick evolution indicates the level of excitement and development effort behind Android. On the other hand, the speedy evolution means that many devices now in use don't have the latest version installed. Application developers must deal with this diversity.

Google tracks the distribution of platforms as observed by accesses to the Android Market. A recent snapshot is posted at `http://developer.android.com/resources/dashboard/platform-versions.html` and shown in Figure 4-2 below.

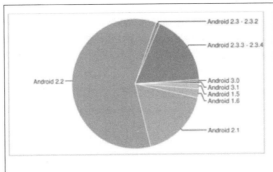

Platform	API Level	Distribution
Android 1.5	3	1.4%
Android 1.6	4	2.2%
Android 2.1	7	17.5%
Android 2.2	8	59.4%
Android 2.3 - Android 2.3.2	9	1%
Android 2.3.3 - Android 2.3.4	10	17.6%
Android 3.0	11	0.4%
Android 3.1	12	0.5%

Figure 4-2:
Distribution
of Android
versions.

For example, in July 2011, about 60 percent of Android devices accessing the Android Market were running SDK version 2.2 while 18 percent were still running the previous version, 2.1. Versions of SDK version 2.3 (including maintenance releases) made up 19 percent of the devices. Devices with the latest Android version (3.0) were slowly coming into use. Conversely, about 4 percent of devices were still using the even older SDK version 1.5, which had been superseded a full two years earlier!

Why should you care about all these different versions and API levels? As an application developer, you decide the minimum API level suitable for your application to run (and set it in the `AndroidManifest.xml` file — see the section below). This API level is used by the standard app downloaders (such as the Android Market application) to decide whether your app should be allowed to be purchased and installed on a user's machine. Pick too low of a number and you have to test more thoroughly, and perhaps limit the features you can offer. Pick too high of a number and you limit your market. Incidentally, Eclipse also looks at the minimum API level to decide whether an app can be downloaded onto an active emulator or device.

The *API level identifier* (see Table 4-1) can be used to mark the minimum level needed for an application to run. This identifier may also be used to indicate two of the additional SDK levels: the preferred level and the maximum level of the SDK in your application properties. Once again, you set minimum, maximum, and target API levels in the `AndroidManifest.xml file`; an example is shown below:

```
<uses-sdk
    android:minSdkVersion="6"
    android:targetSdkVersion="11"
    android:maxSdkVersion="11"
/>
```

Table 4-1	API Levels for Major SDK Releases	
SDK Version	*Name*	*API Level*
3.2	Honeycomb maintenance release	13
3.1	Honeycomb maintenance release	12
3.0	Honeycomb	11
2.3.3	Gingerbread maintenance release	10
2.3	Gingerbread	9
2.2	Froyo	8
2.1	Eclair maintenance release	7
2.0	Eclair	5
1.6	Donut	4
1.5	Cupcake	3

Notice the gap between API levels 5 and 7. API level 6 had no major release — instead, an intermediate release, 2.0.1, was assigned level 6. (We don't list API levels earlier than 1.5 because there's no need.)

Examining the Differences between SDK Versions

Every major SDK release has generally added, rather than removed, features and supported devices. Thus, an application built on an earlier release is *forward compatible* with a later release. For example, an app developed for Android 2.1 also runs on Android 2.3.

The following sections describe the features that were added in each release.

The earliest Android release documented by Google is Android 1.1. Both 1.0 and 1.1 well-supported the Android Application Model (see Chapters 1 and 3) in that they both had the capability to support Activities, Services, Menus, and so on. In other words, the foundation for all the stuff that you see in this book was in place with Android 1.0. Android 1.1 fixed quite a few bugs, added Locale support (so that Android could handle multiple languages), and added the first set of built-in applications (beyond the telephone dialer). Most importantly, 1.1 added support for external libraries. This meant that starting with this version, Google Map functionality was supported.

Android 1.5 — Cupcake

Cupcake released new features in these categories:

- ✔ **Communications:** Support for stereo audio streaming (A2DP) and remote control of Bluetooth-enabled media devices (AVRCP); automatic connection to Bluetooth headsets within range
- ✔ **Data entry:** A new soft keyboard with text completion
- ✔ **Multimedia:** The ability to record and watch videos in Camcorder mode and upload videos to YouTube and pictures to Picasa from the phone
- ✔ **User interface:** New widgets and folders that can populate the Home screens; animated screen transitions

Complete details on Cupcake are here: `http://developer.android.com/sdk/android-1.5.html`.

Android 1.6 — Donut

Released on September 15, 2009, Donut included an improved Android Market experience and improvements in these categories:

✔ **Accessibility:** A text-to-speech engine (which we're experimenting with in order to build apps for folks with visual impairments)

✔ **Applications:** Free turn-by-turn navigation from Google

✔ **Communications:** Updated support for the CDMA/EVDO and 802.11x Wi-Fi standards, and virtual private networks (VPNs)

✔ **Multimedia:** An integrated camera, camcorder, and gallery interface; better performance for camera applications

✔ **Search:** Updated voice search; better speed and integration with native applications, including the ability to dial contacts and search bookmarks, history, contacts, and the web from the Home screen

✔ **User interface:** Support for WVGA screen resolutions, the gesture framework, and the `GestureBuilder` development tool

Complete details on Donut are here: `http://developer.android.com/sdk/android-1.6.html`.

Android 2.0 — Eclair

Released on October 26, 2009, Eclair included these improvements:

✔ **Applications:** New contact lists; Microsoft Exchange support, searchable SMS messages

✔ **Communications:** Bluetooth 2.1 with new Bluetooth profiles

✔ **Data entry:** Improved virtual keyboard

✔ **Mapping:** Improved Google Maps 3.1.2

✔ **Multimedia:** Built-in flash support, digital zoom, and other enhancements for the Camera app

✔ **System and performance:** Optimized hardware speed

✔ **User interface:** Support for more screen sizes and resolutions; new browser user interface and HTML5 support; better contrast ratio for backgrounds; `MotionEvent` class enhanced to track multitouch events; live (animated, interactive) wallpapers

Note: The 2.0.1 SDK was released on December 3, 2009, and the 2.1 SDK was released on January 12, 2010. These maintenance releases had bug fixes but no additional features.

Details on the 2.0 version of the SDK are here: `http://developer.android.com/sdk/android-2.0.html`.

Android 2.2 — Froyo

Released on May 20, 2010, Froyo (*frozen yo*gurt) included these features:

- ✔ **Applications:** Better Microsoft Exchange support (autodiscovery, calendar synchronization, global address list look-up, remote wipe, security policies,); updated Market application with batch and automatic update features; support for file upload fields in the built-in browser, which can now also display animated GIFs (rather than just the first frame)

- ✔ **Communications:** USB tethering and Wi-Fi hotspot functionality; the option to disable data access over a mobile network (to prevent unexpected data charges); voice dialing and contact sharing over Bluetooth

- ✔ **Data entry:** Quick switching between multiple keyboard languages and their dictionaries; support for numeric and alphanumeric passwords

- ✔ **System and performance:** General Android operating system speed, memory, and performance optimizations; application speed improvements in the Dalvik VM from the use of just-in-time (JIT) compilation; support for installing applications to the expandable memory

- ✔ **User interface:** Integration of the Chrome V8 JavaScript engine into the Browser application; improved application launcher with shortcuts to the Phone and Browser applications; Adobe Flash 10.1 support in the browser

Details on the 2.2 version of the SDK are here: `http://developer. android.com/sdk/android-2.2.html`.

Android 2.3 — Gingerbread

On December 7, 2010, Gingerbread (2.3.3 is the generally available) was released with these new features:

- ✔ **Applications:** Improved social networking features

- ✔ **Application development:** Faster, concurrent garbage collection and faster event distribution, making possible the development of higher-performing applications (such as for gaming); the ability of native code (applications in C and C++) to directly gain access to sensor inputs; a new `Activity` subclass, `NativeActivity`, allowing life cycle callbacks to be implemented in native code

- ✔ **Communications:** Internet calling; near-field communications (NFC) capability (which allows the device to act as an RFID-like reader, for example)

- **Multimedia:** Support for the VP8 open video-compression format and the WebM open container format; AAC encoding and AMR wideband encoding (in software) so that applications can capture higher-quality audio than narrowband; access to multiple cameras and mixable audio effects

- **User interface:** Improved copy-and-paste functionality

Details on Gingerbread are here: `http://developer.android.com/sdk/android-2.3.3.html`. Note that documentation for the base 2.3 version is no longer on Google's site.

Android 3.0 — Honeycomb

On February 22, 2011, the Android 3.0 (Honeycomb) SDK was released. The changes in this release of Android included

- **Applications:** Support for video chat using Google Talk

- **Application development:** Enhanced input device and USB support (in 3.1), API for interacting with connected cameras (in 3.1)

- **Communications:** Background Wi-Fi networking

- **System and performance:** Refined multitasking, hardware acceleration, and support for multicore processors

- **User interface:** Optimized tablet support with a new fragments-based user interface; an Action Bar that can be used to enhance the previously available Menu functionality; a 3D desktop with redesigned widgets with new themes; system clipboards and drag-and-drop; enhanced App Widgets; animation of UI components (in 3.0 and enhanced in 3.1); compatibility zoom for fixed-size apps (in 3.2), that is, apps written for smaller devices

We are underselling 3.0 and its incremental releases 3.3 and 3.4 with the bland descriptions above. 3.0 was a major release that has essentially revamped the Android SDK, in particular, the way user-interfaces can be built for Android by decoupling the UI from the activity, and giving each its own separable life cycle.

And beyond

The next major version of the Android SDK (expected in the third quarter of 2011) will continue the push towards a single, unified platform for both phones and tablets. At the time this book was published, the name of this new SDK had not been officially announced. To no one's surprise, Google has hinted that the new version "will start with an I, and be named for a dessert." Whether the next version ends up being named Ice Cream, or perhaps Ice Cream Sandwich, it's likely to be delicious!

Dealing with API Levels

Given this information, what should be your general strategy? We recommend choosing the minimum-level API that your application needs. The conventional wisdom is that a balance exists: Pick the smallest version number to reach the highest number of devices, but pick the largest number to minimize the amount of testing. We'll go out on a limb and add that because Android adoption is deep into the growth phase, don't worry about sinking below SDK version 2.1 (API Level 7) — there's enough of a market to sell to. (Ninety percent or more of the current market is at version 2.1 or later. Google maintains a current snapshot of devices accessing the Android Market; see http://developer.android.com/resources/dashboard/platform-versions.html.)

Never assume that a device has the current SDK installed. In fact, if you want the broadest possible reach, you should assume the opposite.

The above guidelines apply, of course, when you first develop your app. How do you deal with the fact that, over time, the Android SDK will evolve, with new features being added and old capabilities being improved? To begin with, most apps will be forwardly compatible (that is, an app built for an earlier version of Android will mostly work just fine on a later version). That is, though applications designed on previous SDK versions won't take advantage of all the features added to future SDK versions, they should work mostly as well as they did on older SDK versions. However, don't rely completely on this compatibility. As each version comes out into the market, test your application against it, if only to make sure that all the features at least superficially work. In particular, make sure that the user interface is usable because as new versions come out on new devices, there are likely to be changes in the way the API handles the new display sizes and new resolutions.

You will also have to worry about "deprecated" elements of the API. Most changes in the SDK from one version to the next involve additions. For example, new classes are added to control new types of phone sensors, or a range of possible values is extended to account for more types of phones. Occasionally, however, a method or class is marked as *deprecated* (for more on deprecation, see http://download.oracle.com/javase/1.5.0/docs/guide/javadoc/deprecation/deprecation.html).

Though a deprecated method or class is still present, it may disappear in future releases.

So what do you do about deprecated methods or classes? To begin with, don't use deprecated functionality when you are developing a new application. After your app has been released, if the method or class becomes deprecated, and your app doesn't work quite right because of its reliance on the deprecated API, you simply have to redo and re-release your app. The good news is that the SDK is, by and large, *backward compatible,* and newer SDK versions should still be able to run all applications that worked on previous SDK versions, so you won't have to do this redoing very often.

Finally, you also have to deal with backward compatibility. That is, you will most likely target a version to develop against that is higher than the minimum version you want the software to support. This is because, even though you are supporting a minimum version, your goal is not to develop for that version (and simply let the forward compatibility of the Android SDK take care of the app working properly on the later versions you are targeting). Rather, you want to target a version in-between the minimum and the latest version where you have the best tradeoff between backward compatibility and features you can exploit in the API to make your application really cool. We won't go into techniques for ensuring backward compatibility here, because these techniques are not Android specific (but just plain old Java techniques — such as using the "factory" pattern). If you e-mail us, though, we'll be happy to give you some pointers.

Chapter 5

Designing a User-Friendly Application

. . . .

In This Chapter

▶ Introducing `View`, the base class of all widgets

▶ Understanding Android support for graphical user interface (GUI) layouts

▶ Recognizing the relationship between XML layout files and Android classes

▶ Understanding key layout classes

▶ Creating good user interfaces

. . . .

The computer, including the smartphone and similar devices (such as the tablet), is now an integral part of society. Users have little tolerance for poor or complicated user interfaces. A user's view of the computer isn't the same as your — the developer's — view. Users don't want to — and shouldn't have to — focus on the computer's CPU, network card, memory usage, or any other component.

The success of your Android application depends significantly on its ease of use. The interaction between human and computer is a widely studied field, with many textbooks and research papers written on the subject. Though we can't cover all elements and issues that govern the creation of a good user interface, we discuss specific design choices and rules of thumb and provide a detailed overview of the support that Android provides for user interaction.

This chapter focuses on the elements, such as buttons, in a traditional, two-dimensional (2D) graphical user interface (GUI) and traditional interaction techniques, such as clicking and typing.

 Chapter 6 covers 2D drawing support. Later chapters also discuss Android support of accessibility, for individuals who have visual or hearing impediments, and Internationalization. *Internationalization* incorporates not only using different languages or currencies in your GUI but also understanding other cultures and their use of specific colors and phrases and the circumstances that can produce different interpretations.

Things to Know Before Creating a User Interface

Android apps are conceptually organized as a set of *activities* — one cohesive step within an Android application along with its user interface. (See Chapter 1 for more on activities.) Every activity also has an associated user interface, which is the activity's *view,* and you specify the view either programmatically (within your program, for example) or by using an XML-based layout file.

The user interface is typically created when the activity is created (when the onCreate() method is called). If an XML file defines the view, the following bit of code loads the view layout:

```
@Override
public void onCreate(Bundle savedInstanceState) {
            super.onCreate(savedInstanceState);
            setContentView(R.layout.main);

}
```

Within the development environment, you can specify several XML files that contain resources and parts of the user interface. When the app is built, these XML files are processed and a set of resource IDs is associated with the layouts. In the preceding example, the R.layout.main resource indicates the root of the layout defined in the XML file, which we cover in detail throughout this chapter.

In this chapter, you use XML layout files for contact information, a calculator, and other applications. We start by describing the key classes for the visual presentation of the user interface — the View class and its descendants. In Chapter 6, we tell you how to create the user interface programmatically.

Understanding views

The View class is the base class for all visible user interface elements. Though View has no appearance and is rarely used directly, it provides the framework and support for the various complex processes that comprise a rich user experience. The View class is responsible for its own measurement, layout, drawing, focus change, scrolling, and key or gesture interactions for the rectangular area of the screen in which it resides.

Software engineers say that the View class has *weak cohesion.* (It has responsibility for many disparate tasks, rather than being solely focused on a single task.) View is perhaps the most complicated class in the Android framework because of the degree of coupling between functionality — a level or coupling that exists because the behaviors in an object-oriented system (for example, resize, measure, and draw) should be associated with the object or class.

For an element such as a button, the designers of Android asked several questions about the `View` class hierarchy, including

- ✔ What are the behaviors of a button?
- ✔ How does a textbox present itself?
- ✔ Can the appearance of a form change over time (for example, for different states of an application)?
- ✔ What happens when the user clicks the button?
- ✔ What happens when the user presses Enter?
- ✔ What happens when the user hovers the cursor over the button?

A simple button encompasses more than just its appearance — it also has a complex set of interactions. In this chapter, we describe many of these interactions in order to illustrate the Android framework in action, so that you can determine where to find a particular method (or behavior) in a widget's hierarchy.

Android has taken the tried-and-true traditional approach of user interface class design, found in almost all GUI toolkits, such as Java Swing. Before we describe the various widgets available in Android, we need to demonstrate this level of complexity to help you see how the world of user interfaces has seemingly "gone bananas" and designed the user interface classes upside down. To help you better understand this concept, the next section dissects the `android.widget.Button` class, its location in the `View` hierarchy, and the classes in this hierarchy chain.

In software engineering, the user interface classes in Android follow a *specialization hierarchy — each derived class restricts the overall functionality rather than extending it.*

Taking a detailed look at the View hierarchy

Figure 5-1 shows the class hierarchy of `View` and its descendants. (We omit the descendants of `ViewGroup` because of space limitations.) The classes in Figure 5-1, covered in Chapter 6, are used to create widgets. Within each class shown in Figure 5-1 is a number indicating the version number of the API in which the class was introduced. For now, you should simply understand that many widgets dealing with text are derived from the `TextView` class, which is derived from the `View` class.

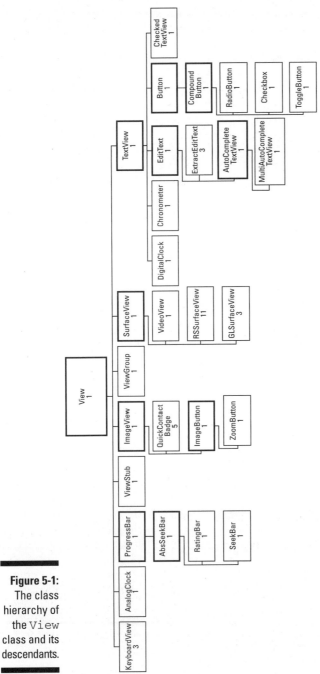

Figure 5-1:
The class
hierarchy of
the `View`
class and its
descendants.

The Button class, which we talk about next, can use text, so it's derived from TextView. If a class name begins with the prefix *Abs*, it's a *base class* — one that provides common functionality for the classes that derive from it, which are the full-featured classes you want to use.

The class AbsoluteLayout is deprecated — don't use it directly. The class SurfaceView and the classes that derive from it are essentially blank canvases that can be used to place or draw media. GLSurfaceView provides a blank canvas that uses OpenGL ES in an Android app. ImageView has been propagated to its own level, directly deriving from View, and has several customizations derived from it.

In this chapter, we describe the top structure of the user interface — layouts. Figure 5-2 shows the classes derived from the ViewGroup class and their descendants; these classes are used for layouts. You can see in the figure that a class such as SlidingDrawer is derived directly from ViewGroup and has no classes derived from it — this class is customized for a specific purpose. Helper classes such as FragmentBreadCrumbs and AdapterView are used with other layouts in advanced situations. The remaining three classes, FrameLayout, LinearLayout, and RelativeLayout (AbsoluteLayout is deprecated), are quite useful alone and are quite general and flexible. For common situations such as a group of radio buttons, the Android SDK provides a few customized layout classes, such as RadioGroup and ViewFlipper.

You can understand the relationships of one of these specialization classes and the View class by carefully analyzing the Button widget and how it fits into the hierarchy of Android classes and interfaces. Button extends the TextView class. The editing capabilities of the fully functional TextView text editor are disabled. TextView (which extends View) and classes derived from it are used anywhere that text is presented to the user, including the digital clock and, of course, buttons. The design of this class hierarchy is intended to put much of the functionality in the base classes and provide hooks (a callback method) to allow derived classes to change how the base class typically responds.

The large and complicated TextView class has hundred of methods, some of which deal with data such as setText() and length(). Other methods deal with the presentation, such as setTextColor(), setHorizontally Scrolling(), setTextSize(), setEllipsize(), and setTypeface(). Still other methods support the interaction, such as setSelected(), set CursorVisible(), and setKeyListener(). This is just a small sampling of TextView methods — and, therefore, its state. (Whew!)

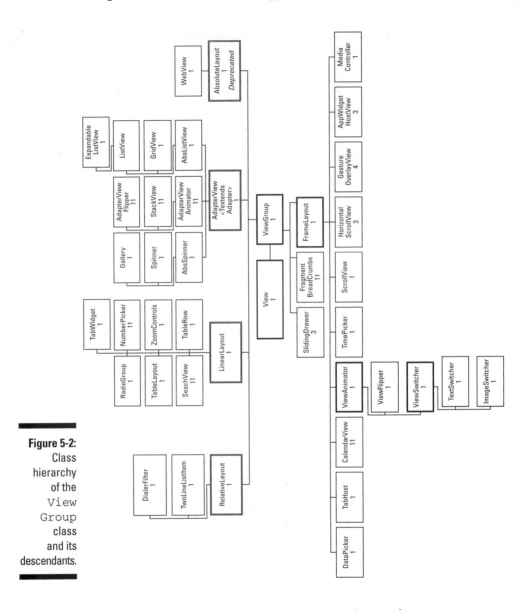

Figure 5-2:
Class
hierarchy
of the
`View`
`Group`
class
and its
descendants.

Wait, there's more: `TextView` also implements the interface
`ViewTreeObserver.OnPreDrawListener`, which has one method:

```
public abstract boolean onPreDraw()
```

The method `onPreDraw()` provides a hook that's called before `TextView`
is drawn. This method is called after all views in the tree have been mea-
sured but before any views in the tree have been drawn. `TextView` uses the
`onPreDraw()` method to adjust its *scroll bounds,* which indicate the portion
of text that's displayed when a large amount of text is scrolled.

As we mention earlier in this section, `TextView` extends `View`, so it inherits all (more than 250) public and protected `View` methods. The more than 400 methods available to `Button` overwhelm even the most seasoned developer, and it's virtually impossible to understand everything that a simple little button does. Unfortunately, all these methods are exposed to you by the Eclipse autocompletion feature, which provides a list of all possible method calls for a class or instance of a class. Figure 5-3 shows autocompletion for an instance of `Button`.

If you look at the SDK documentation for the `Button` class, you see that it adds no new methods — everything needed to define its appearance and behavior and to measure it, for example, is defined in the base classes. All `Button` does is redefine some basic `TextView` behavior. To find out how much, you can look at the Android open source code for `Button`:

```
public class Button extends TextView {
    public Button(Context context) {
        this(context, null);
    }

    public Button(Context context, AttributeSet attrs) {
        this(context, attrs, com.android.internal.R.attr.buttonStyle);
    }

    public Button(Context context, AttributeSet attrs, int defStyle) {
        super(context, attrs, defStyle);
    }
}
```

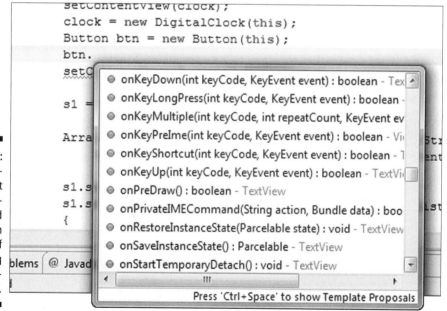

Figure 5-3: Eclipse provides the list of acceptable method calls for an instance of Button using autocompletion.

Buttons are defined by the last argument in the constructor (which you can override).

The workhorses (at least for `Button`) are the `View` and `TextView` classes. This common specialization of base classes in the user interface APIs lets you do almost anything with a button. After you understand the class hierarchy, you're ready to look at the available user interface components and the classes that help with the layout of the user interface. The rest of this chapter focuses on the higher-level layout (or flow) components. Chapter 6 covers the individual widgets available in the Android framework.

Working with views and layouts

An application or activity contains the `View` and `ViewGroup` classes. More precisely, an activity contains a rooted tree of elements, where every element is either a widget, a container of widgets with layout behaviors, or another, special element that controls the appearance or behavior of either widgets or layouts, such as one that animates the initial presentation.

One or more occurrence of `View` can be combined into a `ViewGroup`. This special type of `View` provides a layout for a set of views. The following sections present every possible layout in Android version 13 (API 3.2).

`ViewGroup` has these 33 classes:

- ✔ `AbsListView`
- ✔ `AbsSpinner`
- ✔ `AdapterView<T extends Adapter>`
- ✔ `AppWidgetHostView`
- ✔ `DatePicker`
- ✔ `DialerFilter`
- ✔ `ExpandableListView`
- ✔ `FrameLayout`
- ✔ `Gallery`
- ✔ `GestureOverlayView`
- ✔ `GridView`
- ✔ `HorizontalScrollView`

✔ ImageSwitcher

✔ LinearLayout

✔ ListView

✔ MediaController

✔ RadioGroup

✔ RelativeLayout

✔ ScrollView

✔ SlidingDrawer

✔ Spinner

✔ TabHost

✔ TableLayout

✔ TableRow

✔ TabWidget

✔ TextSwitcher

✔ TimePicker

✔ TwoLineListItem

✔ ViewAnimator

✔ ViewFlipper

✔ ViewSwitcher

✔ WebView

✔ ZoomControls

You use many of these classes in conjunction with other layouts. ViewGroup can also be (and usually is) nested, so FrameLayout may contain Relative Layout and ScrollView, which contains TableLayout.

Several of these layouts are meant not to be used in isolation but, rather, as components added to other layouts. For example, ViewAnimator is used to add flair when switching from one layout to another or at the initial presentation of the view. Layouts, which are extensions of the ViewGroup class, are used to position *child controls* (widgets contained within the ViewGroup) for the user interface. Because layouts can be nested, you can create arbitrarily complicated interfaces by using a combination of layouts.

You typically define a user interface by using an XML file, such as main.xml, located in the res/layout folder. A simple example that produces the text string "hello" looks like this:

```xml
<?xml version="1.0" encoding="utf-8"?>
<LinearLayout xmlns:android="http://schemas.android.com/
        apk/res/android"
    android:orientation="vertical"
    android:layout_width="match_parent"
    android:layout_height="match_parent"
    >
    <TextView
        android:layout_width="match_parent"
        android:layout_height="wrap_content"
        android:text="hello"
        />
</LinearLayout>
```

When you compile an app and the compiler reads its XML files, every element tag in the XML file corresponds to an associated instance of an Android GUI class, or `View`. Each element is thus associated with an instance of a Java class. As indicated earlier in this chapter, these instances are presented onscreen when the activity is loaded and the content is set. The XML description in the preceding chunk of code uses two classes: `LinearLayout` and `TextView`.

The loading and processing of the XML files at compile-time differs from Windows Presentation Foundation, for example, where the XML (or XAML) is processed at runtime, allowing the GUI to be changed after installation.

The following section walks you through the process of creating user interfaces. Separating the appearance of the user interface from the behavior, or code-behind (the programming to tell the app what to do, for example, if a particular button is clicked), lets you focus on only the presentation aspect. The XML facilitates this separation, specifying the appearance in the XML and leaving the behavior to the java implementation. Here, the focus will be only on the appearance.

Sampling Some Android Layouts

The Android SDK includes an extensive and useful set of layouts to help construct user interfaces. Because layout managers play a fundamental role in arranging the pieces of your user interface, you should develop a good understanding of at least a couple of the layout classes so that you can work effectively. This section examines in depth a few key layouts supported by Android. These layouts enable an application to look "polished" as it moves from device to device (or even from portrait to landscape orientation) by gracefully adapting to new font metrics, component styles, component shapes, and even themes. You simply select the right combination of layouts to make an interface easy to understand and use. Begin by sketching your interface on paper and considering whether you should

✔ Group widgets into separate tasks

✔ Present all tasks at one time

✔ Simplify the user interface to show common tasks first

✔ Hide less common tasks at first but make them easily accessible

✔ Present the spatial relationships between various tasks

✔ Present the spatial relationships between the widgets within each task

✔ Change the layout if the phone is rotated

✔ Change the behavior of the app if a larger or smaller screen is used

✔ Choose the best widget for every necessary input or piece of information

One key benefit of using XML for the generation and definition of a user interface is that you can mock up and test the user interface outside the code logic. In the next section, we look at this topic in more detail by mocking up several user interfaces.

Mocking up a contact display

The simple mock-up we present in this section is a view to display a name and an address. For this task, you need widgets for the name, two address lines, a city, a state, and a zip code. The `LinearLayout` class is useful when a simple sequential set of widgets is needed. Here's the XML file `contact.xml` (the line in bold is described in the following section):

```xml
<?xml version="1.0" encoding="utf-8"?>
<LinearLayout
        xmlns:android="http://schemas.android.com/apk/
        res/android"
    android:orientation="vertical"
    android:layout_width="match_parent"
    android:layout_height="wrap_content"
  >
  <TextView
    android:layout_width="wrap_content"
    android:layout_height="wrap_content"
    android:text="Name"
    />
  <EditText
    android:layout_width="match_parent"
    android:layout_height="wrap_content"
    android:text="Enter Name ..."
    />
  <EditText
    android:layout_width="match_parent"
    android:layout_height="wrap_content"
    android:text="Address:"
```

```
      />
    <EditText
      android:layout_width="match_parent"
      android:layout_height="wrap_content"
      android:text="    ..."
      />
    <EditText
      android:layout_width="wrap_content"
      android:layout_height="wrap_content"
      android:text="State"
      />
    <EditText
      android:layout_width="wrap_content"
      android:layout_height="wrap_content"
      android:text="Zip Code"
      />
  </LinearLayout>
```

Figure 5-4 shows the result of this view. Note that we don't program anything yet (and don't, in this exercise). To create this application, create a new Android project in Eclipse and modify the res/layout/main.xml file to contain the preceding code sample. The onCreate() loads this file in the template generated by using the Eclipse tools. This user interface example is somewhat unpleasant to look at, but we show you how to fix the problem later in this chapter. Later chapters in this book also cover themes and the code-behind that makes the user interface functional.

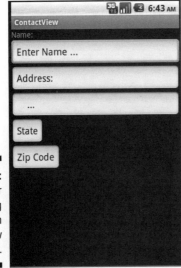

Figure 5-4:
A GUI for entering information about a new contact.

Examining the XML code closely

If you look at the XML code carefully in the preceding section, you see that it has a single LinearLayout enclosing a single TextView and five EditText widgets. You control the display of these widgets by using various layout parameters included in the XML. All occurrences of View must have a layout_width and layout_height specification — without them, the app crashes. You can use one of two special constants for this purpose which allow the system to make decisions on how best to display the widgets:

✔ **–1:** The system should make the widget as large as its containing parent, represented by the symbolic constant match_parent (or fill_ parent).

✔ **–2:** The system should shrink-wrap the widget to fit the content of the widget, represented by the symbolic constant wrap_parent.

The layout constant fill_parent was renamed in version 8 to match_ parent, and fill_parent was marked as deprecated.

You can use a third option to specify a precise size for the width or height, by using a numerical value with a unit specification. Possible values for the units are

✔ **dp:** Density-independent pixels

✔ **in:** Inches

✔ **mm:** Millimeters

✔ **px:** Pixels

✔ **sp:** Scaled pixels based on preferred font size

For example, to change the State EditText widget to measure only a half-inch, you replace Line 27 of the code (indicated by boldface) in the preceding section with this line:

```
android:layout_width="0.5in"
```

In general, use one of the special constants match_parent or wrap_ content. If a user's screen is smaller than expected, the field (or any field that was supposed to follow it on the same line) may get truncated. A user's screen that's larger than expected may have large, unsightly, empty spaces, possibly causing confusion.

Always use the match_parent or wrap_content constants for the width and height whenever possible, to ensure consistent results across different hardware.

Another XML tag is the `LinearLayout`'s orientation tag. It can be either horizontal or vertical. The vertical setting works best for applications such as the one in the example. Horizontal is useful for toolbars or applications that have several small widgets you want laid out horizontally. For the vertical setting, each child widget is placed on a separate line. It's an optional parameter, and the default is horizontal.

Understanding the relationship between XML and the Android SDK

Every XML tag corresponds to an attribute of the widget. For `layout_width` and `layout_height`, these attributes aren't direct attributes of `TextView` or `EditView` (or the base class `View`) but are, rather, shorthand for the `LayoutParams` class (defined in the `View` class) associated with this widget. All widgets (all instances of a `View`) have an associated `LayoutParams`. The `layout_width` and `layout_height` are the only attributes in the base class `ViewGroup.LayoutParams`. Several derived classes from `ViewGroup.LayoutParams` provide additional control and functionality. `LinearLayout.LayoutParams` is used by the `LinearLayout` layout class and is derived from the `ViewGroup.MarginLayoutParams` class.

Specifying extra features provided by ViewGroup.MarginLayoutParams

The `ViewGroup.MarginLayoutParams` class provides attributes for specifying extra space on the outside of the particular view. You can specify the top, bottom, left, and right margins individually by using the attributes `android:layout_marginTop`, `android:layout_marginBottom`, `android:layout_marginLeft`, and `android:layout_marginRight`, respectively. Alternatively, you can specify the attribute `android:layout_margin` to set all four margins to the same value. The value you assign to these attributes must be a dimension value, which is a floating-point number appended with a unit such as *14.5sp*. Available units are

- dp: Density-independent pixels
- in: Inches
- mm: Millimeters
- px: Pixels
- sp: Scaled pixels based on preferred font size

You can also use a reference to a resource or theme attribute. Themes are covered in Chapter 6.

Specifying extra features provided by LinearLayout.LayoutParams

`LinearLayout.LayoutParams`, which extends the `ViewGroup.MarginLayoutParams` class, has two additional attributes to specify the *gravity* and *weight* of every child widget. The attribute `android:layout_` `gravity` is similar to the *justification* effect in text publishing, where lines are spaced to come out even at the margins. From the Android SDK Reference pages, gravity may take on the values listed in Table 5-1.

Table 5-1		LinearLayout.LayoutParams Constants
Constant	*Value*	*What It Does*
`top`	0x30	Pushes object to the top of its container, not changing its size.
`bottom`	0x50	Pushes object to the bottom of its container, not changing its size.
`left`	0x03	Pushes object to the left of its container, not changing its size.
`right`	0x05	Pushes object to the right of its container, not changing its size.
`center_ vertical`	0x10	Places object in the vertical center of its container, not changing its size.
`fill_ vertical`	0x70	Grows the vertical size of the object, if necessary, so that it completely fills its container.
`center_ horizon- tal`	0x01	Places the object in the horizontal center of its container, not changing its size.
`fill_ horizon- tal`	0x07	Grows the horizontal size of the object, if necessary, so that it completely fills its container.
`center`	0x11	Places the object in the center of its container in both the vertical and horizontal axes, not changing its size.
`fill`	0x77	Grows the horizontal and vertical size of the object, if necessary, so that it completely fills its container.
`clip_ vertical`	0x80	An additional option that can be set to have the top or bottom (or both) edges of the child clipped to its container's bounds. The clip is based on the vertical gravity: top gravity clips the bottom edge; bottom gravity clips the top edge; neither clips both edges.
`clip_ horizon- tal`	0x08	An additional option that can be set to have the left or right edges (or both) of the child clipped to its container's bounds. The clip is based on the horizontal gravity: left gravity clips the right edge; right gravity clips the left edge; neither clips both edges.

Several of these attributes can be combined, using the | operator. For example, to specify the State field in the lower-right corner, you might rewrite the State widget this way:

```
<EditText
    android:layout_width="wrap_content"
    android:layout_height="wrap_content"
    android:layout_gravity="bottom|right"
    android:text="State"
    />
```

This snippet indeed pushes the State EditText box to become right-justi-fied. However, the bottom setting is ignored by LinearLayout with the ver-tical orientation. If you were using horizontal orientation, the box would be at the bottom, but not right-justified. The system takes all information from its children and determines the best layout using this information as well as its own rules and settings.

Setting a particular attribute (such as a margin) is only a suggestion to the system. It may be ignored or altered.

The layout_weight attribute is useful to evenly space controls either hori-zontally or vertically. For it to work, all widgets within a container (a layout) should define a weight. If the weights are all equal, you *may* achieve uniform distribution. We say *may* because (as we state elsewhere) the system consid-ers it part of its overall strategy, not as gospel. If you give five widgets a weight of one and a sixth widget a weight of two, the sixth widget is, ideally, twice as large as the other five. In practice, this seems to be weak guidance if using unequal weights or widgets with different content sizes. If the amount of data causes the shrink-wrap size to increase, it overrides the weight setting.

You should try your layouts on several devices that have different resolutions. The Android SDK and AVD Manager let you do this by allowing you to create virtual devices with different screen sizes and resolutions. Be sure to try your interface with a normal amount of data, a minimal amount of data, and a maxi-mum amount of data in only a few of the widgets and then in all of the widgets.

Remember that the margin controls in ViewGroup.MarginLayoutParams, the justification and scaling controls in LinearLayout.LayoutParams, and the fill or wrap controls for the width and height in ViewGroup. LayoutParams set the value of only one field in the LinearLayout class — the LayoutParams field. Many more attributes may be able to be set to control the appearance (and behavior) of the individual widgets. A few more attributes for controlling the layout exist — most notably, the android:baselineAligned attribute of LinearLayout. By default, it's set to true and the widgets are aligned with a baseline (the Text field's base-line for widgets, such as TextView). Setting this attribute to false allows the widgets to be aligned at their tops. The android:layoutAnimation in the ViewGroup class specifies an animation to be used when the particular ViewGroup is first displayed.

In the next section, we beautify this simple GUI as much as we can by using `LinearLayout`. Later sections in this chapter explore alternative layouts that offer more control and flexibility. As you can soon see, `LinearLayout` is useful as a part of the overall GUI being displayed.

If you find yourself fighting the layout, consider using a different layout class.

Enhancing the look of the contact View

The bulk of the attributes we use to spruce up the simple Contact application are in either the `View` class or the `TextView` class. Because `EditText` is a thin veneer on `TextView`, it adds no attributes of its own — instead, `EditText` specializes `TextView`.

Figure 5-5 shows the intended finished result. Compare this image to Figure 5-4 (the original implementation) to see how many differences you can spot.

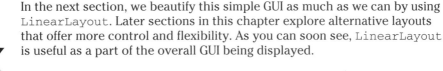

Figure 5-5:
An improved version of the GUI to enter a contact.

The only structural difference lies in the State and Zip Code widgets lying on the same line. Having these two widgets on the same line is impossible to do with a single `LinearLayout`, which places each `View` below the preceding `View`. To accomplish this task, you need a hierarchy. After you place the State and Zip Code widgets into a separate container or layout, this container can then be treated as a single `View` element in the top `LinearLayout`. We know of only one container so far — `LinearLayout`.

You want the state and zip code to appear on the same line, so you set the android:orientation attribute to horizontal. Structurally, you have replaced the original State and Zip Code EditText widgets with the following snippet (simplified from the final result to illustrate the structural differences):

```
<LinearLayout              android:orientation="horizontal"
    android:layout_width="match_parent"
    android:layout_height="wrap_content"
    >
    <EditText
        android:layout_width="wrap_content"
        android:layout_height="wrap_content"
        android:layout_weight="1"
        android:text="State"
        />
    <EditText
        android:layout_width="wrap_content"
        android:layout_height="wrap_content"
        android:layout_weight="1"
        android:text="Zip Code"
        />
</LinearLayout>
```

By placing the State and Zip Code widgets within a LinearLayout that is oriented horizontally and making their weights the same, together they span the view. Note that both layout widths are set to wrap_content.

The other enhancements revolve around setting colors and fonts and a background image. To create this new, improved version now, follow these steps:

1. **Start Eclipse and create a new project. Select Android Project as the project type.**

2. **Name the project** ContactView, **select version 8 (at least), and fill in the other parameters to name your activity and namespace or package.**

3. **Open the** main.xml **file in the** res/layout **directory by double-clicking the filename within Eclipse.**

4. **Delete the existing** TextView, **leaving only the first line.**

5. **Add a** LinearLayout.

   Because the LinearLayout is the first (or root) element, you define the Android namespace here. This step is required because the system wouldn't know LinearLayout or any of the Android widgets.

6. **Insert the following line immediately after the** LinearLayout **prefix:**

```
xmlns:android="http://schemas.android.com/apk/res/android"
```

The attributes are customarily included within the XML tag while placing the child views between the beginning and ending tags. So, for `LinearLayout`, you place the closing bracket (>) after the namespace declaration on either the same line or a new line. When you close the bracket, Eclipse automatically generates an end tag for you. Press the Return key on your keyboard to place the end tag on its own line. Unfortunately, Eclipse doesn't indent your XML code well. Proper indentation aids in comprehension and reduces errors, so indent the closing bracket (not the end tag). In front of the closing bracket, insert the required attributes (`layout_width` and `layout_height`) as well as the orientation attribute. Use `vertical` for the orientation and `match_parent` for the layout width and height. Your solution should look like this:

```
<?xml version="1.0" encoding="utf-8"?>
<LinearLayout xmlns:android="http://schemas.android.com/apk/res/android"
              android:orientation="vertical"
              android:layout_width="match_parent"
              android:layout_height="match_parent"
              >
</LinearLayout>
```

Start practicing some good design and programming habits. If you want to reference the instance of this `LinearLayout` within your Java code, a unique identifier greatly simplifies the process of gaining access to the instance. Add an `android:id` attribute to the `LinearLayout` this way:

```
android:id="@+id/mainLayout"
```

The special syntax of the `@+` characters within the string indicates that you want to add to the ID pool a new resource named `mainLayout` and associate the `id` attribute to it.

Because every XML tag corresponds to a class in the R file, every instance of the tag creates a new instance of that class. The ID is similar to a dictionary look-up to access a handle to this instance. See Chapter 2 for more on the R file.

Granted, the default background is a little boring — you can add an image as the background for this view. All `View` classes (and, therefore, all GUI classes) have the `android:background` attribute. This attribute can take a color or a drawable. Use the background image for this chapter (named `backdrop.jpg`), located on this book's companion website (at `www.dummies.com/go/android3sdkprogramming`), or your own preferred image. On a Windows computer, simply drag the image file from its folder into Eclipse and on top of the `res/drawable-mdpi` folder. In the dialog box that asks whether you want to copy or link to this file (see Figure 5-6), select Copy Files and click OK.

Figure 5-6:
In this
dialog box,
you add an
image to the
project.

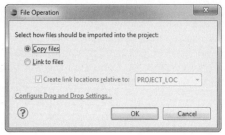

Three folders with the prefix `drawable` are in the `res` folder. They correspond to resources for devices that have low dots-per-inch (dpi) measurement, medium dpi, and high dpi, and they're named `res/drawable-ldpi`,
`res/drawable-mdpi`, and `res/drawable-hdpi`, respectively. If you have
only one resource, copy it to the appropriate folder; the system builds the
others for you. In any case, you access this resource by using `drawable/`
`filename` in the XML code, where `filename` doesn't include the file exten-
sion. Now add an attribute to set this image as the background:

```
android:background="@drawable/backdrop"
```

The resulting project should produce the result shown earlier, in Figure 5-5.

You add the `EditText` widgets between the `LinearLayout` closing bracket
and the end tag. Good design practice dictates a consistent look and feel.
Android assists in this goal by allowing custom resources and access to
these resources in both the code and the XML. We just showed you this strategy in setting the background attribute. Now you can look at adding string
resources, color resources, and dimension resources for your text boxes.

You can add resources within Eclipse in three primary ways (in addition to
the external drag-and-drop method):

- ✔ Using the Resource editor
- ✔ Editing the xml file directly
- ✔ Using Eclipse's code refactoring

All these resources are placed into the `res/values/strings.xml` file.
Open the `res/values` folder in the Eclipse Package Explorer window and
double-click the `strings.xml` file. The file opens with two views (denoted
by the tabs near the bottom of the window; see Figure 5-7). In the Resources
view, you can add a resource, delete a resource, and reorder resources. (Why
reorder? Because you can.) Click the Add button. A dialog box opens, asking
you to select the type of resource you want to add. Selecting the type lets the
system validate the resources so that they can be used wherever a value of
that type is needed. Select the Dimension entry and click OK. A new resource
has been added to the bottom of the list. You give it a name and value (or

change the name and value) by using the text fields to the right. Enter **fontSize** for the name and **9pt** for the value. When you save the `strings.xml` file, the changes appear in the list pane. If you switch views to the `strings.xml` view by using the `strings.xml` tab at the bottom, you can see that all you did was place a new entry in the `strings.xml` file — in this case, the following line:

```
<dimen name="fontSize">9pt</dimen>
```

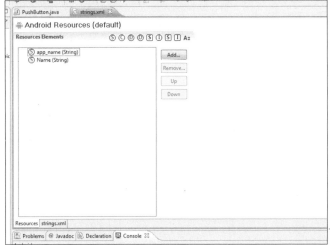

Figure 5-7:
Examining
the
`string.`
`xml`
resource
file.

Go back to Resources view and add a new resource. This time, select a `Color` resource and name it `textColor` and give it a value of `#ff0000` (scarlet). Returning to the `strings.xml` file, notice that a new tag has been added — except that this time it's a color tag. You use the tag string to reference the resource, so the font size is indicated by `"@dimen/fontSize"`, not by `"@Dimension/fontSize"`. In addition to adding the resources from Resource view, you can edit the `strings.xml` file directly.

A third technique for adding a resource is to use the refactoring tools within Eclipse. In XML, you have only one good option: Convert a string to a string resource.

Suppose that you add the following attribute to one of the `EditText` widgets:

```
android:text="Hello"
```

You want to remove the literal, "Hello," from the file and make it a resource because it might allow for internationalization later. You can easily accomplish this task by double-clicking `"Hello"` to select it and then choosing Android⇨Extract Android String from the Refactor menu.

Add the necessary resources to the `strings.xml` file to ensure that your file looks like this:

```
<?xml version="1.0" encoding="utf-8"?>
<resources>

    <string name="app_name">ContactView</string>
    <color name="textColor">#000000</color>
    <dimen name="fontSize">9pt</dimen>
    <dimen name="topMargin">0.1in</dimen>
    <dimen name="indent">0.1in</dimen>

</resources>
```

By storing the font size (`textSize`) in a resource, you need to change only the resource value to have the change propagated to all text boxes. This strategy greatly simplifies experimenting with the design while keeping the font characteristics consistent.

To make use of these resources, add an `EditText` component within the `LinearLayout`. Here's the description for the Name field in the example:

```
<EditText
    android:id="@+id/nameWidget"
    android:layout_width="match_parent"
    android:layout_height="wrap_content"
    android:hint="Enter Name ..."
    android:textStyle="bold"
    android:textSize="@dimen/fontSize"
    android:textColor="@color/textColor"
    android:layout_marginTop="@dimen/topMargin"
    android:singleLine="true"
    />
```

Note that the `textSize`, `textColor`, and `layout_marginTop` all make use of resources. You also added an ID resource for this widget. Because a name shouldn't span multiple lines of text, you set the `singleLine` attribute to `true`. In addition, you changed the `text` attribute to a `hint` attribute. Now there's no text, so if the user starts typing, no text needs to be deleted first. The `hint` attribute sets the text for a hint to be displayed instead of setting the text field. The hint is displayed whenever the text box is empty and appears (by default) in a grayed-out color.

To end our discussion of `LinearLayout` and how to customize the view, here's the final `main.xml` code:

```xml
<?xml version="1.0" encoding="utf-8"?>
<LinearLayout xmlns:android="http://schemas.android.com/
          apk/res/android"
    android:id="@+id/mainLayout"
    android:orientation="vertical"
    android:layout_width="match_parent"
    android:layout_height="match_parent"
    android:background="@drawable/backdrop"
    >
    <EditText
        android:id="@+id/nameWidget"
        android:layout_width="match_parent"
        android:layout_height="wrap_content"
        android:hint="Enter Name ..."
        android:textStyle="bold"
        android:textSize="@dimen/fontSize"
        android:textColor="@color/textColor"
        android:layout_marginTop="@dimen/topMargin"
        android:singleLine="true"
        />
    <EditText
        android:id="@+id/addressWidget"
        android:layout_width="match_parent"
        android:layout_height="wrap_content"
        android:layout_marginLeft="@dimen/indent"
        android:textSize="@dimen/fontSize"
        android:textColor="@color/textColor"
        android:hint="Address ..."
        android:gravity="top|left"
        android:lines="2"
        />
    <LinearLayout
        android:orientation="horizontal"
        android:layout_width="match_parent"
        android:layout_height="wrap_content"
        android:layout_marginLeft="@dimen/indent"
        >
        <EditText
            android:id="@+id/stateWidget"
            android:layout_width="wrap_content"
            android:layout_height="wrap_content"
            android:layout_weight="0.2"
            android:capitalize="characters"
            android:singleLine="true"
            android:textColor="@color/textColor"
            android:textSize="@dimen/fontSize"
            android:hint="State"
            />
        <EditText
            android:id="@+id/zipcodeWidget"
            android:layout_width="wrap_content"
```

```
                android:layout_height="wrap_content"
                android:layout_weight="0.5"
                android:layout_marginLeft="20sp"
                android:textColor="@color/textColor"
                android:textSize="@dimen/fontSize"
                android:singleLine="true"
                android:hint="Zip Code"
                android:numeric="integer"
                />
        <TextView
                android:layout_width="wrap_content"
                android:layout_height="wrap_content"
                android:layout_weight="0.1"
                android:gravity="center_horizontal"
                android:textColor="#ffffff"
                android:textSize="@dimen/fontSize"
                android:textScaleX="2"
                android:text="-"
                />
        <EditText
                android:id="@+id/zipExtWidget"
                android:layout_width="wrap_content"
                android:layout_height="wrap_content"
                android:layout_weight="0.4"
                android:textSize="@dimen/fontSize"
                android:textColor="@color/textColor"
                android:singleLine="true"
                android:digits="0123456789"
                android:hint="Ext"
                />
    </LinearLayout>
    <EditText
            android:id="@+id/phoneWidget"
            android:layout_width="match_parent"
            android:layout_height="wrap_content"
            android:layout_marginLeft="@dimen/indent"
            android:textSize="@dimen/fontSize"
            android:textColor="@color/textColor"
            android:hint="Phone number ..."
            android:singleLine="true"
            android:phoneNumber="true"
            />
</LinearLayout>
```

Whew! That's a nice little application. Well, not quite. Recall that it's just a mock-up — you've done no Java programming. However, now you have a firm grasp of LinearLayout and the attributes associated with layouts, views, and resources. There's even a phone number attribute for TextView. The LinearLayout is generally a good choice for small components of your user interface (such as the state and zip code). The next few sections describe some other choices that should be preferred for the top layout in the hierarchy.

LinearLayout is the base class for several other layouts, including TableLayout and its helper, TableRow, which are discussed in the following section. The RadioGroup layout is used to arrange a group of radio buttons, and though ZoomControls should be considered a widget rather than a layout, it's derived from LinearLayout. ZoomControls provides a good example of creating your own, custom widgets; it provides two customized buttons and the long-click behavior for continuous zooming. Similarly, TabWidget, covered later in this chapter, extends LinearLayout and should be considered a widget more than a layout.

Mocking up a simple calculator

To begin to understand why one layout might be preferred over another, you can take a look at different layout styles. In this section, we tell you how to create the user interface for a simple calculator. We have you use a single TableLayout to present the entire calculator because it lets us illustrate some table controls (rather than simply present the best solution).

Consider nesting a couple of layouts in your production code. For example, a text window on top of a grid of buttons suggests perhaps a LinearLayout containing two children: TextView and TableLayout. Two other good choices are RelativeLayout and FrameLayout.

Figure 5-8 shows the result you're shooting for. It makes sense that TableLayout extends the LinearLayout class, because a table is a set of TableRows stacked on top of (or underneath) each other. The basic structure of a table is shown in Figure 5-9.

Figure 5-8:
A calculator interface.

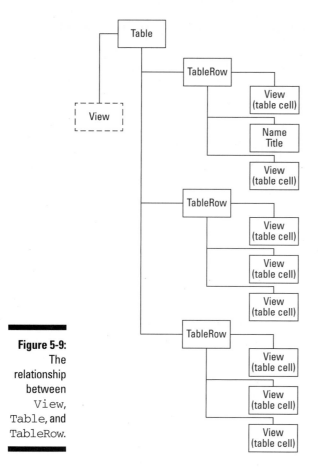

Figure 5-9:
The
relationship
between
`View`,
`Table,` and
`TableRow`.

Deciphering the structure of a table

The `TableLayout` in XML is similar to the HTML `<table>` element. A `TableLayout` contains a collection of `TableRows`, each of which is similar to the `<tr>` element in HTML. For individual cells, you can use any kind of `View` element, including another layout element. Here's the code for the table row in the bottom row of the calculator:

```
<TableRow>
    <Button
        android:id="@+id/btnNum0"
        android:text="0"
        android:layout_width="match_parent"
        android:layout_height="wrap_content"
```

```
            android:layout_weight="1" />
    <Button
        android:id="@+id/btnClear"
        android:text="C"
        android:layout_width="match_parent"
        android:layout_height="wrap_content"
        android:background="@drawable/clearbutton"
        android:textColor="#ffffff"
        android:layout_weight="1" />
    <Button
        android:id="@+id/btnEqual"
        android:text="="
        android:layout_width="match_parent"
        android:layout_height="wrap_content"
        android:layout_weight="1" />
    <Button
        android:id="@+id/btnAdd"
        android:text="+"
        android:layout_width="match_parent"
        android:layout_height="wrap_content"
        android:layout_weight="1" />
</TableRow>
```

This code snippet adds the Zero, Clear, Equals, and Addition buttons. You assign each button a layout weight of 1 to achieve equal spacing. Every button is assigned an ID so that you can respond properly to the button being clicked. The text color of the Clear button changes to white, and its background is set to the `drawable` resource named `clearbutton`. We tell you how to produce this red button in Chapter 6.

Using Greedy widgets that take up multiple columns

The first row in the table contains a single `TextView` item to display the result. However, it must span the entire table. How many columns does the table have? The number of columns is determined by the maximum number of children in each row. If one `TableRow` has 12 children, the table has 12 columns. Every row of the table can have a different number of children, and every child can be a different size. In other words, the `TableLayout` isn't a 2D grid or *n*-by-*n* matrix. It's simply a collection of Views with some coordination among rows. Each `View` element is typically a `TableRow`, but even this constraint isn't enforced. (See the later sidebar "Jumbled table karma" for more insights and technical details for controlling the table column sizes — or not.)

The table in the Calculator app spans four columns. It has six rows, and all except the results widget row and the line below it have four columns. For the result window, `TextView` spans all four columns of the table. You accomplish this task by using the `android:layout_span` attribute within `TextView`.

Here's the definition for the `TableRow` containing the result window `TextView` (we added a 20-space margin for aesthetic purposes):

```
<TableRow>
    <!-- The Result Window -->
    <TextView
        android:id="@+id/resultView"
        android:background="#000000"
        android:textColor="#ffffff"
        android:typeface="monospace"
        android:text="0.0"
        android:gravity="right"
        android:textSize="12pt"
        android:layout_span="4"
        android:layout_width="match_parent"
        android:layout_margin="20sp"
    />
</TableRow>
```

The results widget also has a black background with white text using a 12-point monospace font. Again, you would be wise to place these font characteristic decisions in the `strings.xml` file or another resource file.

Adding non-TableRow elements

Another portion of the calculator is the red, horizontal line below the result window. You create this effect by adding a naked `View` to the table. Because the heavyweight `View` class is fully functional, it can be used as a blank canvas for adding space or other occurrences of `drawable`. In this example, the background is set to a constant color. To create the appearance of a line, you set the height of `View` to a small value — in this case, five *pixels*. The following code snippet creates the second row of the table:

```
<View
    android:layout_height="5px"
    android:background="#990000"
    android:layout_marginBottom="10sp"
    >
</View>
```

This example adds a margin to push the buttons away from the line. You can find the complete source code for the Calculator app on this book's web page.

Jumbled table karma

Table layout construction can be cumbersome and tricky with cells containing differing amounts of content, because an intense negotiation battle for precious screen real estate is taking place between each widget and the table logic. Fundamentally, the goals of automatic layout algorithms are to present as much of the content as possible, by contracting or expanding space as necessary. If an individual widget in a table cell suddenly needs more space, it's preferable to remove some air (empty space) from certain columns and adjust other column sizes to include (use) that space. Column widths were previously specified upfront and fixed, leading to a great deal of frustration. Machine intelligence can reason only so far and is based on the information provided by the designer. A single `TableLayout` can cause so much confusion to the layout manager that no sane person would even call it a table. The layout manager has to decide what to do with empty cells and how to handle large content while also accommodating every widget's `layout_weight` and the table attributes `android:stretchColumns` and `android:shrinkColumns`.

Keeping things consistent

The lack of a rigorous table specification and the lax "anything goes" mentality of `TableLayout` allows for great flexibility. By now, you may have an appreciation of the complexity of the decision-making process that takes place in a layout manager. The old adage "garbage in, garbage out" applies well to table construction. Because the table has been around since the early days of HTML and office publishing, it's often considered the layout manager of choice, even if the data or widget to be presented isn't tabular.

Figure 5-10 shows an app with a single `TableLayout` view as the root. It may be difficult to see, but it has seven columns. Trying to line up any of these columns with the various empty cells and the lack of spanning and shrinkable and stretchable settings is quite difficult.

When using `TableLayout`, try to follow these guidelines (because the system doesn't make you follow them):

- ✔ Ensure that every occurrence of `TableRow` has the same number of columns.

- ✔ If a `TableRow` must have fewer columns, use the `layout_span` attribute to consume the same number of columns.

- ✔ Mark only a few columns as shrinkable.

- ✔ Mark all columns as stretchable or reduce the `TableLayout` width.

✔ Set the `TableLayout` width to `wrap_content` for small tables.

✔ Limit to a single column any content that drastically changes its size. If this column isn't the last one, mark it as shrinkable and allow it to span multiple lines.

Figure 5-10:
A messy,
jumbled
table.

The table can be a useful part of your user interface. In the next few sections, we cover some higher-level layouts that typically contain `LinearLayout` and `TableLayout` — one of the most important is `RelativeLayout`. After you have a solid understanding of layouts, we can present the remaining available layouts in more of a reference style.

Allowing columns to shrink whenever necessary

Every column in a table can be *shrinkable*, which shrinks a child of a `TableRow` if none of the children in the row fits. This situation is different from `wrap_content` in that `shrinkable` pushes the column to a size smaller than its data and increases the row height. The following figure shows you several tables measuring 2-rows-by-3-columns (separated by text labels, or `TextView` elements). In the first table, no column is set to be shrinkable. In this case, whether a column is shrinkable is immaterial because all the data fits within the parent view, the `TableLayout`.

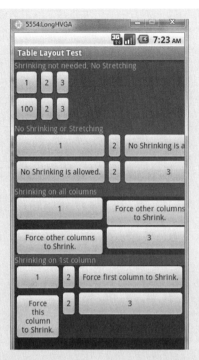

The second table in the figure has two buttons, which require more space than an individual TableRow can handle. Without shrinkable columns, the last column is pushed off the edge of the view.

If you set all columns willy-nilly to be shrink-able, the layout manager tries to be fair and trims some space from every control equally. It does this after it determines each control's minimum size, so the third table in the figure shows the first column being compressed and the second column apparently being removed (or simply trimmed away!). The width of the column shrunk too much to display even a single character and couldn't even display itself. You set all columns to be shrinkable by using the TableLayout attribute:

```
android:shrinkColumns="*"
```

Because Columns 1 and 3 in this table were also shrunk to less than their desired size, they were forced to push their data onto additional lines (which Column 2 couldn't do with a single character). And now, being able to set the android:baselineAligned attribute in the LinearLayout class to false is useful. In the sidebar figure, the TableRow (which extends LinearLayout) tries to maintain the alignment of the baseline of the first line of text, which causes the buttons with multiple text lines to shift down as their text is shifted up within the button.

A final experiment is to set one column as shrinkable (which is how you should use this feature). You're saying that the data in this column isn't critical and can be compressed or clipped. The last table in the sidebar figure has the first column as shrinkable, which causes the second and third columns to return to their desired sizes, sacrificing Column 1. You do this by using the following line:

```
android:shrinkColumns="0"
```

The baseline attribute was set to false in both TableRow definitions to align the tops of the buttons.

Allowing columns to stretch to fill space

In addition to being shrinkable, a column can be set to stretchable. Then the layout manager tries to give this column more space if the set of columns doesn't fill the entire parent view (TableLayout). Recall that all children of the TableLayout (the TableRows) have their layout widths changed to match_parent (fill_parent). All rows must therefore span the table width. We aren't saying that the display of the controls must span the width. The following figure shows five 2 x 3 tables. The first table has no stretchable columns. Every control is granted the space it requested, and no columns are expanded. The remainder of the TableRow is padded to fill the TableLayout.

In the second table in this figure, all columns are set to be stretchable by using the following attribute in the TableLayout tag:

```
android:stretchColumns="*"
```

This setting, typically a useful one, tells the layout manager to give all columns their desired sizes plus an equal amount of extra padding. The first column in this table has more content (more text on the button, resulting in a wider button), so it had an initial desired size larger than the other columns. Hence the first column occupies more space.

In the third table, only the second column (Column 1) is allowed to stretch, so it receives all the extra padding. Again, you indicate it in XML by using the `TableLayout` attribute:

```
android:stretchColumns="1"
```

The first and third columns are exactly the same size as the first table without stretching. For applications such as this one, and in our calculator example, an equal size for every column often looks better.

To do this, you must "trick" the layout system:

For a uniform column size, you need a third option for setting the width of a widget. We typically use either of these attributes:

`android:wrap_content` adjusts the size of the control to the minimum that's needed.

`android:match_parent` adjusts the size to the maximum amount of remaining available space in the parent (so far) and the amount returned by `wrap_content`.

A control (or widget) can also have its width and height specified using a dimension, such as `0.1in`. The dimension overrides any of the calculations just mentioned and sets the size of the control to the specified amount. If the data display needs more space than the specified size, it's either clipped or (for some, such as `TextView`) wrapped to another line and the height adjusted if the size isn't fixed.

For the fourth and fifth tables in the preceding figure, all controls (`Button`'s, in this case) have a small fixed value (such as 0) that tells the system, "I need only this amount of space." In the fourth table, no stretching is allowed, so every column gets the maximum fixed amount

that's specified for that column. Here's the XML code for this table:

```xml
<TableLayout
    android:layout_
    width="match_parent"
    android:layout_
    height="wrap_content"
    android:background="@
    color/line1"
    >
    <TableRow
        >
        <Button
            android:text="1"
            android:layout_
    width="20dip" />
        <Button
            android:text="2"
            android:layout_
    width="20dip"/>
        <Button
            android:text="3"
            android:layout_
    width="20dip"/>
    </TableRow>
    <TableRow>
        <Button

    android:text="10000"
            android:layout_
    width="10dip" />
        <Button
            android:text="2"
            android:layout_
    width="10dip" />
        <Button
            android:text="3"
            android:layout_
    width="10dip" />
    </TableRow>
</TableLayout>
```

In this case, every column has a desired size of 20 device-independent pixels *(dip)* because that's the maximum size between the two rows. Every `Button` is then expanded to this size, so even though the second row wants only 10dip per button, it receives 20dip per button. The

(continued)

(continued)

Button with the text string "10000" spans multiple lines even though the numbers aren't visible.

Setting all columns to be stretchable adds an equal amount of space to every column. Because in this example every column is the same size, a uniform column size that spans the table is created, as shown in the last table of the preceding figure. Finally, if a column has, for example, a fixed size that's twice the size of the other columns, the column, when expanded, is twice the size of the others.

It might seem that weights would provide the same control, but they don't. They simply provide a hint to the system. If content amounts differ, this necessary size overrides the weights. However, if stretching is turned off, weights perform stretching. So combining a fixed size with stretching or a fixed size with weights produces the same effect of uniform or proportional column sizes. The proportions can be specified in either the size or the weights. In any case, if your content exceeds the column size, data is clipped and isn't presented.

RelativeLayout: Flexibility du Jour

The most flexible of the standard layouts, Relative Layout allows every child View position to be defined relative to its siblings or the parent's boundaries, or both. Here's the example from the RelativeLayout tutorial on the Android SDK website:

```xml
<?xml version="1.0" encoding="utf-8"?>
<RelativeLayout xmlns:android="http://schemas.android.com/apk/res/android"
    android:layout_width="match_parent"
    android:layout_height="match_parent">
    <TextView
        android:id="@+id/label"
        android:layout_width="match_parent"
        android:layout_height="wrap_content"
        android:text="Type here:"/>
    <EditText
        android:id="@+id/entry"
        android:layout_width="match_parent"
        android:layout_height="wrap_content"
        android:background="@android:drawable/editbox_background"
        android:layout_below="@id/label"/>
    <Button
        android:id="@+id/ok"
        android:layout_width="wrap_content"
        android:layout_height="wrap_content"
        android:layout_below="@id/entry"
        android:layout_alignParentRight="true"
        android:layout_marginLeft="10dip"
        android:text="OK" />
    <Button
        android:layout_width="wrap_content"
```

```
        android:layout_height="wrap_content"
        android:layout_toLeftOf="@id/ok"
        android:layout_alignTop="@id/ok"
        android:text="Cancel" />
</RelativeLayout>
```

This example results in the view shown in Figure 5-11. In a nutshell, you have `TextView` with `EditText` below it, which has, in turn, the OK and Cancel buttons below it. The OK button is also anchored to the right of the overall view (`RelativeLayout`). The Cancel button is anchored to the left of the OK button and its top is aligned with the OK button (which places it below `EditText`). Every widget (except Cancel) has an ID associated with it, which the other widgets can reference in their alignment specifications.

Figure 5-11:
Using
Rela-
tive-
Layout.

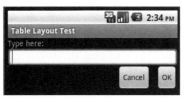

`RelativeLayout` defines the `RelativeLayout.LayoutParams` class, which extends `MarginLayoutParams`. It adds the attributes listed in Table 5-2, which the children of a `RelativeLayout` can use to control their positioning.

Table 5-2   Attributes for the RelativeLayout.LayoutParams Class

Attribute Name	What It Does
`android:layout_above`	Positions the bottom edge of this view above the specified anchor view ID
`android:layout_align-Baseline`	Positions the baseline of this view on the baseline of the specified anchor view ID
`android:layout_align-Bottom`	Makes the bottom edge of this view match the bottom edge of the specified anchor view ID
`android:layout_align-Left`	Makes the left edge of this view match the left edge of the specified anchor view ID
`android:layout_align-ParentBottom`	If set to `true`, makes the bottom edge of this view match the bottom edge of the parent

(continued)

Table 5-2 *(continued)*

Attribute Name	What It Does
android:layout_align-ParentLeft	If set to true, makes the left edge of this view match the left edge of the parent
android:layout_align-ParentRight	If set to true, makes the right edge of this view match the right edge of the parent
android:layout_align-ParentTop	If set to true, makes the top edge of this view match the top edge of the parent
android:layout_align-Right	Makes the right edge of this view match the right edge of the specified anchor view ID
android:layout_alignTop	Makes the top edge of this view match the top edge of the specified anchor view ID
android:layout_align-WithParentIfMissing	If set to true, parent is used as the anchor when the anchor cannot be found for layout_toLeftOf and layout_toRightOf, for example
android:layout_below	Positions the top edge of this view below the specified anchor view ID
android:layout_center-Horizontal	If set to true, centers this child horizontally within its parent
android:layout_center-InParent	If set to true, centers this child horizontally and vertically within its parent
android:layout_center-Vertical	If set to true, centers this child vertically within its parent
android:layout_toLeftOf	Positions the right edge of this view to the left of the specified anchor view ID
android:layout_toRightOf	Positions the left edge of this view to the right of the specified anchor view ID

These attributes allow an alignment with any sibling as long as you gave them IDs (using the android:id attribute) as well as alignment with the parent edges or centering within the parent. Think of them as snap-on parts. If you're familiar with Windows .NET Forms or WPF, this concept is similar to the Anchor properties.

As every new view is added to RelativeLayout, it defines two vertical gridlines (one for the left edge of the widget and one for the right edge) and three horizontal gridlines (top, bottom, and baseline). Any new view can use these (abstract) gridlines to request its position. As it's added, it introduces its own gridlines, some of which are co-located with existing gridlines. This concept is shown schematically in Figure 5-12.

Figure 5-12:
Snapping
widgets to
align with
other
widgets.

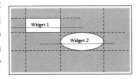

In Figure 5-12, after Widget 1 is placed, all future widgets position themselves horizontally to align one of their edges to the left or right edge of Widget 1. Thus, there are four possible choices for horizontal alignment (one for each edge) for the new widget, Widget 2 — left and right; you can align the widget with either of the two vertical edges from Widget 1:

✔ Align Widget 2's left edge with the left edge of Widget 1.

✔ Align Widget 2's left edge with the right edge of Widget 1.

✔ Align Widget 2's right edge with the left edge of Widget 1.

✔ Align Widget 2's right edge with the right edge of Widget 1.

Vertical alignment (with the horizontal gridlines) gives you five possible choices to align with another widget:

✔ top-top

✔ top-bottom

✔ bottom-top

✔ bottom-bottom

✔ baseline-baseline

The use of the `Baseline` constant aligns the first row of text with the baseline of the specified widget's text.

Edge refers not to the edge of the displayed widget but, rather, to the edge of the widget plus any margins.

You may recall that the layout manager determines the positions of every gridline based on such factors as the widget size and margins, for example. As the content of one widget grows, it forces the other widgets to maintain its alignment.

Avoid creating a chicken-and-egg situation in which one widget needs another widget's position to determine its position but the position can't be calculated because it requires (eventually) the first widget's position. For example, if `RelativeLayout` has its height set to `wrap_content` and a child is set to `align_parent_bottom`, a circular dependency exists, which results in a run-time error.

`RelativeLayout` is useful for both high-level design and smaller components, such as a standard right-aligned Okay or Cancel confirmation, a login component, or the `TwoLineListItem` widget, which derives from `RelativeLayout`. Though both `TableLayout` and `RelativeLayout` manage the 2D spatial relationships between the many widgets in its hierarchy, `FrameLayout` (described in the following section) allows only one of its children at a time to be seen but reserves enough space to show each one seamlessly.

The FrameLayout layout

The important `FrameLayout` class, which forms the base for many other classes, simply pins every child view to the upper-left corner. Adding multiple children stacks each new child on top of the one before it, with each new child obscuring the last. If the new child is transparent or smaller, it may only partially obscure its previous siblings.

The size of the frame layout is the size of its largest child (plus padding), visible or not. All children, when rendered, are basically given this size but pinned to the upper-left corner. Using the `layout_gravity` of a child widget allows the widget to appear to move away from the upper-left corner. Thus, `FrameLayout` is often used to provide an overlay effect. The following XML code (taken from `http://developer.android.com/resources/articles/layout-tricks-merge.html`) places a text label centered near the bottom of the view over the much larger image being displayed:

```
<FrameLayout xmlns:android="http://schemas.android.com/apk/res/android"
    android:layout_width="match_parent"
    android:layout_height="match_parent">

    <ImageView
        android:layout_width="match_parent"
        android:layout_height="match_parent"

        android:scaleType="center"
        android:src="@drawable/golden_gate" />

    <TextView
        android:layout_width="wrap_content"
        android:layout_height="wrap_content"
        android:layout_marginBottom="20dip"
        android:layout_gravity="center_horizontal|bottom"

        android:padding="12dip"

        android:background="#AA000000"
```

```
            android:textColor="#ffffffff"

            android:text="Golden Gate" />

    </FrameLayout>
```

The result is shown in Figure 5-13. This layout works and adjusts the sizes of the widgets, regardless of the image sizes or the amount of text in the caption label.

Figure 5-13:
An
example of
using the
Frame-
Layout
class.

The `FrameLayout` class is used as the base for the `ScrollView`, `ImageSwitcher`, `TabHost`, and `ViewAnimator` layouts and the date and time picker widgets, and for many more layout and widget classes. It has associated with it a `FrameLayout.LayoutParams` class that derives from the `MarginLayoutParams` class and adds the gravity layout attribute.

Chapter 6 covers more user interface support to make these more functional.

Choosing the Right Layout

The layout manager you should choose is the one that makes your life easiest, of course, while still providing your users with the functionality they require. The same design can probably be implemented using several approaches and top-level layout managers. In this section, we help you consider which layout managers work best in which situations. Though you should follow general guidelines, exceptions to the rule always exist, so use your best judgment. Fundamentally, your choices are dictated by the data to be gathered or presented and when it's needed:

- ✔ If your application has a fairly linear progression of user interaction, `ScrollView` with `RelativeLayout` or `TableLayout` may be your best bet.

- ✔ For applications with several activities, each with its own user interface, consider using `ImageSwitcher`, `SlidingDrawer`, `TabHost`, `TextSwitcher`, `ViewFlipper`, or `ViewSwitcher`. They allow the layout to be changed (and often replaced), presenting an entirely new set of widgets.

The best user interface presents the most important information in a way that's clearly visible and easy to use while allowing less-often-used items to be accessed.

Use the command-line tool `layoutopt` in the Tools SDK to find inefficiencies in your XML-based layouts.

Here are several more guidelines you should follow when developing your Android apps:

- ✔ **Buy a physical Android phone or tablet.** In fact, buy several. The experience of installing and running your application on a physical device is different from running it on the emulator.

- ✔ **Design for big fingers.** Many people have large fingers and clicking small buttons can be an adventure.

- ✔ **Design for both horizontal and vertical screen orientations.** The layout on many mobile devices changes as the orientation of the device changes or the keyboard is used.

- ✔ **Avoid putting too much information on a tiny screen.** Hide features that aren't used most of the time.

- ✔ **Scrolling can be confusing in a user interface, so try to make your data fit on the screen.** If you can't, logically group functionality and split it into several windows or tabs. Save scrolling for long chunks of data that cannot be broken into several pieces.

- ✔ **Don't overload the menu.** The contextual menu has to be used quickly. If you have a lot of information, create one entry for a submenu named More, as Google does on its main page (at `www.google.com`).

- ✔ **Always notify the user whenever an app may be consuming resources that aren't free.** For example, an app may be sending data across the network that consumes a user's data plan quota.

↙ **The user experience with your app should be consistent with other apps they commonly use.** Don't try to be clever by introducing nonstandard behaviors. The following behaviors should be consistent:

- *Pressing the Back button cancels the current action.* Pressing Back saves the state, quits the app, and waits for you to return, a behavior that's fundamentally different from most desktop applications. It's similar to minimizing the window on a desktop, except that, to restore the window, you launch the application again.

- *A tap typically performs an action.* Confirmation screens that ask you to save or confirm actions are even more annoying on a small device than they are on a desktop. If a user taps a setting, the setting should change. If a user makes a change and taps the Back button, the setting's change should persist.

- *When you reopen an app, it should return to the last state it was in.* Tapping the Back button doesn't close an app. You return it to the same state it was in by using the `onResume/onCreate/onPause` method.

- *If a long pause occurs between the time an app was last used and then reopened, starting the app from an initial default state is reasonable.* The rationale is that a long pause implies a new task or "train of thought" and, therefore, a clean slate. This concept is, of course, application dependent, but consider it in your design.

Chapter 6

Enhancing Your Layout with Widgets, Styles, and Themes

Designing the overall layout is only one piece of the puzzle involved in creating a user interface for your app. In this chapter, we describe the basic views used for individual data entry or selection. You can modify these views for your own app's style or allow users to apply their own themes. If this level of control isn't sufficient for you, the entire suite of drawing tools is available to create your own, custom controls.

Beholding the Power of the Framework: Built-In Views

The Android SDK provides a rich and fairly comprehensive set of components for you to use in your apps. Figure 6-1 shows the class hierarchy of the built-in widgets. (The children of `ViewGroup` have been omitted, for brevity.) All are available in the `Android.widget` package. Most of them have been in the framework beginning with version 1. `KeyboardView` and `GLSurfaceView` were added in version 3, and `QuickContactBadge` was added in version 5. The `RSSurfaceView` class is the new addition to version 11 (Android 3.0). `RSSurfaceView` is not a true widget but, rather, a raw surface on which to draw and, in this case, an OpenGL ES surface for Renderscript. `RSSurfaceView` replaces `GLSurfaceView`.

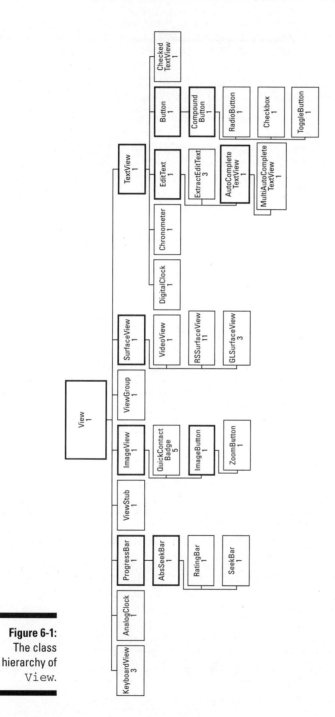

Figure 6-1:
The class
hierarchy of
View.

New widgets can be created by deriving and extending any of these classes. In deciding which widget to use for your application, consider these two questions:

✔ Which View is the easiest for your users to use in performing the necessary action?

✔ Which View will lead to the fewest number of errors?

It may be difficult to believe, but early computer applications had no menus, no combo boxes, no date pickers, and no buttons — and the mouse didn't enter the scene until even later. You had to memorize various keystrokes or keywords in order to interact with an application, a situation that still exists on many command-line applications. Typing the wrong command can lead to frustration and unwanted results. One helpful feature of a *combo box,* for example, is that it limits user choices to ones that the application knows about, which prevents syntactical errors. Much like a menu, a *combo box* also provides the user with information about the permissible choices, allowing the exploration of options that may not be obvious in a legacy application.

An individual GUI component is often referred to as a *widget* — not to be confused with an Android App Widget, which can be hosted in a special class of apps. They're similar in that an Android widget is supposed to be small enough to be considered a single component. You also see widgets referred to as *components* (as we have done here) or *elements* of the GUI.

Chapter 5 covers the nitty-gritty details of a button and its relationship to the View class. In this chapter, we look at the higher-level functionality of a button, including its behavior and the different appearances it can take on.

Working with a push button

You might already know (if you read Chapter 5) that a GUI component can be added either programmatically or by using XML-based layout files. In honor of Homer, from *The Simpsons,* we show you how to create a giant button to override the local nuclear power plant. Create a new app and, in the onCreate method, add a button, like this:

```
@Override
public void onCreate(Bundle savedInstanceState) {
    super.onCreate(savedInstanceState);
    LinearLayout layout = new LinearLayout(this);
    Button dohButton = new Button(this);
    dohButton.setText("In case of meltdown, Push Me!");

    layout.addView(dohButton);
    setContentView(layout);
}
```

This code snippet creates a button, sets the text of the button to *In case of meltdown, Push Me!,* and adds the button to LinearLayout, which is then set to the View content of the app. You can change the appearance of this button quite simply. If you add the following statements after you create the button (but before you set the app's content), your button is sized and colored, as shown in Figure 6-2:

```
dohButton.setText("In case of meltdown, Push Me!");
dohButton.setWidth(400);
dohButton.setPadding(30,45,30,45);
dohButton.setTextColor(0xFFFF0000);
dohButton.setTypeface(Typeface.DEFAULT_BOLD);
```

Figure 6-2:
The result
of program-
matically
creating
Button
and setting
some of its
attributes.

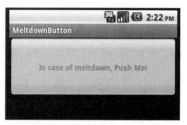

This example sets the width of the Button in terms of pixels so that it's 400 pixels wide. The text color is set to red using a hexadecimal number in the format #AARRGGBB. A regular base-10 number could have been used here, but would actually be more difficult to read, as the digits in the number would not relate to the individual color channels: alpha, red, green, and blue.

The *alpha channel* in a color controls its transparency. An alpha of 255 (#FF, in hexadecimal format) implies an opaque color, and a 0 alpha is transparent (invisible).

The example also sets the padding to create a bigger button. Though you can set the background color just as easily as you set the text color, it destroys the "look" of a button. In fact, the Button class is more specifically called a *push button* (because its three-dimensional appearance makes the button look like it's "popping out" of the phone, like a keyboard key). Pushing the button changes its appearance temporarily, verifying for the user that the push button is valid. Unfortunately, setting the background color destroys this process. The button has no 3D look and doesn't change colors when it's pushed.

Two methods set the font and typeface of text. The method just described uses the default font and only specifies bold. All these customizations are in either the base class, `TextView`, or the `View` class.

`Button` has no method to set an image or icon for a button. You can use the `ImageButton` class (derived from `ImageView`, not `Button`) for buttons with images only. If you want a button with a stylized background and text, you replace the entire background of the button using a *drawable resource.* (See "Pretty in pink: Creating custom buttons," later in this chapter). The following section helps you make this button useful.

Creating Tic-Tac-Toe using push buttons

In this section, we show you how to rework the Tic-Tac-Toe application (see Chapter 2) to use buttons so that you can programmatically control whether the text is displayed, whether the button is enabled (or can be pushed), and how to handle the game logic when a button is pressed.

You start by making a layout with nine large buttons. As we explain in Chapter 5, you can use several layouts for this task. The following chunk of XML uses a set of three `LinearLayout`s with horizontal orientation inside a `LinerLayout` with a vertical orientation. Every button is given a weight equal to 1, as is every internal `LinearLayout`, to provide uniform button spacing. The following code example produces this layout by using XML:

```xml
<?xml version="1.0" encoding="utf-8"?>
<LinearLayout xmlns:android="http://schemas.android.com/apk/res/android"
    android:orientation="vertical"
    android:layout_width="fill_parent"
    android:layout_height="fill_parent"
    >
  <LinearLayout
    android:orientation="horizontal"
    android:layout_width="fill_parent"
    android:layout_height="fill_parent"
   android:layout_weight="1"
      >
      <Button
        android:hint="play"
        android:layout_width="fill_parent"
        android:layout_height="fill_parent"
        android:layout_weight="1"
        />
      <Button
        android:hint = "play"
        android:layout_width="fill_parent"
```

```
                    android:layout_height="fill_parent"
                    android:layout_weight="1"
                    />
          <Button
                    android:hint = "play"
                    android:layout_width="fill_parent"
                    android:layout_height="fill_parent"
                    android:layout_weight="1"
                    />
    </LinearLayout>

    <LinearLayout
      android:orientation="horizontal"
      android:layout_width="fill_parent"
      android:layout_height="fill_parent"
    android:layout_weight="1"
          >
          <Button
                    android:hint="play"
                    android:layout_width="fill_parent"
                    android:layout_height="fill_parent"
                    android:layout_weight="1"
                    />
          <Button
                    android:hint = "play"
                    android:layout_width="fill_parent"
                    android:layout_height="fill_parent"
                    android:layout_weight="1"
                    />
          <Button
                    android:hint = "play"
                    android:layout_width="fill_parent"
                    android:layout_height="fill_parent"
                    android:layout_weight="1"
                    />
    </LinearLayout>

    <LinearLayout
      android:orientation="horizontal"
      android:layout_width="fill_parent"
      android:layout_height="fill_parent"
    android:layout_weight="1"
          >
          <Button
                    android:hint="play"
                    android:layout_width="fill_parent"
                    android:layout_height="fill_parent"
                    android:layout_weight="1"
                    />
          <Button
```

```
            android:hint = "play"
            android:layout_width="fill_parent"
            android:layout_height="fill_parent"
            android:layout_weight="1"
            />
        <Button
            android:hint = "play"
            android:layout_width="fill_parent"
            android:layout_height="fill_parent"
            android:layout_weight="1"
            />
    </LinearLayout>
</LinearLayout>
```

Every `Button` is given a hint with the text string `"play"`. Recall that the hint is displayed whenever the text is empty. In this example, it's used to indicate that the square hasn't yet been played. (Figure 6-3 shows the result of using this layout.) If you prefer an empty space, simply delete the hint attributes.

Figure 6-3:
The initial state of the tic-tac-toe board using push buttons: No text in the button and the Hint property set to play.

Creating a GUI with Java

Our purpose in this chapter is to illustrate code-based GUI control, so you should also look at how to create the Tic-Tac-Toe application entirely programmatically. When you set the content for the view of the activity by using the following call in the `onCreate` method of the `Activity`, it uses an XML-based layout (that was compiled into an R file — see Chapter 2).

```
setContentView(R.layout.main);
```

Replace the preceding line with the following two lines:

```
View ticTacToe = createTicTacToe();
setContentView(ticTacToe);
```

The createTicTacToe method is a new method you need to write in order
to create the content. The layout requires four LinearLayout instances and
nine Buttons. To increase code readability, the createTicTacToe method
creates three rows using the createRow method, which creates three
Buttons. Continuing a top-down design, the createTicTacToe method
looks something like this:

```
private View createTicTacToe()
{
                        LinearLayout root = new
        LinearLayout(this);
                        LinearLayout row1 =
    createRow(0);
                        LinearLayout row2 =
    createRow(1);
                        LinearLayout row3 =
    createRow(2);

                        root.addView(row1);
                        root.addView(row2);
                        root.addView(row3);

                        root.
        setOrientation(LinearLayout.VERTICAL);
                        return root;
}
```

This example creates a LinearLayout instance that's eventually returned
as the variable root. Another helper method, createRow, is used to create
each row of the tic-tac-toe board. It returns an instance of a LinearLayout
which is added to the base LinearLayout, root. The default orientation
for LinearLayout is horizontal, and the method setOrientation is used
to change it to vertical, which provides the basic layout for the tic-tac-toe
board.

The method createRow takes in a single Integer parameter to indicate
which row is being created. You use this row number to assign a unique
identifier to every button. You also use the row number to set a Hint for the
Button, changing the XML design slightly. Here's the first implementation:

```
private LinearLayout createRow(int rowNumber)
{
                        int index = 3 * rowNumber+1;
                        LinearLayout.LayoutParams layout
        = new LinearLayout.LayoutParams(-1,-1,1.0f);

                        LinearLayout row = new
        LinearLayout(this);
                        row.setLayoutParams(layout);

                        Button space = new Button(this);
                        space.setId(index);
                        space.setHint(Integer.
        toString(index));
                        space.setLayoutParams(layout);
                        row.addView(space);

                        space = new Button(this);
                        space.setId(index);
                        index++;
                        space.setHint(Integer.
        toString(index));
                        space.setLayoutParams(layout);
                        row.addView(space);

                        space = new Button(this);
                        space.setId(index);
                        index++;
                        space.setHint(Integer.
        toString(index));
                        space.setLayoutParams(layout);
                        row.addView(space);

                        return row;
}
```

Several packages need to be imported — in particular, the following:

```
import android.view.View;
import android.widget.Button;
import android.widget.LinearLayout;
```

Build and run this application now. You should see a board similar to the one shown in Figure 6-3, except the hint is now a number for each button. Note the ordering of the numbers: They increase across the row and then down the columns. This is the order in which you added the Buttons to LinearLayout and the order in which LinearLayouts were added to the top-level LinearLayout. The margins and cell padding remain at the default setting. Going forward, the appearance of the button is controlled depending on its state (playable, occupied by X, or occupied by O).

After you have specified the app's basic appearance, you can look at handling its basic behaviors (refer to Chapter 3), such as a large X being placed in a square after the user clicks a button.

Handling basic Button behaviors

For an application such as Tic-Tac-Toe, a Button should change its state whenever it's pushed, which is exactly what the ToggleButton is designed for. Tic-Tac-Toe has the added constraint of a button being allowed to be pressed only once. You use the default Button to accomplish this task. As you can see, many classes deeper in the class hierarchy are simple customizations of the base class — in this case, Button.

To handle button clicks (or taps, on modern touchscreens), the interface OnClickListener needs to be implemented. This interface, defined in the View class, has one method that must be implemented. The onClick method takes as input the View, which occupies the screen where the click event happened. The system doesn't automatically call the onClick method that you define in the Activity class. Good software engineering principles may require you to have one or more classes that handle click (or tap) events. In this case, every class would implement the OnClickListener interface. To determine which onClick method should be called, you have to explicitly tell the system for every widget which onClick method (or instance of OnClickListener) should be called. View has the setOnClickListener method to accomplish this. Passing it an instance of the View.OnClickListener performs two tasks:

- Sets the Clickable property to true
- Saves a reference to the OnClickListener, whose onClick method is called whenever a click occurs in View

The specification of the OnClickListener can occur for a parent or container, such as a LinearLayout in the application, but then that View is passed to the onClick method. For the Tic-Tac-Toe application, having the actual Button passed to the onClick method tells you precisely which square was selected. To do this, you add the following line every time a Button is created in the createRow method:

```
space.setOnClickListener(this);
```

Redefine Activity to implement the OnClickListener interface, similar to this line:

```
public class TicTacToeButtons extends Activity implements OnClickListener
```

Finally, add the implementation for the `onClick` method. You add a helper class to handle the button logic, named `GameLogic`. To use this class, you must cast the incoming `View` into a `Button`. (Programmatic error detection would also be wise at this point, but you've wired up only `Button`s so far, so this strategy should work well.) Here's the `onClick` method:

```
@Override
public void onClick(View view) {
    Button button = (Button) view;
    gameLogic.playSquare(button);
}
```

The next section looks at this `GameLogic` class to see how it works with the `Button`s it has passed.

Writing the GameLogic class

In addition to keeping track of which squares have already been played and by whom, the `GameLogic` class changes the state of the button when it's played. Separating these concerns would be ideal — in particular, separating button updates from the game logic, but for now you can put all this logic into the game logic.

The `Button` class can be used as a base class. Consider specializing this class even further and create a `TicTacToeButton` class that keeps track of its own state (playable, X, O).

The `GameLogic` class, which takes a `Button` to play a turn, tracks whose turn it is to play. Provide a parameter on the constructor to indicate whether the person playing X or O should go first, like this:

```
public class GameLogic {

    public GameLogic() {
        this(false);
    }
    public GameLogic(boolean oGoesFirst) {
        currentPlayer = 0;
        if( oGoesFirst) currentPlayer = 1;
    }
    private int currentPlayer = 0;
}
```

Two constructors are provided: a default or parameter-less constructor, which simply calls a constructor that takes a single `boolean` value to indicate whether O should go first (`true`) or X should go first (`false`).

As mentioned, the `playSquare` method takes a `Button` as a parameter. This method is the main interface with the game logic. It needs to determine which square is selected and change the `Button` appearance and state for that square. `playSquare` must also remember every player's turn in order to identify whether someone has won the game. Finally, it tracks which player plays next and updates the class for the next turn. Here's the implementation of `playSquare`:

```
public void playSquare(Button button)  {
    int id = button.getId();
    setButtonState(button);
    markSquare(id, currentPlayer);
    currentPlayer = (currentPlayer + 1) % 2;
}
```

The routine `setButtonState` takes as input a `Button` and changes:

- ✔ The `Button`'s clickable state to `false`
- ✔ The text of the button to either X or O based on the current player
- ✔ The text size of the button

Setting the button's clickable state to false ensures that the `Button` can be clicked only once. Setting the text indicates which player clicked the `Button`. Here's the implementation for `setButtonState`:

```
private void setButtonState(Button button) {
    button.setText(symbols[currentPlayer]);
    button.setTextSize(64);
    button.setClickable(false);
}
```

Using *scaled pixel* units to specify the text size lets the application ignore the details of the screen resolution. (The article about supporting multiple screens at `http://developer.android.com/guide/practices/screens_support.html` covers this topic in more detail.) The `setButton State` routine uses a simple variable, `symbols`, to set the `Button` text:

```
private String[] symbols = {"X", "O"};
```

Figure 6-4 shows the result of this logic after a player has taken two turns.

Figure 6-4:
Changing
the appear-
ance of a
Button.

The rest of the game logic — keeping score and determining a winner — is left as an exercise. If you run this application, note that after a Button is clicked, it cannot be clicked again.

A drawback of this application is that the tic-tac-toe board looks like a collection of buttons! The raised or three-dimensional appearance of buttons traditionally conveys to users that they should push them. Android users also receive feedback whenever they click buttons. We describe this concept in more detail in the following sections and tell you how to change the appearance of the Tic-Tac-Toe application.

Pretty in pink: Creating custom buttons

A better solution for the TicTacToe application is to derive a new button: TicTacToeButton. It provides a specialization that separates the behavior of a Tic-Tac-Toe square implemented as a button from the game logic. Virtually any View class can be used as a base class to derive your own user interface class.

Attempting to create a custom TicTacToeButton

In this section, you specialize the Button class — which is a specialization of the TextView class, which is a specialization of the View class. Though the Button class doesn't know which square it's on in the tic-tac-toe grid, it provides an easy-to-use set of methods that can set the state. Start with this example:

```
package com.wiley.fordummiessdk;

import android.content.Context;
import android.graphics.Canvas;
import android.graphics.Color;
import android.graphics.Paint;
import android.graphics.Paint.Align;
import android.widget.Button;
import android.widget.LinearLayout;

public class TicTacToeButton extends Button {
    private static String emptyString = "play";
    private static String xString = "X";
    private static String oString = "O";
    private static int emptyColor = Color.BLACK;
    private static int xColor = Color.WHITE;
    private static int oColor = Color.BLACK;
    private static int emptyBackgroundColor = Color.LTGRAY;
    private static int xBackgroundColor = Color.RED;
    private static int oBackgroundColor = Color.WHITE;
    private static float emptyFontScale = 16;
    private static float markedFontScale = 64;

    public TicTacToeButton(Context context) {
        super(context);
        LinearLayout.LayoutParams layout = new LinearLayout.LayoutParams(-1,-
                1,1.0f);
        this.setLayoutParams(layout);
        reset();
    }

    public void markX() {
        this.setText(xString);
        this.setTextSize(markedFontScale);
        this.setTextColor(xColor);
        this.setBackgroundColor(xBackgroundColor);

        this.setClickable(false);
    }

    public void markO() {
        this.setText(oString);
        this.setTextSize(markedFontScale);
        this.setTextColor(oColor);
        this.setBackgroundColor(oBackgroundColor);

        this.setClickable(false);
    }

    public void reset() {
```

```
        this.setText("");
        this.setHint(emptyString);
        this.setTextSize(emptyFontScale);
        this.setTextColor(emptyColor);
        this.setBackgroundColor(emptyBackgroundColor);

        this.setClickable(true);
    }

    public static void setTextColors(int empty, int x, int o) {
        emptyColor = empty;
        xColor = x;
        oColor = o;
    }

    public static void setBackgroundColors(int empty, int x, int o) {
        emptyBackgroundColor = empty;
        xBackgroundColor = x;
        oBackgroundColor = o;
    }

    public static void setFontSizes(float emptyScale, float markedScale) {
        emptyFontScale = emptyScale;
        markedFontScale = markedScale;
    }

    public static void setTextStrings(String empty, String x, String o) {
        emptyString = empty;
        xString = x;
        oString = o;
    }
}
```

This class has a set of static methods to set the default properties of
`TicTacToeButton`. These methods allow the user to set these properties
once and then create several instances. Having a default set of appearances
allows for easier customization of the button. Reasonable defaults were
already specified when these variables were defined.

Calling either of the two main routines `markX` and `markO` disables the button
(by setting its `Clickable` property to `false`) and sets the text, text scale,
and text color to the appropriate values. These routines also set the background color for the button. A button uses a drawable that by default provides a color gradient with some padding around this gradient. There is a
different default gradient for each of a button's three states: enabled, pushed,
and disabled. Setting the background color replaces all these default drawables, including the padding. Figure 6-5 shows the result: the grid associated
with a tic-tac-toe board is gone.

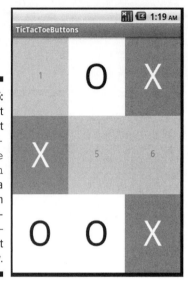

Figure 6-5:
A first
attempt at
TicTac-
Toe
Button
with a
custom
back-
ground —
not
satisfactory.

This problem is easily solved by creating new drawables that have the colors and styles you want. Alternatively, any class derived from View can specify its own onDraw method. This is the approach we will look at in the next section.

Overriding the onDraw method for custom drawing

The onDraw method is called whenever a control needs to be presented. Every widget can be thought of as a drawing. The system normally defines the drawing style and every class typically provides an implementation of the onDraw method. If the TicTacToeButton class were derived from View rather than from Button, you would have to provide your own implementation of onDraw. Because Button has an implementation, the example in the preceding section used it instead.

The onDraw method is passed a parameter of type Canvas. This Canvas provides the context for any drawing, as well as a rich set of methods for drawing. The Canvas class, which has methods to draw pictures, circles, lines, rectangles, and text, works closely with the Paint class, which provides colors and text attributes for the drawing calls.

For the TicTacToeButton class, a solid-colored rectangle centered in the view is needed for the background. The size of this rectangle needs to be slightly smaller than the size of the button. When you add a 12-pixel border around the "button," the background is shown outside this rectangle. In addition, the text needs to be centered using the specified text, scale, and color. The implementation of the onDraw method is similar to this example:

```
@Override
protected void onDraw(Canvas canvas) {
    super.onDraw(canvas);

    float width = getWidth();
    float height = getHeight();
    float padding = 12;

    Paint backgroundPaint = new Paint(Paint.ANTI_ALIAS_FLAG);
    backgroundPaint.setColor(currentColor);
    canvas.drawRect(padding, padding, width-padding, height-padding,
            backgroundPaint);

    float x = 0.5f * width;
    float y = 0.5f * height;
    Paint paint = new Paint(Paint.ANTI_ALIAS_FLAG);
    paint.setColor(currentTextColor);
    paint.setStrokeWidth(2);
    paint.setTextSize(currentFontScale);
    paint.setTextAlign(Align.CENTER);
    canvas.drawText(currentString, x, y, paint);
}
```

Using the current size of the button, this method draws a rectangle centered within a 12-pixel border using paint with the background color (in this case, black). A new paint object is then created to draw the text using the draw-Text method of the Canvas class.

Because the onDraw method is called whenever a control needs to be displayed, not whenever a square is marked, a change to the overall structure of the class is required. Rather than set properties of the underlying Button and then query them in the draw, the implementation simply tracks the key settings. The currentString, currentTextColor, currentColor, and font scales are set in the mark routines. Here's a new implementation of the markX, markO, and reset methods:

```
public void markX() {
    currentColor = xBackgroundColor;
    currentTextColor = xColor;
    currentString = xString;
    currentFontScale = markedFontScale;

    this.setClickable(false);
}

public void markO() {
    currentColor = oBackgroundColor;
    currentTextColor = oColor;
```

```
        currentString = oString;
        currentFontScale = markedFontScale;

        this.setClickable(false);
    }

    public void reset() {
        currentColor = emptyBackgroundColor;
        currentTextColor = emptyColor;
        currentString = emptyString;
        currentFontScale = emptyFontScale;

        this.setClickable(true);
    }


    private int currentColor = emptyBackgroundColor;
    private String currentString = emptyString;
    private float currentFontScale = emptyFontScale;
    private int currentTextColor = emptyColor;
```

Figure 6-6 shows the final implementation using red for squares marked X and using white for squares marked O. Empty spaces have a gray background.

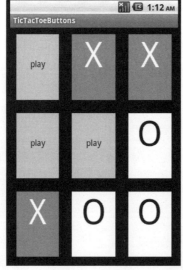

Figure 6-6:
A custom-drawn
TicTac-
Toe-
Button.

Although this section describes how to use the `Canvas` and `Paint` classes to provide a `View` with its own, custom drawing so that you can give any piece of the user interface your own, creative touch, one major concern when providing custom appearances is allowing for user-defined styles and themes. Android is supplied with support for styles, which we cover in the next section.

Simplifying Attribute Settings with Styles

The `View` class has many attributes that can be set to control its appearance, and `TextView` adds several more attributes. Some of the more common attributes of the `View` class that you may want to change include the ones described in this list:

- ✔ `android:id`: Specifies an identifier name for this `View`.

- ✔ `android:clickable`: Specifies whether this `View` receives click events.

- ✔ `android:keepScreenOn`: Specifies whether to keep the screen from turning off while this `View` is displayed.

- ✔ `android:background`: Specifies a drawable resource to use as the background for this `View`.

- ✔ `android:padding`: Sets the amount of padding in pixels surrounding this `View`.

- ✔ `android:visibility`: Specifies whether this widget is displayed.

- ✔ `android:tag`: Allows an arbitrary string to be supplied with the widget. This string can be retrieved by using the `getTag` method and searched for by using the `findViewWithTag` method.

The `TextView` class adds many attributes to control the appearance of the text as well as how the text is entered:

- ✔ `android:editable`: If set, allows the user to enter input into this control. Text boxes are typically editable; labels and buttons are not.

- ✔ `android:autoLink`: Controls whether URLs, phone numbers, map addresses, and e-mail addresses are automatically converted to clickable links.

- ✔ `android:autoText`: If set, corrects some common misspellings when entered.

- ✔ `android:ellipsize`: If set, when the text doesn't completely fit within the `TextView`, the text includes an ellipsis (. . .) to indicate the inclusion of more text.

- ✔ `android:numeric`: Changes the input method to a numeric keypad.

- ✔ `android:phoneNumber`: Changes the input method to a phone number input method.

- ✔ `android:digits`: Changes the input method to a numeric keypad and allows only the specified set of characters to be entered.

  ✔ android:password: When set, obscures the entered text and replaces every character with a dot.

  ✔ android:hint: If the text string has not been set or the user has not entered any text, then this string will be displayed.

  ✔ android:text: The string of text to display.

  ✔ android:singleLine: Restricts the display of text to a single line.

  ✔ android:lines: Restricts the display to the specified number of lines.

  ✔ android:textColor: Specifies the color to use when displaying the text.

  ✔ android:textSize: Specifies the size of the text, such as 18sp, where sp stands for *scaled pixels*, a standard dimension unit.

  ✔ android:textStyle: Can be set to a combination of normal, bold, or italic using the or (|) operator (for example, android:textStyle= "bold|italic").

  ✔ android:typeface: Can be set to a combination of normal, sans, serif, or monoscript by using the or (|) operator.

This list contains only about one-tenth of the possible attributes that can be set. See the Reference page for TextView on the Android SDK web page (http://developer.android.com/reference/android/widget/TextView.html).

Creating your own style

A collection of numerous appearance settings (see the preceding section) with similar values is known as a *style* for presenting the TextView. Changing these appearance settings every time a Button or TextView is created can be tedious and painstaking. Android helps solve this problem by supporting styles. You can create your own style by placing all these settings into a separate XML file. You place this file in the res/values directory. A style allows the following layout:

```
<EditText
    android:layout_width="match_parent"
    android:layout_height="wrap_content"
    android:background="#000000"
    android:textColor="#FFFFFF"
    android:textStyle="bold|italic"
    android:text="Hello"
/>
```

to be simplified to this:

```
<EditText
    style="@style/DarkBold"
    android:text="Hello"
/>
```

To simplify a layout, you must create as a resource a new XML file that defines the style. A style contains a set of item names (value pairs), where the name is any of the standard attributes. For the preceding example, the resulting resource looks like this:

```
<?xml version="1.0" encoding="utf-8"?>
<resources>
    <style name="DarkBold">
        <item name="android:layout_width">
            match_parent
        </item>
        <item name="android:layout_height">
            wrap_content
        </item>
        <item name="android:background">
            #000000
        </item>
        <item name="android:textColor">
            #FFFFFF
        </item>
        <item name="android:textStyle">
            bold|italic
        </item>
    </style>
</resources>
```

This example allows the application of the same style across a set of `TextView`s (including `Button`s and other derived classes).

Adding inheritance to a style

To keep a style consistent, all attributes need to be set to a value. Furthermore, a new style is needed for every permutation of appearances. Fortunately, the Android SDK provides a simple mechanism to tweak an existing style by using *inheritance*. Using inheritance, one style is used as the default values for another style. The new style needs to change only the attributes which differ from this default. Suppose that you want to use the `DarkBold` style (see the preceding section) for entering and displaying phone numbers. You can do it easily by defining a new style with the `phoneNumber` attribute set to `true`:

```
<style name="DarkPhone" parent="@style/DarkBold">
    <item name="android:phoneNumber">true</item>
</style>
```

For similar situations, Android provides a slightly easier inheritance mecha-nism. Just prefix a style with a user-defined style and the dot operator (for example, `DarkBold.Phone`), similar to Java-nested classes or namespace scoping rules. The example would then be written this way:

```
<style name="DarkBold.Phone">
    <item name="android:phoneNumber">true</item>
</style>
```

Note that because the name changes from `DarkPhone` to `DarkBold.Phone`, you enter the name of the style as `DarkBold.Phone`:

```
<EditText
    style="@style/DarkBold.Phone"
    android:text="Hello"
/>
```

This example isn't just a shortcut — it's good practice for naming styles. Clearly, `DarkBold.Phone` is now used with the `DarkBold` style.

Now you can create that long-admired fuchsia-colored background with lav-ender text style. However, because you're reading this book, you're probably more interested in programming than in designing pleasing color schemes. Fortunately (as you find out in the next section), Android provides a selec-tion of polished styles that can be applied to provide pleasing results — a big win for anyone who is, like us, artistically challenged!

Taking advantage of the built-in Android styles

Android ships with a fairly rich set of styles for you to use (or inherit from). Its SDK contains resources for these styles in the `R.java` documentation. (Visit `http://developer.android.com/reference/android/R. style.html` for more information.) Android 3.0 (version 11) ships with the new Honeycomb holographic styles. For text appearance, the main style is defined in `android:style/TextAppearance`.

Several variations of this style are available and make good starting points for your own, custom styles:

✔ android:style/TextAppearance.Large

✔ android:style/TextAppearance.Medium

✔ android:style/TextAppearance.Small

✔ android:style/TextAppearance.Inverse

✔ android:style/TextAppearance.Inverse.Large

✔ android:style/TextAppearance.Inverse.Medium

✔ android:style/TextAppearance.Inverse.Small

Unless you define all attributes, you should use best practices to inherit your custom styles from one of these predefined styles. You do this in the same way as you inherit from a custom style, by using the parent element. The resource file in the precious sections should be changed as follows:

```xml
<?xml version="1.0" encoding="utf-8"?>
<resources>
    <style name="DarkBold"
        parent="@android:style/TextAppearance.Large">
        <item name="android:layout_width">
            match_parent
        </item>
        <item name="android:layout_height">
            wrap_content
        </item>
        <item name="android:background">
            #000000
        </item>
        <item name="android:textColor">
            #FFFFFF
        </item>
        <item name="android:textStyle">
            bold|italic
        </item>
    </style>
</resources>
```

For more information and a complete list of attributes that can be set, see this page at the Android SDK developer's website: http://developer.android.com/guide/topics/ui/themes.html. Happy styling!

Using Themes to Maintain a Consistent Style

One problem with using styles is that a style must be applied to every widget. It would be nice if you had a way to say, "Here's my *default* style." You can, by using a theme. The only difference between a style and a theme is how they're applied: You can apply any style to the application, but you apply the theme to the application in the application's manifest. Modify the application tag in the `ApplicationManifest.xml` file to indicate the theme, like this:

```
<application android:theme="@style/DarkTheme">
```

Rather than use the style `DarkBold`, which has attributes applied only for the appearance of text, define a new style that inherits from a standard Android style. The following style definition inherits from the new Holographic theme:

```
<style name="DarkTheme" parent="@android:Theme.Holo">
    <item name="android:background">
        #000000
    </item>
    <item name="android:textColor">
        #FFFFFF
    </item>
    <item name="android:textStyle">
        bold|italic
    </item>
</style>
```

Providing compatibility for older devices

The problem with the approach in the preceding section is that older phones may not support the Holographic theme. You can define the same style multiple times by using the same style name if the resources are placed into a version-specific folder. So, if the style definition in the preceding section is placed in the `res/values-v11` folder and the following example is placed in the `res/values` folder, the application automatically switches to the Holographic theme on devices supporting Android 3.0 or higher:

```
<style name="DarkTheme" parent="@android:Theme.Light">
    <item name="android:background">
        #000000
    </item>
    <item name="android:textColor">
        #FFFFFF
    </item>
    <item name="android:textStyle">
        bold|italic
    </item>
</style>
```

The theme lets you change settings for application-specific appearances and behaviors, including the new `ActionBar` in Android 3.0. The complete list of attributes that are defined in a theme is available in the `R.stylable` documentation under the Theme section (`http://developer.android.com/reference/android/R.styleable.html#Theme`) on the Android SDK website.

Differentiating activities by using specific themes

If different activities within a single application need to use different themes — or if you simply want one or more of your activities to have a different style (theme) — you set them on the `activity` tag in the manifest file, rather than on the `application` tag. The following line applies the Android standard `Dialog` theme to `AccountActivity`:

```
<activity android:theme="@android:style/Theme.Dialog"

          android:name="AccountActivity">
```

The `BackgroundActivity` can set its default style to `DarkTheme` by added the following line to the manifest file.

```
<activity android:theme="@style/DarkTheme"
          android:name="Background">
```

As with most operating systems, a large community of users works to develop themes and then share them with the developer community. These themes range in complexity from a simple change to the background image to controlling the animations when `Views` are first displayed. Most device manufacturers and many phone carriers provide their own themes to enhance the user experience.

Chapter 7

Designing Your Application's Logic and Data

In This Chapter

▶ Applying object-oriented design techniques and guidelines and design patterns in your Android app

▶ Incorporating your design into the Android framework and the Android Application Model

*E*arlier in this book, we illustrated the capabilities of the Android SDK. But simply showing you its capabilities leaves out an essential portion of your understanding — how you can, starting from just an idea about what your app is supposed to do, design and implement it. In other words, we walk you through the use of all the ingredients in your kitchen but don't show you how to cook something good to eat! Therefore, we now interrupt our regularly scheduled programming to segue into how to design an Android application.

This chapter is, in a sense, a complement of Chapter 3, where we explained what the Android Application Model and the Android framework are, using the Tic-Tac-Toe example as the medium). In this chapter, we show you how to design Tic-Tac-Toe from scratch and implement it within the Android framework.

Understanding Best Practices in Application Design

As college professors, we have seen literally thousands of students develop software. When we began writing this book, we pondered what special value we could bring to the project. We determined that we could best contribute by providing a lesson on how to write good software — in particular, software written within a framework such as the Android SDK.

184

When writing an app while learning to use a new framework, most programmers understandably focus on simply making it work. They might also focus on making the app look good, but concentrate on its user interface alone. After a programmer's first app or two begin to work, mastery of the framework becomes the programmer's next goal. This goal is a good one in itself. Also, because most frameworks are developed somewhat thoughtfully, following the framework's guidelines (implementing activities and views in the Android framework, for example) results in mostly good design. However, a framework takes you only so far because its guidance has to be generic *because it's aimed at supporting all kinds of applications, not just yours.* You have to design your app given the specific factors that make your app *your* app. Take plenty of time to complete this task and not only will your app have fewer bugs but you can also reuse and maintain more code.

The design techniques and guidelines you can use are object-oriented, or O-O, design techniques (see the following section) that fall under the general category of responsibility-driven design (a concept originated by Dr. Rebecca Wirfs-Brock). We also heavily borrow from documented standard software design practices known as design patterns.

Though we specify that you should follow the framework guidelines, simply following them doesn't result in a completely well-designed app, because the framework can offer only generic guidelines. These standard O-O techniques and design patterns *also* go only part of the way, for the *opposite* reason that they don't state how to fit these techniques into your technology framework. We try to address these gaps in this chapter. In other words, we show you how to design your app, in the context of the Android SDK and the Android Application Model, by using these well-established design techniques.

The progression of this chapter is as follows. First, we briefly cover standard object-oriented design techniques. Then we walk you through the design of the Tic-Tac-Toe example.

Applying object-oriented design

The idea behind object-oriented design is that programs are intended to solve problems in the real world. Basing software components on real-world entities — both concepts as well as physical things — makes the software easier to figure out (analyze) as well as design. Further, because the components have been modeled on the real world, they're stable (they won't change quickly, because the real world isn't changing quickly) and more capable of capturing variation and evolving in a more understandable manner. This is because the variation that naturally happens in the real world is captured in the application.

We reiterate that, by *real world,* we don't necessarily mean only physical elements. For example, a tic-tac-toe game consists of a board, moves, players, and *(X* and *O)* symbols. Some elements are physical (such as players and the board), and some are not (such as moves). But all these elements are real-world entities. O-O design specifies that when you write a software app to play tic-tac-toe, you have classes that represent these items — classes named `Board`, `Game`, and `Symbol`, for example.

Understanding the basic elements of object-oriented design

The following list reviews basic object-oriented terminology:

- **Object:** The primitive element of an object-oriented program. An object *encapsulates* (retains) data and provides methods (operations or functions) that implement what the class is supposed to do — its responsibilities. Thus, a `Stack` encapsulates the elements of the stack and provides `push` and `pop` methods to insert *and* extract elements in accordance with how the stack is supposed to work: Elements inserted last are extracted first.

- **Class:** Implements an object and contains the necessary data structures and method code (in our stack example, the method code is that which implements the push and pop operations).

- **Type:** An object specification that describes how to interact with it — by using its methods. An object essentially may have multiple types because its class can implement more than one related set of functionality. In Java, the type of an object is specified by the interfaces it implements. Because an object may implement multiple interfaces, an object has multiple types. (Incidentally, rather than think of an object as having multiple types, you can think of an object's single type as the union of the interfaces it implements.)

- **Subclass:** A class that inherits all functionality from another class (known as the *superclass*). A subclass can either override specific functionality by providing its own implementation of certain methods or it can extend the functionality of the superclass by providing additional methods and using additional member variables.

    Similarly, a type (that is, an interface) may also be extended by defining a subtype. In this case, no functionality is overridden; the subtype simply has more methods that any object of that subtype must implement.

- **Abstract and concrete classes:** You cannot create objects from certain classes. These classes are known as *abstract classes.* Classes from which you can create objects are known as *concrete classes.* Of course, interfaces are always abstract.

✔ **Collaborator:** Objects (for example, instances of classes) interact with each other to implement the features of the application (an application is defined below). Thus, each class has a set of *collaborators* that it interacts with.

✔ **Application:** An application consists of a collection of collaborating classes of various types.

The tasks involved in using object-oriented design are identifying and defining appropriate classes and types and then designing their collaborations so that the application can do what it needs to do. *Capiche?* Simple enough? Read on.

Extracting and defining objects, classes, responsibilities, collaborators, methods, and signatures

In order to identify and define appropriate classes and types and then design their collaborations so that the application can do what it needs to do, you need to start with something that describes the application. Use whatever material you have available — a concept document, a requirements document, or a storyboard, for example, or even notes on a whiteboard. If you have none of these items, create them now. Trained software developers developing large applications do this task formally, in a process known as *requirements analysis.* For small apps and simple systems, however, informal methods work just fine. So simply write up a couple of pages on what you want your app to do, who its users are, and how you want them to interact with it. You can use paper or type a document into the computer. It's your call.

After you create the write-up, review it carefully to identify and record on paper the nouns; these nouns become candidate (not final) classes. Also identify and record the verbs; these verbs become candidate (not final) responsibilities. Systematically review the nouns and verbs you used and write down their definitions. If you have just a few nouns and verbs, you might even keep track of their definitions in your head. (Notice that we suggest only that *you* might track them in your head — *we* have to write everything down!)

If your definitions have two nouns or two verbs that have more or less the same meaning, remove the one that least captures the meaning you want to capture. If a noun doesn't have a single definition, try splitting the noun into two, to define each one cohesively. Repeat this process with the verbs.

Incidentally, feel free to rename nouns and rewrite verbs so that they better fit your definitions of them.

Also, reject any nouns and verbs that are in the environment in which your system operates (and, as a result, outside the context of your system).

Next, allocate the consolidated set of verbs (for example, the candidate responsibilities) among the nouns (for example, the candidate classes) so that every class has only the responsibilities that "properly" belong to it. To quickly test for proper allocation, ensure that the responsibilities don't cause the definition of the class to lose cohesiveness.

You test for cohesiveness of a class as follows. Ask the question (to yourself), "Who or what does this class represent?" If your answer indicates that it represents a *single* well-understood entity, then the class is cohesive.

Now create a few detailed scenarios that capture the essential capabilities of your app. Use these scenarios to identify the collaborations by walking through the steps of the scenario in detail, to identify which class and which method enable the step. You can also find missing classes and methods this way.

To ensure that every class is a good one, review the questions in this checklist:

- ✔ Does the class have a suitable name?
- ✔ Does the class represent exactly one well-understood entity?
- ✔ Does the class have responsibilities (methods)?
- ✔ Does the class have collaborators?
- ✔ Does the class (or its components) maintain state?

The next step is to consolidate and clean up the class hierarchy. In this step, you look for classes that encapsulate similar data and responsibilities. You may create superclasses as needed to encapsulate common responsibilities (refer to the earlier section "Understanding the basic elements of object-oriented design"), but make sure that each superclass passes the cohesiveness test. The original classes can then inherit from and extend the superclasses.

Before you create a superclass, however, perform the "is a" test, by speaking the sentence "The *<subclass>* is a *<superclass>*" (replacing the italicized place-holders with the names of the classes you're testing). If the sentence doesn't completely make sense, the creation of the superclass is incorrect.

As the final step, specify (or at least understand) what every method is supposed to do, what it creates as output, and what it needs as input in order to perform its function. In other words, working class by class, and method by method, define its input parameters and output result — known as its *signature*.

Applying design patterns

The 1994 book *Design Patterns: Elements of Reusable Object-Oriented Software* (published by Addison-Wesley and written by Erich Gamma, Richard Helm, Ralph Johnson, and John Vlissides — known as the IBM Gang of Four) strongly influenced the field of software design and became an important resource for learning object-oriented design. Because the book described common ways to design classes and their interactions for solving common software design problems, software developers could look up a "catalog" of designs to see whether a particular design pattern provided a template to begin their own designs. (Programmers could say, essentially, "Aha! My problem seems similar to the problem that this pattern is supposed to solve.") However, note that a design pattern is *not* a canned solution that you can simply plug into your own code. It is (again) simply a place to *start* your design.

The well-known *model-view-controller* (MVC) design pattern, shown in Figure 7-1, shows itself in many different kinds of applications — in particular, in web applications. The idea behind this pattern is to isolate the domain logic of the application from the way the application is presented to the user (the application's user interface) so that these two vital application components can be designed, implemented, and maintained separately. For example, the logic of playing a tic-tac-toe game based on its game rules is the domain logic of the Tic-Tac-Toe application, and hence the model. The tic-tac-toe grid presented to users (for their interaction) is the user interface and, hence, the view. The controller is a component, interposed between the two, that

🖛 Receives user actions (such as "The user clicked here")

🖛 Translates commands into actions on the model

🖛 Updates the resulting model and notifies the user interface that it must update itself

Figure 7-1:
The
model-view-
controller
design
pattern.

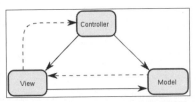

If this discussion makes sense at a high level but you're unsure how to connect it to development using the Android SDK and the Android Application Model, well, that's what the next section is for!

Understanding software frameworks

A software framework may be defined as follows:

> *A software framework is collection of related software components providing generic functionality that can be selectively overridden or refined by user-provided code or components, thus providing functionality specific to an application or domain.*

In object-oriented software frameworks, the functionality provided by the framework can be "selectively overridden" or "specialized," by using a set of object-oriented techniques that implement the concept known as inversion of control. *Inversion of control* means that the program's flow of control — the way the program runs — isn't dictated by the user of the framework but, rather, by the framework itself (as default behavior). This default behavior is intended, however, to be extended or modified by code that the user supplies. The user supplies this code in the form of classes that extend the base classes of the framework (which are usually abstract classes) and either override certain methods or provide implementations of virtual methods. The user's classes may also implement specific interfaces that are then passed to and invoked by the framework. (Incidentally, this concept distinguishes frameworks from software libraries that simply provide computational capabilities that can be invoked from your application — such as the string manipulation routines provided by the `java.lang` package.)

The Android SDK is, in fact, a framework. As we describe in Chapters 1 and 3, it provides a set of base classes that you extend with your own classes and code.

Among other things, the default functionality provided by frameworks implements patterns (or variations of patterns). For example, a core component of the Android framework (for example, the Activity class and its subclasses) implements the MVC pattern. The activity serves as the controller between its `View` and the application logic (the domain logic) that's supposed to take place in that activity. Although this domain logic can be implemented directly in the activity itself, if the domain logic is complex, a better option from a design perspective is to extract it into a separate class or set of classes, which essentially comprises the model.

So far we've given you a bunch of definitions. We now illustrate the concepts we covered in this section in the next section, using the Tic-Tac-Toe example.

Illustrating Android App Design by Using the Tic-Tac-Toe Example

In this section, we walk you through the process (outlined in earlier sections of this chapter) of designing the Tic-Tac-Toe app. The first step is to extract objects, classes, responsibilities, and collaborations from descriptions of the game and the application. We begin with a description of tic-tac-toe and add to it an informal specification of the software-based game to create the following description of the Tic-Tac-Toe app:

> Tic-tac-toe, also spelled tick-tack-toe, or noughts and crosses, as it is known in the Commonwealth countries, is a pencil-and-paper game for two players, who take turns marking the spaces in a 3×3 grid with the symbols X and O, respectively. The X player usually goes first. The player who succeeds in placing three respective marks in a horizontal, vertical, or diagonal row wins the game. Tic-Tac-Toe for Android implements the tic-tac-toe paper game as an Android app. In it, human users can play tic-tac-toe against a computer. Multiple games can be played in a session, with either the computer or the human playing first on an electronic board that's displayed on the device's touchscreen. Session scores are accumulated. If the user quits the session, scores are reset.

Discovering classes, responsibilities, and collaborators for Tic-Tac-Toe

From the description of the tic-tac-toe game, you proceed in the following order:

1. Examine nouns to extract candidate objects, classes, and attributes

2. Examine verbs to extract responsibilities

3. Identify collaborations

This process results in the following list:

- **Nouns (candidate objects and classes):** pencil, paper, game, nought, cross, player, X, O, space, symbol, grid, mark, vertical row, horizontal row, diagonal row, human user, human, computer, session, board, touchscreen, score

- **Verbs (candidate responsibilities):** take turn, mark, goes, place, win, implement, play, playing first, display, accumulate, quit, reset

From this list, merge, remove, and refine the nouns into classes, as described in the following list (we have omitted the rather obvious definitions):

✔ *Pencil* and *paper* are physical items that are not relevant to an Android-based game. These are removed from the list of candidate classes.

✔ Observe that *symbol* and *mark* are identical and retain *symbol.*

✔ Observe that *nought* and *O* and *cross* and *X* are identical and, for simplicity, leave *O* and *X*. Further, note that *O* and *X* appear to be either instances or subclasses of `Symbol`.

✔ After comparing *user* and *player,* retain *player* as the player in the game (*user* is the person using the Android device). Note that *human user* and *human* might be identical concepts, and also note that they (and *computer*) are instances or subclasses of *player.*

✔ Realize that *board* and *grid* have similar enough meanings that one of them can be removed. In this example, keep *grid* and, in fact, rename it to *game grid.*

✔ Because *touchscreen* appears to refer to a physical component of the phone, your first inclination might be to remove it. On the other hand, you need a class to handle the visual display of the board. You can choose this element to be the board itself, or perhaps separate the data structure that represents the board from its visual manifestation. (We chose to retain it as the representative of the visual display, but renamed it *board.*)

✔ Consider *row* as a component of *game grid* and consider *vertical row, diagonal row,* and *horizontal row* as essentially different subclasses or instances of *row.* (You don't yet know which.)

✔ Consider *session* an instance of *game,* with *score* an attribute of either *game* or its two players.

Continue this process with the verbs:

✔ Remove *take turn* and *goes* as terms similar to *play,* and retain *play.* For now, retain *playing first* and the missing *playing second* as potential refinements of *play.* (The final design will show that they're unnecessary.)

✔ Remove the verb *mark* because it's similar to *place.* Retain *place* but rename it *place symbol.*

✔ Remove *implement* for not being a responsibility relevant to the game, but rather to the process of building it.

✔ Retain *display, accumulate, exit,* and *reset* as valid responsibilities.

The following potential classes, instances, and responsibilities remain:

- **Classes:** Symbol, Player, Human, Computer, Board, Row, and Game (with the attribute Score)

- **Instances:** O, X, of the class `Symbol`

- **Responsibilities (which later become methods):** play, place, display, accumulate (scores), quit, and reset

Now tentatively assign responsibilities to classes in a manner as rational as possible:

- The class `Game` is allocated the responsibilities play, accumulateScores, quit, and reset.

- The class `Board` has Display responsibilities.

- The class `GameGrid` has Place.

- The classes `Symbol`, `Player`, `Human`, `Computer`, and `Row` have no responsibilities (yet). You will find out in the next section, "Walking through scenarios to discover collaborators and missing classes and responsibilities," whether to delete them.

Walking through scenarios to discover collaborators and missing classes and responsibilities

After you discover the classes, responsibilities, and collaborators for our Tic-Tac-Toe example, as described in the previous section, you can consider different scenarios to ensure that every one is supported by a method of a class (or, more accurately, a method of *an object of* the class). Also, as a side effect of this walk-through, you should identify and understand the collaborations.

Because tic-tac-toe is a simple game, we describe a single, simple, and somewhat generalized scenario. (When you build a complex app, be sure to have detailed scenarios, each exploring a new set of interactions with the app.)

Here's the scenario:

1. Start a new game.

2. Specify who plays first (human or computer). The first player is assigned the X as a symbol; the second player, the O.

3. The first player places his (or its) symbol at an empty location on the board, followed by the second player placing his symbol.

    Repeat this step until one player has three symbols in a row, column, or diagonal or until no more squares can be played, in which case the game ends in a draw.

4. Accumulate players' scores. The winning player has 1 added to his score. No change is made to a losing player's score. (Both players' scores remain the same if the game ends in a draw.)

5. If the user wants to start a new game, do so. Otherwise, quit.

The following list walks you through every step of the scenario to see which class will handle it:

1. **Start a new game.**

    Ouch! You ran into trouble in the first step. No class supports the responsibility of starting a new game. This responsibility doesn't seem to belong in either the Game or Board class, so you have to create a new GameController class to start a new game (by creating a new instance of Game). GameController and Game are thus collaborators (because GameController creates an instance of Game).

2. **Specify who plays first (human or computer). The first player is assigned the X as a symbol; the second player, the O.**

    Specifying who plays first and second can seemingly also be a responsibility of the GameController class. Because all these responsibilities are internal, they don't have to be implemented as externally visible methods of this class (although they can certainly be private methods).

3. **The first player places his symbol at an empty location on the board followed by the second player placing his symbol.**

    Repeat this step until one player has three symbols in a row, column, or diagonal or until no more squares can be played, in which case the game ends in a draw.

    A symbol has to be (visually) placed on the board. Creation of the symbol is covered by the Symbol class. The Board class can cover placement of the symbol, if you add the method placeSymbol to it. Then Play is invoked on Game, which causes Grid to be updated.

    After a symbol is placed, you have to evaluate whether the game has ended with a win or a draw. This looks like it is a Game responsibility, and because Game likely collaborates with GameGrid to see whether a row, column, or diagonal has been completed, Game needs a responsibility — checkResult. Note that the classes Board, GameGrid, and Game are now collaborators. If no win has occurred and the board still has empty locations, the game continues.

Next, you have to switch to the second player. If this player were the machine and you wanted to know what handles the logic, you would let Game handle it. To do this, Game must collaborate with GameGrid to produce a list of empty squares to choose from, so GameGrid needs the responsibility getEmptySquares.

4. **Accumulate players' scores. The winning player has 1 added to his score. No change is made to a losing player's score. (Both players' scores remain the same if the game ends in a draw.)**

At first blush, you might want to make the Game class responsible for accumulating scores. However, you will probably quickly realize that the Game class represents a single game, and that scores are accumulated across games in a session. So Game doesn't seem a suitable class for accumulating scores, but perhaps GameController does. After you determine that this decision is appropriate, you rename GameController to GameSession. It creates a new game, specifies the players, plays the game, and accumulates scores.

5. **If the user wants to start a new game, do. Otherwise, quit.**

It seems appropriate that GameSession handle starting a new game and quitting the session; this assignment gives the GameSession symmetric responsibilities. The updated scores have to be shown somewhere, perhaps by using the Board class. To do so, you add the ShowScores method to Board. With the assignment of ShowScores, Board represents more than the tic-tac-toe board. Hence, you rename it to GameView.

Now you have these classes, responsibilities, and collaborators:

- **Game:** Represents a single tic-tac-toe game.
  - *Responsibilities:* play, checkResult
  - *Collaborators:* GameSession, GameView, Grid
- **GameView:** Represents the visual display of a tic-tac-toe game.
  - *Responsibilities:* placeSymbol, showScores
  - *Collaborators:* Game
- **GameGrid:** Represents the 3 x 3 tic-tac-toe grid.
  - *Responsibilities:* placeSymbol, getEmptySquares
  - *Collaborators:* Game
- **GameSession:** Represents a tic-tac-toe session in which multiple games are played.
  - *Responsibilities:* playNewGame, quit, decidePlayers, accumulateScores
  - *Collaborators:* Game, GameView

✔ **Symbol:** Represents the tic-tac-toe symbol X or O.

- *Responsibilities:* None

- *Collaborators:* Game

Note the transition of responsibility names from English-like to Java-method-like names.

Your final step is to run each class through the checklist below. We presented this checklist earlier in this chapter (in the section "Extracting and defining objects, classes, responsibilities, collaborators, methods, and signatures). Verify that every class has the items in the following list and that the class maintains — or its components maintain — state:

✔ A suitable name

✔ A cohesive description

✔ Responsibilities

✔ Collaborators

You will clearly see that the Tic-Tac-Toe classes meet these criteria.

Defining method signatures

When you have identified the classes and methods and you know which classes collaborate, the next step is to specify (or at least understand) what each method is supposed to do, what outputs it creates, and which inputs it needs. We explain this task class by class, method by method, starting with Game. (If you complete the scenario walk-throughs we describe in the earlier section "Walking through scenarios to discover collaborators and missing classes and responsibilities," you can work in any order because you know what each method is responsible for.)

The first method in Game is play, which is called whenever an X or an O is played on a square, identified by its coordinates. Because this method needs a Grid, a Symbol, and a coordinate (*x, y*) position, its signature is play(Grid, Symbol, x, y). It can return two disjoint sets of values:

✔ An error code indicating whether the move was legal (and, therefore, successful) or illegal

✔ The state — Win, Draw, or Active — that the game remained in after the move

Play returns the Boolean value of true if the move was correctly played. It returns false if an incorrect move was made. (For example, by someone trying to play a square that was already filled.)

The second method in `Game` is `checkResult`. You need to examine the Grid, so its signature is `checkResult(Grid)`. You want it to set the state of the game to Win (for the player who just played), Draw, or Active. Because you also want it to *set* the state of the game, you rename this method `checkResultAndSetState(Grid)`. Finally, because you realize that you need methods that return the state of the game, you add the three methods `isActive()`, `isWon`, and `isDrawn()` to the class.

Systematically reviewing all classes identified so far produces the following set of methods and signatures:

✔ **Game**
- *play (Grid, Symbol, x, y):* Returns true for success or false for failure
- *checkResultAndSetState (Grid):* Returns nothing
- *isActive():* Returns true or false
- *isWon():* Returns true or false
- *isDrawn():* Returns true or false

✔ **GameView**
- *placeSymbol(Symbol, X, Y):* Returns Success or Failure
- *showScores(PlayerOneScore, PlayerTwoScore):* Returns nothing

✔ **Grid**
- *placeSymbol (Symbol, x, y):* Returns Success or Failure
- *getEmptySquares ():* Returns a set of coordinates

✔ **Symbol**
- This class has no methods, and hence no signatures.

✔ **GameSession**
- *playNewGame()*
- *quit()*
- *decidePlayers()*
- *accumulateScores(WinningPlayer)*

There you have it: classes and methods with method signatures! Hooray! But if you're wondering whether you've finished designing so that you can start implementing, the answer is (unfortunately) "not yet!"

If you were the ancient Paladin of computing (have compiler, will travel) and were developing an application from scratch, you could potentially start coding (after you add a main program, incidentally). But you aren't the Paladin — you're a modern-day knight in Android armor and you must fit your design inside the Android Application Model to take advantage of the framework wherever possible but also to compromise wherever the framework doesn't quite fit your design (at least not without lots of extra work). In the following sections, we show you an example of how you might do this.

Incorporating your design into the Android Application Model

If you already read our spiel about design patterns and the model-view-controller (MVC) pattern in the earlier section "Applying design patterns," this section will make more sense to you. An Android *activity* is simply an "Android-ization" of the MVC pattern, with generic view and controller capability provided by the Android framework. Views are supported by the `View` class (imagine that!), and the controller is supported by the `Activity` class. The model segment comes from you because it's a component that is specific to your app.

In case you're asking what the model, view, and controller components of Tic-Tac-Toe (Aha!) are, this list has the answers:

- ✔ `GameView`: The view
- ✔ `GameSession`: The controller
- ✔ `Game`: The model

In other words, `Game` will become a pure Java class, `GameView` will extend `View`, and `GameSession` will extend `Activity`.

In the following section, we describe these respective classes in the `Tic-Tac-Toe` code — you might want to follow along in Eclipse, too. By the way, for a refresher on all elements of the Android Application Model, read (or review) Chapter 3.

Understanding the model component of Tic-Tac-Toe

In this section, we present the model (the `Game` class), shown with only its member variables and its method skeletons:

```
package com.wiley.fordummies.androidsdk.tictactoe;

import java.util.ArrayList;

public class Game {
```

```
private enum STATE { Inactive, Active, Won, Draw };
private STATE state=STATE.Inactive;;
private Symbol currentSymbol=null;
private enum PLAYER {Player1, Player2};
private PLAYER currentPlayer=PLAYER.Player1;
private PLAYER winningPlayer=PLAYER.Player1;
private String PlayerOneName=null, PlayerTwoName=null;
private GameGrid gameGrid=null;
private int playCount=0;

Game(){ //Constructor - creates gameGrid, initializes game state}
GameGrid getGameGrid(){// Accessor method for gameGrid}
void setPlayerNames(...){// setter for player names}
String getPlayerOneName(){//accessor method}
String getPlayerTwoName(){//accessor method}
String getCurrentPlayerName(){//accessor method}
String getWinningPlayerName(){//accessor method}
public Symbol getCurrentSymbol(){//accessor method}

public boolean play(int x, int y){// handles one turn of TicTacToe}

private void checkResultAndSetState(){//used to check after each move if the
        game has been won or drawn and set the state of the game}

boolean isActive(){//is the game still active - i.e. not been won or drawn}
boolean isWon(){//the game has been won by a player}
boolean isDrawn(){//the game has been drawn}
}
```

This class, which is a pure model of the tic-tac-toe game, has a bunch of
getter methods prefixed with `get`. The setter method is `setPlayerName`. An
important method here — `play(int x, int y)` — handles one turn in tic-
tac-toe. It automatically alternates between players (which is why you don't
need two play methods, one for each player) and calls the method `check-
ResultAndSetState()` after every play to check on whether the game
should continue or has been won, lost, or drawn. The `checkResultAndSet-
State()` method is private because it is called only internally by `play(...)`.

Next come the methods `isActive()`, `isWon()`, and `isDrawn()` (their function should be clear to you from their names or from the discussion in the
previous section):

We now show you the implementations of the key methods `play(...)` and
`checkResultAndSetState(...)`. The `play(...)` method is shown first below:

```
public boolean play(int x, int y){
    boolean successfulPlay=false;
    if ((gameGrid.getValueAtLocation(x, y)==Symbol.SymbolBlankCreate())){
        successfulPlay = true;
        playCount++;
        gameGrid.setValueAtLocation(x, y, currentSymbol);
```

```
         checkResultAndSetState();
         if(gameState == STATE.Active){// if the game is still active
             // Swap symbols and players
             if(currentSymbol == Symbol.SymbolXCreate())
                 currentSymbol=Symbol.SymbolOCreate();
             else
                                 currentSymbol=Symbol.SymbolXCreate();
             if(currentPlayer==PLAYER.Player1) currentPlayer=PLAYER.Player2;
             else currentPlayer=PLAYER.Player1;
         }
     }
     return successfulPlay;
}
```

The method `play(...)` does four things:

✔ Places the symbol on the tic-tac-toe grid

✔ Increments the play count

✔ Determines whether the move caused the game to be ended (by being won or drawn)

✔ If the game is still active, swaps the players and the symbols in preparation for the next move

Finally, take a look at `checkResultAndSetState(...)`:

```
private void checkResultAndSetState(){
    if(gameGrid.isRowFilled(0)||
       gameGrid.isRowFilled(1)||
       gameGrid.isRowFilled(2)||
       gameGrid.isColumnFilled(0)||
       gameGrid.isColumnFilled(1)||
       gameGrid.isColumnFilled(2)||
       gameGrid.isLeftToRightDiagonalFilled()||
       gameGrid.isRightToLeftDiagonalFilled()){
        winningPlayer = currentPlayer;
        gameState = STATE.Won;
    }else if (playCount==9){
        gameState = STATE.Draw;
    } /* else, leave state as is */
}
```

This chunk of code checks every row, column, and diagonal to see whether any are completely filled. If so, it sets the state of the game as won. If nine successful plays have been made without the game being won, the game is declared a draw.

Understanding the controller component of Tic-Tac-Toe

The controller component of Tic-Tac-Toe is the `GameSession` activity. Here are its member variables and method skeleton:

```
public class GameSession extends Activity {
    private Board board;
    private Game activeGame=null;
    private GameView gameView=null;
    int scorePlayerOne=0;
    int scorePlayerTwo=0;
    String firstPlayerName = null;
    String secondPlayerName = null;
    /** Called when the activity is first created. */

    public void onCreate(Bundle savedInstanceState){}

    private void startSession(){// a new session consists of multiple games }
    private void playNewGame(){//handles one complete game}
    private void setPlayers(Game theGame){// sets player names in the game}
    private void quitGame(){//abandon a game}
    private void proceedToFinish() {}
    private void accumulateScores(String winningPlayerName){}

    private void scheduleAndroidsTurn(){// introduces a random delay in machine
            play}
    private void androidTakesATurn(){//handles machine play}
    protected void humanTakesATurn(int x, int y){// handles a human's turn}


    public boolean onCreateOptionsMenu(Menu menu) {}
    public boolean onOptionsItemSelected(MenuItem item) {}
}
```

The `onCreate(...)` method is the one that's called when this `Activity` is kicked off by the Android framework. With regard to the Tic-Tac-Toe app, `onCreate(...)` kicks off a new game session.

The next set of methods in `GameSession` is specific to Tic-Tac-Toe. The role of several of these methods is straightforward, such as `startSession(...)`, `playNewGame(...)`, `setPlayers(...)`, `quitGame(...)`, `proceedTo Finish(...)`, and `accumulateScores(...)`. But three other methods are worth describing in more detail. We first examine the pair of methods `schedule AndroidsTurn(...)` and `androidTakesATurn(...)`, which collaborate to handle machine play. Take a look at `androidsTurn(...)`:

```
private void scheduleAndroidsTurn() {
    Random r = new Random();
    board.disableInput();
    Handler handler = new Handler();
    handler.postDelayed(
        new Runnable() {
            public void run() {
```

```
            androidTakesATurn();
        }
    },
    500 + r.nextInt(2000)
);
}
```

This method disables the screen so that the human cannot play and then posts a task (consisting of the method `androidTakesATurn()` that implements the machine play). The task is posted with a random delay, after which the task executes. This task enables the screen display again. Note that a new thread is needed in order to implement the delay so that the application remains active. Note also that input has to be enabled in the *posted* task and not in `scheduleAndroidTurn(…)`, or else the screen becomes active before the machine completes its turn. Here's `androidTakesATurn()`:

```
private void androidTakesATurn(){
    GameGrid gameGrid = activeGame.getGameGrid();
    ArrayList<Square> emptyBlocks = gameGrid.getEmptySquares();
    int n = emptyBlocks.size();
    Random r = new Random();
    int randomIndex = r.nextInt(n);
    Square picked = emptyBlocks.get(randomIndex);
    activeGame.play(picked.x(), picked.y());
    gameView.placeSymbol(picked.x(), picked.y());
    board.enableInput();
    if(activeGame.isActive())
        gameView.setGameStatus(activeGame.getCurrentPlayerName() + " to play.");
    else
        proceedToFinish();
}
```

As you can see, `androidTakesATurn()` first gets a list of empty blocks from the game grid and then picks one at random to play. Then it enables input to the screen and checks to see whether the game is still active. If the game is over, `proceedToFinish(…)` is called, which checks to see whether the session should continue or the user has finished.

Understanding the view component of Tic-Tac-Toe

Turn your attention to the view component of Tic-Tac-Toe. It's composed of the `GameView` class, which is small enough that we can show you the entire class:

```
package com.wiley.fordummies.androidsdk.tictactoe;

import android.widget.TextView;

public class GameView {
    private Board gameBoard=null;
    private TextView statusView=null;
    private TextView sessionScoresView=null;
```

```
        public void setGameViewComponents(Board theBoard,
                                          TextView theStatusView,
                                          TextView theSessionScoresView){
            gameBoard = theBoard;
            statusView = theStatusView;
            sessionScoresView = theSessionScoresView;
        }

        public void setGameStatus(String message){
            statusView.setText(message);
        }

        public void showScores(String player1Name, int player1Score,
                               String player2Name, int player2Score){
            sessionScoresView.setText(player1Name + ":" + player1Score +
                                   "...." +
                                   player2Name+":"+player2Score);


        }

        public void placeSymbol(int x, int y){
          gameBoard.placeSymbol(x, y);
        }
    }
```

Most of the work in this class is done by its components — `Board` and the two `TextView` components (covered in the next section). Also note that the `GameView` class is true to the principle that it's a view and *only* handles user interface responsibilities.

Understanding the support data structures in Tic-Tac-Toe

You now need to examine the supporting data structures used in Tic-Tac-Toe. You start with `Symbol` and `GameGrid`, which is shown here:

```
public class GameGrid {
    public static final int SIZE=3;
    private Symbol[][] grid=null;

    GameGrid(){// Constructor. Initializes the grid to blanks}
    public void setValueAtLocation(int x, int y, Symbol value{…}
    public Symbol getValueAtLocation (int x, int y){…}
    public boolean isRowFilled (int row){//Entire row has the same symbol}
    public boolean isColumnFilled (int col){//Entire column has the same symbol}
    public boolean isLeftToRightDiagonalFilled(){//Left diagonal has the same
            symbol}
    public boolean isRightToLeftDiagonalFilled(){(){//Right diagonal has the
            same symbol}
    public ArrayList<Square> getEmptySquares(){//Get the unfilled squares}
}
```

The `GameGrid` data structure is shared between `Game`, `GameView`, and `GameSession`. `Game` needs `GameGrid` to implement tic-tac-toe game logic, such as placing symbols and evaluating whether the game has been won or drawn or is still active. `GameView` needs `GameGrid` because it contains the symbols `GameView` needs to show on the screen. `GameSession` needs it to implement human- and machine-playing logic.

Here's the `Symbol` class:

```
package com.wiley.fordummies.androidsdk.tictactoe;

public class Symbol {
    private enum MARK { X, O, Blank }
    private MARK value=null;
    private static Symbol SymbolX=null;
    private static Symbol SymbolO=null;
    private static Symbol SymbolBlank=null;

    private Symbol(){/* Empty PRIVATE constructor to enforce Singleton */}

    public static final Symbol SymbolXCreate() {}
    public static final Symbol SymbolOCreate() {}
    public static final Symbol SymbolBlankCreate() {}
    public String toString(){}
}
```

You might wonder why you even need a class for representing Symbols. In other words, maybe you could have used `Strings` (using an X and an O to represent the tic-tac-toe characters). The reason you create a class is to illustrate two kinds of design elements:

- ✔ The first design element is a simple optimization to think about when you write code for resource-constrained mobile devices.

- ✔ The second design element is the use of another pattern (the *Singleton pattern*) to reduce the number of identical classes that are created and to make these instances easily accessible to all methods with a program.

The optimization that we want you to consider is the avoidance of string comparisons in your code. String comparisons are slow because they have to be done character by character. Instead, you use an enumerated type of comparison to represent an X and an O, which represents them as numbers (while still retaining expressivity). When you check to see whether a row is filled, for example, you're making numeric comparisons rather than string comparisons. Incidentally, there are string comparisons in many other places in the Tic-Tac-Toe code, but they were left in because they do not have much impact on performance, relatively speaking.

To ensure that you don't unnecessarily create large numbers of objects containing Xs and Os, we next introduce a scheme whereby only one instance of an X and one instance of an O is created and they're shared by all the code. To show you how to do it, check out the following code snippet (which uses ellipsis dots to separate the segments that don't appear together in the actual code):

```
private static Symbol SymbolX=null;
...
private Symbol(){/* Empty PRIVATE constructor to enforce Singleton */}
public static final Symbol SymbolXCreate() {
    if (SymbolX == null){
        SymbolX = new Symbol();
        SymbolX.value = MARK.X;
        return SymbolX;
    }
}
```

To begin with, the default constructor for `Symbol` is made private so that a `Symbol` class cannot be instantiated by using `new Symbol()` outside the class itself. Any instances of the `Symbol` class thus *must* be created by using one of the three methods `SymbolXCreate()`, `SymbolOCreate()`, or `SymbolBlankCreate()`.

Now take a look at the code that implements `SymbolXCreate()`. The first time it's called, it creates and returns a new instance of an X (and saves it in `SymbolX`). Every subsequent time it's called, it returns the *same* instance. Note that each method *thinks* it's getting a new instance!

Note one last thing about `Symbol`: Because symbols must be displayed as strings in certain methods, you give the `Symbol` class a `toString()` method.

The following `TextView` class is a built-in Android class. Its use in the `GameView` class is shown here:

```
private TextView statusView=null;
...
public void setGameStatus(String message){
    statusView.setText(message);
}
```

You declare a `TextView` variable as shown in the code just above and then use the `setText` method to make it display a message.

Finally, the following snippet walks you through the skeleton of the `Board` class:

```
package com.wiley.fordummies.androidsdk.tictactoe;

import com.wiley.fordummies.androidsdk.tictactoe.R;

import android.content.Context;
import android.content.res.Resources;
import android.graphics.Bitmap;
import android.graphics.BitmapFactory;
import android.graphics.Canvas;
import android.graphics.Paint;
import android.graphics.Rect;
import android.graphics.Paint.Cap;
import android.util.AttributeSet;
import android.view.MotionEvent;
import android.view.View;

public class Board extends View {
    private final GameSession gameSession; // game context (parent)
    private float width;
    private float height; // will be same as width;
    private final float strokeWidth = 2;
    private final float lineWidth = 10;
    private GameGrid grid=null;
    private boolean enabled = true;

    public Board(Context context, AttributeSet attributes) {/* Constructor */}
    protected void onDraw(Canvas canvas) {/* Draws and re-draws the Board */}
    protected void onSizeChanged  (int w, int h, int oldw, int oldh){/* handles
            size changes of the Board */}
    public boolean onTouchEvent(MotionEvent event) {/* handles any interactions
            with the Board */}

    private void invalidateBlock(int x, int y) {/* marks a segment of the board
            as to be re-drawn */}
    protected void disableInput(){/* disables user input */}
    protected void enableInput(){/* Enables user input */}

    public void setGrid(GameGrid aGrid){/* Sets the gameGrid member variable */}
    protected boolean placeSymbol(int x, int y){/* places a symbol on the board
            */}

    public Bitmap getBitmapForSymbol(Symbol aSymbol){/* converts a Symbol to a
            bitmap - note: breaks abstraction! */}
}
```

Board is a subclass of the built-in View class. Also, as with GameView, all
Board methods are related to the user interface. Board methods can be
categorized into four sets of methods. The first set is composed of the methods that are required to be implemented by the View class — a constructor,
Board(…), onDraw(…), onSizeChanged(…), and onTouchEvent(…). The
constructor initializes the view and gains access to the GameSession object
by looking up its context. The onDraw method draws the tic-tac-toe grid, and
onSizeChanged(…) handles any size changes to the board.

The important method in this set is the onTouchEvent(..) method, shown here:

```
public boolean onTouchEvent(MotionEvent event) {
    if( !this.enabled ) return false;
    int posX = 0;
    int posY = 0;
    int action = event.getAction();
    switch (action){
        case MotionEvent.ACTION_DOWN:
            float x = event.getX();
            float y = event.getY();
            if( x > width && x < width * 2 ) posX = 1;
            if( x > width * 2 && x < width * 3 ) posX = 2;
            if( y > height && y < height * 2 ) posY = 1;
            if( y > height * 2 && y < height * 3 ) posY = 2;
            gameSession.humanTakesATurn(posX, posY);
            break;
    return super.onTouchEvent(event);
}
```

The onTouchEvent(..) method ignores all except one type of MotionEvent event — ACTION_DOWN. When onTouchEvent(..) receives this type of event, it converts its coordinates into tic-tac-toe grid coordinates and then invokes humanTakesATurn(…) on the parent gameSession object. (And now you know why it needed its context.)

The next set of methods — invalidateBlock(…), enableInput(…), and disableInput(…), respectively — mark a played square on the board to be redrawn (because its value has changed), and permit or disallow human input to the board (that is, when the machine is playing).

The final set of methods — setGrid(…) and placeSymbol(…) — provides a handle to the shared grid. The method placeSymbol(…) places a symbol on the grid. Note that placing a symbol only means invalidating the square on the grid so that it is redrawn.

Understanding design decisions and compromises made in Tic-Tac-Toe

This section explains the design decisions made in the game. These design decisions were the result of the object-oriented design process we described in this chapter. You will also see some of the *compromises* made in the game design, just so you see that it is okay to make compromises in less-important areas as long as the design of the main components is good.

With respect to data structures, you use a two-dimensional array (see grid in GameGrid) to represent the tic-tac-toe board but hide the use of the array inside an abstraction (GameGrid). You do this so that, if you want, you can change the implementation of the grid to a more efficient representation (such as a bitmap) without having to change the code that needed to use it.

You do not use `String` to implement symbol, because you don't want the overhead of string comparisons. You also illustrate the use of a `Singleton` class to reduce the overhead of creating many identical objects and to avoid requiring the passing of a common object to all methods in the program.

You break the `Game` abstraction by allowing access to and directly sharing the `gameGrid` instance. Note that the `gameGrid` is *modified* only in the `Game` class but that other classes need to read it. You can enhance the Game interface to provide read-only access to its grid, but you choose not to do so primarily for convenience and simply pass `gameGrid` around.

Look for design compromises in the application because of the Android framework. You break abstraction principles in at least one place. Note that `Symbols` are displayed in two ways: as strings (see the `isRightToLeft DiagonalFilled(...)` method in the `GameGrid` class) and as bitmaps (see the `onDraw` method in the `Board` class). However, the `toString(...)` method is placed (properly) with the `Symbol` class, but the `getBitmapForSymbol(...)` method is in the `Board` class (because the Android framework has no convenient methods to gain access to the resources for the application from inside a plain old class, such as `Symbol`). The Android framework essentially forces this design compromise on you. We say, "Just live with it!"

Another compromise of this type is that the controller (the `GameSession` class) also implements `View` components, such as the menu and the dialog boxes in `proceedToFinish(...)`. The latter is a design principle broken essentially for convenience — you can implement the various dialog boxes in `GameView`, but the implementation of the menu callbacks in `GameSession` is caused by Menus and Activities being tied together in the sense that they're expected to be used together. (Oh, well!)

What comes next? In addition to designing and implementing the features of an application (the *functional* requirements), you also have to implement qualities such as reliability, scalability, maintainability, and, in particular, security, in order for your app to be considered professional quality. Chapters 8 and 9 walk you through that process.

Part III

Making Your Applications Fit for the Enterprise

The 5th Wave   By Rich Tennant

Well, heck – that's just darn impressive! And you say it's programmed to sew up and dress the incision afterward as well?

In this part . . .

Though Part II is about building the right application, this part of the book is all about building the app right. Chapter 8 talks about making your app fast and responsive (qualities that, by the way, aren't the same thing, as you will see), and Chapter 9 talks about security. Without speed, responsiveness, and security, your app won't be successful when it's released, regardless of how cool its features might be. This part shows you how to make it so.

Chapter 8

Making Your Application Fast and Responsive

In This Chapter

▶ Applying nonfunctional requirements to Android apps

▶ Constructing your app to perform well

▶ Making your application appear responsive

*A*n app that is successful in gaining user acceptance must meet two kinds of requirements: functional and nonfunctional. Functional requirements describe *what* the app must do (the functions it must perform). A wayfinding app, for example, must allow the user to plot a route from one location to another. As another example, the Tic-Tac-Toe application must show you a board and enable you to place Xs and Os on it. These functional requirements describe what is needed to "build the right app."

While most developers realize that their apps must implement these functional requirements, they don't focus enough effort on meeting *nonfunctional* require-ments, which mandate *how* the app must do what it does. Nonfunctional requirements provide guidelines on how to "build the app right."

In this chapter, we focus on nonfunctional requirements and identify three that apply especially to Android apps: performance, battery conservation, and responsiveness. We then show you ways in which to meet these nonfunctional requirements.

Becoming Familiar with Nonfunctional Requirements

It's a statement worth repeating: Nonfunctional requirements (NFR) — also known as *quality* requirements or *design* requirements — provide guidelines on how to *build an app right*. For example, you might consider it appropriate to require a wayfinding app to plot a route in fewer than 30 seconds, or for a computer playing a Tic-Tac-Toe application to mimic a human in order to retain the user's interest.

The list below outlines the important principles about NFR:

- ✔ **Nonfunctional requirements describe *how* to implement an app.** For example, if security isn't a requirement, you can decide to store all app data in unencrypted files and on the SD card. If security *is* an issue, however, you might encrypt the files and store them in the app's private file area so that their content isn't easily accessible and they're deleted when the app is uninstalled.

- ✔ **NFR most commonly occur in the following categories: availability, performance, scalability, usability, security, modifiability, and maintainability. (Cost is also often an important nonfunctional requirement category.)** When you build an app, you have to decide which nonfunctional requirements apply to your app. You have to also refine your NFR so that they're "testable." For example, for a performance NFR, you should be able to measure the speed of your application at the places where the NFR applies (such as during the screen display).

- ✔ **Certain nonfunctional requirements are especially important for mobile devices.** These requirements are performance, battery conservation, and responsiveness, all discussed in the following sections.

- ✔ **Do not attempt to meet all possible nonfunctional requirements in an app.** It's extra work to implement features in ways that users don't value. For this reason, you should also define (and, wherever applicable, *quantify*) to what extent you want to meet the NFR.

- ✔ **NFR fulfillment always involves trade-offs.** In other words, meeting a single nonfunctional requirement often negatively affects the meeting of another. For example, performance and security are often at cross-purposes. For example, you pay a performance overhead for the increased security of encryption and decryption of stored data. The trick is to find the right balance.

Designing Your App at Multiple Levels

When you design an app, you actually design it at multiple levels. At the highest level of design are "architectural" decisions (such as the use of the Android framework, or even the choice of Java as the development language). You have little choice in making certain architectural decisions, such as the use of the Android framework and Java to develop Android apps. Google provides the highest level of support for Java, and so developing apps in Java is significantly easier than using C or C++. Thus the architectural decision to use Java is a no-brainer. In other architectural decisions, however, you have choices, such as the type of encryption to use to secure your data wherever it is stored, retrieved, or transmitted. Architectural decisions are the most difficult to change after you've started building the software. Our translation is that you can't do much about architectural decisions after you make them; so try to make good decisions in the first place.

After the architecture is set (yes, like cement), the next level of design is in the partitioning of your application into classes, the allocation of methods to classes, and then, as a last step, the mapping of the design to the architecture of the first step. We cover this process in detail in Chapter 7. Needless to say, this design, while not quite as hard to change, is still difficult to modify after it has been decided upon.

The third level of design is at the choice of algorithms (say, for sorting) and data structures (using a hash table to find a value in a contact list, such as a phone number, corresponding to a key, say, the name of the contact). Abstracting the data structures and algorithms inside classes or methods so that they are compartmentalized really helps when you try to change out algorithms and data structures.

The final level of design lies in your choice of low-level coding practices. Code is relatively easy to change; all you need is a good editor, a few hours to hack your way through the existing code, and strong coffee to keep you awake throughout the process.

Optimizing Application Performance

In this section, we address app performance in Android, again using the sample Tic-Tac-Toe application.

Architectural choices with respect to performance include elements such as whether you're using SQLite or files (SQLite is slower for many things, however, it's faster if you're retrieving bits of already stored data), building screens using 2D graphics or widgets, or accessing the network every time your app needs data or storing certain data locally, for example. The following list describes the requirements-driven architectural decisions we made in the Tic-Tac-Toe application, and our reasons:

- ✔ **Programming language:** We use Java because its built-in support and easy app development outweigh any performance gains we might make by writing native (C or C++) code, especially considering that our app has no out-of-the-ordinary need for high performance.

- ✔ **Data storage:** We store user preferences using the built-in preference classes because of their programming convenience. We use SQLite to store login and password information because the number of times login information is retrieved (a task that SQLite excels in, like all relational databases) will most likely be much higher than the number of registered users added (a task that SQLite is slower in doing, like all relational databases).

✔ **Remote data transfer format:** Though we show both an XML and a JSON example, the preferred format is likely to be JSON because of its lower overhead.

✔ **Graphics:** We chose raw 2D graphics rather than widgets for the board for speed purposes. (Note that the Tic-Tac-Toe application has simple enough graphics that widgets would have worked as well, as the button-based implementation in Chapter 6 clearly illustrates.)

We also made a couple of deliberate decisions regarding data structures and algorithms in Tic-Tac-Toe. The primary data structure decision is to represent the grid as a two-dimensional array and encapsulate it inside a Grid class *so that we can change this implementation* if it turns out to be slow. (Note that the design process shown in Chapter 7 independently arrives at the conclusion that the grid should be its own class — this connection should serve as a validation for the design process.) The primary algorithm decision is to have the machine randomly pick empty squares to play. Note that this scheme is also abstracted (inside GameSession.androidTakes ATurn()), so if you want to change the way the machine plays, you have to modify only this lone method.

Your coding practices should improve application performance by doing less computation. You can do many things to bring about this result:

✔ **Save intermediate results in variables and then reuse them, especially in loops.** This simple example from GameSession.androidTakesA Turn() demonstrates this technique:

```
…
activeGame.play(pickedX=picked.x(), pickedY=picked.y());
gameView.placeSymbol(pickedX, pickedY);
…
```

✔ **Avoid internal getters and setters.** Access member variables directly within the class instead of using the getters and setters. This avoids the overhead of an additional method call. You can see this process in the GameGrid class, where the locations in the two-dimensional array member variable grid are accessed directly instead of using the accessor methods setValueAtLocation(…) and getValueAt Location(…), which is how the grid is accessed *outside* the class by client classes such as Board and Game.

✔ **Avoid creating unnecessary objects.** Remember that Java Strings (though appearing to be elementary data types) are objects, so limit the number of strings you create as well. We illustrate this tactic in the Symbol class in Tic-Tac-Toe, where we used the Singleton pattern so that only one instance of an X, O, and Blank symbol is ever created, and we defined symbols as enumerated types rather than as strings. Related to this concept is the use of constants (variables declared using static final — see the next item for more on this).

✔ **Use static final for constants.** If constants are simply declared as static, the definitions can be overridden and are therefore treated as variables. Thus, the Java virtual machine (JVM) has to perform extra work to figure out the correct reference and value of the constant. If the constant is declared using static final, the *compiler* knows to substitute the value of the constant where it sees uses of the constant in the code so that no runtime overhead is incurred. For an example, see the declarations shown in the following GameSession.java class:

```
private static final int ANDROIDTIMEOUTBASE=500;
private static final int ANDROIDTIMEOUTSEED=2000;
```

✔ **Know the framework libraries well, and use them wherever possible rather than write your own code.** Because the library-implemented code is usually optimized (say, using assembler code), it's more efficient than equivalent code written by you, even after the compiler has tried to optimize it. The link http://developer.android.com/guide/practices/design/performance.html on the Android website gives the examples String.indexOf(...), System.arraycopy(...), and related methods that can be as much as ten times faster than hand-written code optimized by the compiler.

An excellent set of old-but-gold techniques around low-level coding practices for efficiency is Jon Bentley's rules for writing efficient programs. We've been able to find summaries of these techniques at various places on the web by simply entering the keywords *Jon Bentley writing efficient programs* in a search engine. For an example, see www.crowl.org/lawrence/programming/Bentley82.html.

Using the Profiler for Code Optimization

You can expend a *lot* of time optimizing code, only to see no real impact on the performance of your program. To make your optimization efforts pay off, develop the habit of *profiling,* instrumenting your app's code in order to understand in which methods your program is spending most of its execution time. The Eclipse IDE with the Android SDK installed provides a useful way to do it, as shown below:

1. **Open Eclipse and make the Devices view visible by choosing Window⟳Show View⟳Other and then selecting Devices inside the Android collection.**

2. **Start the Tic-Tac-Toe app on either a device or an emulator.**

   The Devices view starts to show activity, as shown in Figure 8-1.

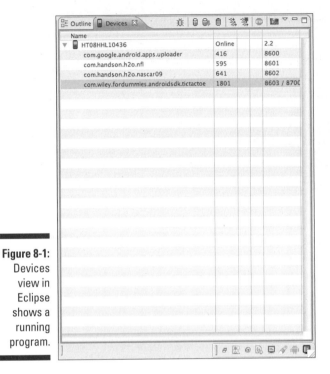

Figure 8-1:
Devices
view in
Eclipse
shows a
running
program.

3. **Log in to Tic-Tac-Toe and navigate to the Options screen, as shown in Figure 8-2.**

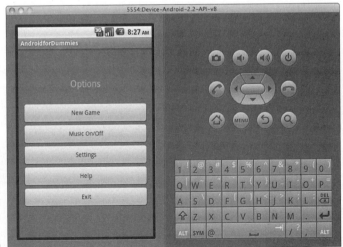

Figure 8-2:
Starting a
new game
in Tic-
Tac-Toe.

4. **Return to Devices view, select the line `com.wiley.fordummies.androidsdk.tictactoe`, and begin profiling by clicking the icon to the left of the Stop sign. (Or, hover the mouse over the icons until you see the Start Method Profiling tooltip.)**

5. **Play four or five games, stretching out every game as far as possible, and then stop the profiling by clicking the same icon as in Step 4. This time, however, notice that it has turned black.**

   The `Traceview` profiler window opens (see Figure 8-3).

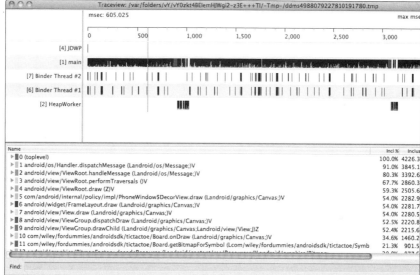

Figure 8-3:
The
`Trace-`
`view`
profiler in
Eclipse.

Now things get interesting. The bottom pane of the profiler window (refer to Figure 8-3) shows a list of methods, ordered by their contribution to overall execution time. As you review this list of methods, you start to come across methods from Tic-Tac-Toe. You will see that `Board.onDraw(...)` and `Board.getBitMapForSymbol(...)` are contributing large chunks of time. Drill into these methods by clicking the arrow to the left, as shown in Figure 8-4, and notice that `Board.getBitMapForSymbol(...)` is the true culprit.

```
...
for(int i = 0; i < GameGrid.SIZE; i++){
    for(int j = 0; j < GameGrid.SIZE; j++){
        Bitmap symSelected = getBitmapForSymbol(grid.getValueAtLocation(i, j));
        offsetX = (int)(((width - symSelected.getWidth())/2) + (i * width));
        offsetY = (int)(((height - symSelected.getHeight())/2) + (j * height));
        canvas.drawBitmap(symSelected, offsetX, offsetY, ditherPaint);
    }
}
...
```

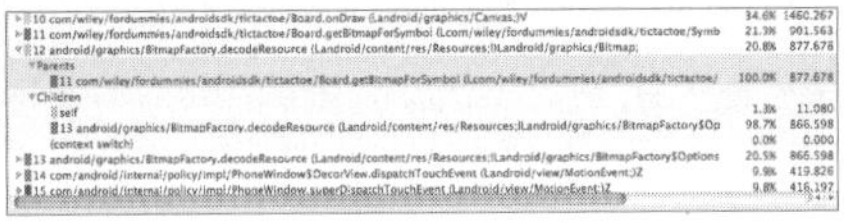

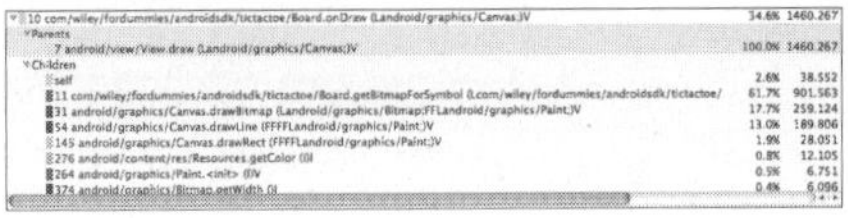

Figure 8-4:
Drilling
down in
the
profiler.
Look first
at `Board.`
`onDraw`
`(...)`. You
can see
that
`get-`
`BitMap-`
`For-`
`Symbol`
`(...)`
is being
called in a
loop from
`Board.`
`onDraw`
`(...)`.

This example explains why `onDraw(...)` is spending a lot of time in `getBit-MapForSymbol(...)`. An examination of the latter function shows that it's calling `getResources()` and `BitmapFactory.decodeResources(...)` for every square on the board, even though the values returned by these methods are invariant (the same) for every call (and for every instance of the game):

```
public Bitmap getBitmapForSymbol(Symbol aSymbol){
    Resources res = getResources();
    Bitmap symX = BitmapFactory.decodeResource(res, R.drawable.x);
    Bitmap symO = BitmapFactory.decodeResource(res, R.drawable.o);
    Bitmap symBlank = BitmapFactory.decodeResource(res, R.drawable.blank);

    Bitmap symSelected = symBlank;
    if (aSymbol == Symbol.SymbolXCreate())
        symSelected = symX;
    else if (aSymbol == Symbol.SymbolOCreate())
        symSelected = symO;
    return symSelected;
}
```

To quickly perform some optimization, you declare a set of private static variables:

```
static Bitmap symX=null, symO=null, symBlank=null;
static boolean bitMapsInitialized=false;
```

You also modify the code of `getBitMapForSymbol(...)` so that it gets the bitmaps only once per application run:

```
public Bitmap getBitmapForSymbol(Symbol aSymbol){
    if (!bitMapsInitialized){
        Resources res = getResources();
        symX = BitmapFactory.decodeResource(res, R.drawable.x);
        symO = BitmapFactory.decodeResource(res, R.drawable.o);
        symBlank = BitmapFactory.decodeResource(res, R.drawable.blank);
        bitMapsInitialized=true;
    }
    Bitmap symSelected = symBlank;
    if (aSymbol == Symbol.SymbolXCreate())
        symSelected = symX;
    else if (aSymbol == Symbol.SymbolOCreate())
        symSelected = symO;
    return symSelected;
}
```

Voilà! When you profile again, you see that `Board.onDraw(...)` and `get-BitmapForSymbol(...)` are no longer the top contributors to app execution time. Now you can move on to the new methods on the list that contribute to execution time.

Though this section explains how to use the profiling tools to judiciously "micro-optimize" application performance, note that your app will run on multiple hardware platforms, with different versions of the Dalvik virtual machine running on different processors at different speeds, with different computational add-ons (such as a video co-processor) that affect the speed of your app on each system. If performance on a specific platform is especially important to you, profile and optimize for that platform.

Maximizing Battery Life

If you own a smartphone or tablet device, you know that battery power is the scarcest resource. The elements that use the largest amount of battery power are the processor, the radio, and the display, so conserving battery power boils down to minimizing computation, minimizing network activity, and not forcing the display to run continuously or at full brightness. *Minimizing computation* essentially means following the techniques described in the previous section on improving performance, so in this section, we focus on reducing network activity.

On a smartphone, two major applications use the network:

- ✔ **Data services:** For example, file downloads, web browsing, and video and audio streaming
- ✔ **Location services:** For example, GPS and 3G and 4G networks

We address both types in the following sections.

Minimizing data services

With respect to data services, the first thing to keep in mind is that trying to make a connection and send or receive data when the connection is poor or non-existent wastes a considerable amount of power. Therefore, you can simply test the network connection in your code before trying to send or receive data. The method hasNetworkConnection() in the Help class in Tic-Tac-Toe shows how to test the various networks available on the device:

```
private boolean hasNetworkConnection(){
    ConnectivityManager connectivityManager =
        (ConnectivityManager) getSystemService(Context.CONNECTIVITY_SERVICE);
    NetworkInfo networkInfo =
        connectivityManager.getNetworkInfo(ConnectivityManager.TYPE_WIFI);
    boolean isConnected = true;
    boolean isWifiAvailable = networkInfo.isAvailable();
    boolean isWifiConnected = networkInfo.isConnected();
    networkInfo =
        connectivityManager.getNetworkInfo(ConnectivityManager.TYPE_MOBILE);
    boolean isMobileAvailable = networkInfo.isAvailable();
    boolean isMobileConnnected = networkInfo.isConnected();
    isConnected = (isMobileAvailable&&isMobileConnnected)||
                  (isWifiAvailable&&isWifiConnected);
    return(isConnected);

}
```

Reducing network use during data transfers is the next step. You can't do much directly about network use because the need for the data transfers is determined by the user. (In other words, users who want to watch YouTube will simply use YouTube.)

However, sometimes you have a choice in how you access that data. For example, several service providers (including Google) provide their data services in XML as well as JSON format. If you have this choice, pick the more compact representation — in this case, JSON — because less data must be transferred in order to receive the same information. In the Tic-Tac-Toe file GeoLocation.java, getNameFromLocation(…) shows you how to get back XML data, and `getGeoPointFromName(…)` shows you how to get JSON data back. As you can see, the amount of processing required is about the same, but with all factors consistent, JSON data is more compact and uses less network bandwidth.

Minimizing location services

In this section we cover the power management aspects of using location services (using location services is described in Chapter 10). You have a couple of different ways to reduce the amount of battery power used by a smartphone or tablet when trying to find location information. One is to use the last known location rather than repeatedly try to determine the current location over the network when it's slow or down or the provider is unavailable. The following code snippet from the method `getBestCurrent Location(…)` from the Tic-Tac-Toe class `GeoLocation.java` shows you how to do it:

```
public Location getBestCurrentLocation(){
    Location myLocation=null;
    myLocation = manager.getLastKnownLocation(bestProvider);
    if (myLocation == null){
        myLocation = manager.getLastKnownLocation("network");
    }
    if (myLocation != null){
        System.out.println("GeoLocation is >"+myLocation.toString()+"<");
        thisLocation = myLocation;
    }
    return thisLocation;
}
```

Another approach is to use a less expensive location provider when possible. You can pick the location provider directly, or you can specify the criteria you care about and have Android give you the appropriate location provider. In Tic-Tac-Toe, we have *not* done this; instead, the code chooses the best provider available, regardless of cost. Take a look at this constructor for the `GeoLocation` class:

```
public GeoLocation(Context theContext){
    thisContext = theContext;
    manager =
      (LocationManager) thisContext.getSystemService(Context.LOCATION_SERVICE);
    Criteria criteria = new Criteria();
    bestProvider = manager.getBestProvider(criteria, true);
    registerForLocationUpdates();
}
```

The following code snippet shows how you would write this method differently if you're looking for the cheapest provider:

```
public GeoLocation(Context theContext){
    Criteria criteria = new Criteria();
    criteria.setAccuracy(Criteria.ACCURACY_COARSE);
    criteria.setPowerRequirement(Criteria.POWER_LOW);
    LocationManager manager =
        (LocationManager)getSystemService(thisContext.LOCATION_SERVICE);
    String cheapestProvider = myLocationManager.getBestProvider(c, true);
    registerForLocationUpdates();
}
```

Be sure to unregister for location updates when your activity is paused, or else these updates will continue to waste battery power, even when the application isn't running.

Certain apps might need to lock the screen and prevent it from dimming or turning off while your application is running (for example, an app that is providing turn-by-turn driving directions). For this task, you use a wake lock. We don't describe wake locks in detail because they're beyond the scope of this book, but check out these two pages for more information:

✔ http://developer.android.com/reference/android/os/
    PowerManager.html

✔ http://developer.android.com/reference/android/os/
    PowerManager.WakeLock.html

Be sure to disable wake locks when your activity is paused. As with location updates, wake locks can continue after `onPause()`.

Ensuring Responsiveness in Your Apps

One nonfunctional requirement (NFR) of special concern in mobile apps is responsiveness. Mobile app developers must ensure that their apps don't even *appear* to freeze, become sluggish, or fail to respond to user input, for example.

Ensuring responsiveness isn't the same as optimizing performance.

Though your app might operate as fast as computationally possible, it must appear to be controllable by the user, even when it's actively working. For example, refreshing a web page might take a long time because the network or the server providing the page is slow. Obviously, your app can do nothing about speeding the refresh, but whenever this type of operation takes place, your app must not freeze ⊠ and it should, for example, allow the user to abandon the sluggish activity.

The primary technique to achieve responsiveness is *threading*. Essentially, the idea is to move from the main thread of the operation that's likely to take a long time and execute its operations on separate (additional) threads using the thread packages in Java. The following simple example shows you how a Java thread can be used to load an image from a network:

```
public void onClick(View v) {
    new Thread(new Runnable() {
        public void run() {
            Bitmap b = loadImageFromNetwork(); // user written method
            // do something with the image
            ...
        }
    }).start();
}
```

Another use of threads is in handling areas in your application where proper operation requires a waiting period. Two examples are in Tic-Tac-Toe. The first is in the `SplashScreen` activity, whose `onCreate(…)` method is listed here:

```
public void onCreate(Bundle savedInstanceState) {
    super.onCreate(savedInstanceState);
    setContentView(R.layout.splash);
    // Launch a new thread for the splash screen
    Thread splashThread = new Thread() {
        @Override public void run() {
            try {
                int elapsedTime = 0;
                while(active && (elapsedTime < splashTime)) {
                    sleep(sleepTime);
                    if(active) elapsedTime = elapsedTime + timeIncrement;
                }
            } catch(InterruptedException e) {
            // do nothing
            } finally {
                finish();
                startActivity(
                new Intent("com.wiley.fordummies.androidsdk.tictactoe.Login"));
            }
        }
    };
    splashThread.start();
}
```

In this code snippet, the splash screen is displayed and a separate thread is launched that sleeps for a while and then launches the `Login` activity. Because the main thread isn't put to sleep, it remains responsive so that the user can exit the splash screen by touching it. A touch event invokes the following `onTouch` method, which lets the app exit the splash screen:

```
public boolean onTouchEvent(MotionEvent event) {
    if (event.getAction() == MotionEvent.ACTION_DOWN) {
        active = false;
    }
    return true;
}
```

We also use threading to implement responsiveness in the implementation of machine play in Tic-Tac-Toe. Take a look at the following method `schedule-AndroidsTurn(...)` in the `GameSession` class:

```
private void scheduleAndroidsTurn() {
    System.out.println("Thread ID in scheduleAndroidsTurn:" +
                        Thread.currentThread().getId());
    board.disableInput();
    if(!testMode){
        Random randomNumber = new Random();
        Handler handler = new Handler();
        handler.postDelayed(
            new Runnable() {
                public void run() {
                    androidTakesATurn();
                }
            },
            ANDROIDTIMEOUTBASE + randomNumber.nextInt(ANDROIDTIMEOUTSEED));
    }else{
        androidTakesATurn();
    }
}
```

The machine pretends to think for a random period and then makes its move. While the computer is "thinking," the user is prevented from making a move. However, while input to the Tic-Tac-Toe board is prevented, other user actions should not be (such as allowing the user to exit the game by choosing Menu⇨End Game). You implement this behavior as described in this list:

- ✔ `board.disableInput()`: Prevents user input from registering on the game board.

- ✔ `Handler.postDelayed(...)`: Posts a delayed callback to the method `androidTakesATurn()` with a randomly generated delay. Thus, `androidTakesATurn()` is called after the random delay (during which the board isn't clickable). This method plays the computer's move and then enables the board. During this process, the main application thread (the user interface thread) is still active and can accept user input, including the directive to end the game, which we just mentioned.

Certain Android framework components automatically launch long-lived operations in separate threads (so that you don't have to do it). Take a look at the extracts of the activity HelpWithWebView:

```
public class HelpWithWebView extends Activity implements OnClickListener {
    protected void onCreate(Bundle savedInstanceState) {
        String URL=null;
        super.onCreate(savedInstanceState);
        setContentView(R.layout.helpwithwebview);
        WebView helpInWebView=null;
        helpInWebView = (WebView) findViewById(R.id.helpwithwebview);
        View buttonExit = findViewById(R.id.button_exit);
        buttonExit.setOnClickListener(this);
        Bundle extras = getIntent().getExtras();
        if(extras !=null){
            URL = extras.getString("URL");
        }
        helpInWebView.loadUrl(URL);
    }
    ...
}
```

helpInWebView.loadUrl(URL) launches a separate thread to load the URL so that the application remains responsive while the page is being loaded.

Understanding the SDK Components Used in This Chapter

This section relates additional details about the components (packages and classes) of the Android framework and its add-ons that provide the functionality covered in this chapter. We don't go into great detail because Google provides web pages that are more comprehensive than we could ever be, but we give you an idea of its components and describe what they can do.

The Android thread model and components

When an Android application is launched, a thread (known as the *main thread* or the *user interface (UI) thread*) is created. The Android user interface isn't thread-safe, so if separate threads are launched, they shouldn't perform user interface operations. (Although the Android runtime throws exceptions in most cases, in cases where your app manages to avoid throwing exceptions, you see some *strange* behavior.) Thus, you have to break your long-lived operation into two tasks:

✔ The intense, long-lived computation is performed.

✔ The result of the computation is shown in the user interface.

The Android framework offers four ways to access the UI thread:

✔ `Activity.runOnUiThread(Runnable myRunnable)` runs the specified runnable object on the UI thread. (See an example of this in `GameSessionTest.java` in the `TicTacToeProject-Test`.)

✔ `View.post(Runnable myRunnable)` causes the runnable to be added to the message queue to be run by the UI thread as it processes all its messages.

✔ `View.postDelayed(Runnable, long)` causes the runnable to be added to the message queue after a specified period.

✔ The `Handler` class lets you perform the preceding `post(...)` and `postDelayed(...)` operations when you don't have access to an active `View`. (See an example of this in `GameSession.java` in the `TicTacToeProject`.)

Look for more details about threading at `http://developer.android.com/resources/articles/painless-threading.html` and on the pages linked to it.

Power management components

Even though we don't describe the power management functionality in the Android SDK because it's beyond the scope of this book, we include a short section about the Android power manager class, which lets you set wake locks that can, for example, maintain full screen brightness while your application is running.

The main class is `PowerManager`, which is documented at `http://developer.android.com/reference/android/os/PowerManager.html`. Acquiring an instance of this class allows you to set wake locks, put the device to sleep, check screen activity, and determine when user activity last took place.

Chapter 9

Making Your Application Safe and Secure

"Eternal vigilance!" is the watchword for developing mobile devices and applications. However, implementing random security techniques in your app as a result of blind panic is hardly a good development strategy. As you design your app, think systematically to see where the security principles described in this chapter apply, and then implement the necessary security using a combination of the techniques also described in this chapter.

In this chapter, we take a holistic look at developing secure Android apps — starting by describing why security is especially important for mobile apps, and then presenting security principles and general security techniques. We then get into Android security specifics.

Recognizing the Importance of Security

Security is an increasingly important consideration for mobile devices (and their applications), for three primary reasons:

✔ **Mobile devices store valuable personal information.** Most people's mobile devices eventually become repositories for all types of personal information — their geographical location, contact names and addresses, financial transactions, and credit card information, for example. Theft of this information can result in significant financial loss to the user.

✔ **Mobile devices have a greater security footprint than applications on your desktop.** Mobile devices have more areas of vulnerability than desktop, and even laptop, applications. Mobile devices are designed to interact with the outside world via the Internet and other networking capabilities, such as Wi-Fi and Bluetooth, so they're exposed to all the consequent dangers. For example, when a user accesses the Internet from the browser on a mobile device, all browser-based vulnerabilities certainly apply — such as phishing, spyware, and viruses (collectively known as *malware*). However, malware poses a greater risk to mobile devices than to desktop computers because websites built to support mobile users are notorious for being security risks themselves (because they have been hurriedly implemented, usually without thought given to making them secure) — which means, of course, that they present a risk to devices that access them.

Because an app is now the primary means of using a device, it creates a security risk. Keep in mind that mobile apps have been authored by a range of organizations and developers and have been installed from diverse locations. Depending on the permissions granted to an app, it may be able to read and create user data on the device. In the Android Application Model, an app can be launched directly from the Home screen *or invoked by another app.* These two characteristics (it can read or create private data and it can be invoked by another app through an Intent — Chapter 3) make every app — including yours — a potential security risk. This is because your app, if it has access to private data and can be invoked by another (malicious) app, can be forced to reveal this data. Creating private data is a problem in itself. If your app creates private data and leaves it on the device in an insecure manner, a malicious piece of code (such as another app) can read it.

✔ **Mobile devices have less ability to protect themselves than desktop computers do.** Even though mobile devices are exposed to a wider set of vulnerabilities than desktop computers are, mobile devices are *less* able to protect themselves because the techniques and best practices used to protect desktop computers often are not feasible on mobile devices. Even if you believe that an Android device is less powerful than a desktop computer because, obviously, it lacks features such as strong encryption, that's not the whole story. A lack of computing power is no longer the primary issue.

Here are some other reasons that mobile devices are more vulnerable than desktop computers:

✔ **Small physical form factor:** Mobile devices are often easily mislaid or stolen because they're small. Someone with bad intentions can easily disassemble them to reach their internal components, such as memory cards, that contain private information.

✔ **No user login required:** A mobile device typically requires no login or other type of authentication in order to use it. A person who steals a user's device has immediate access to all the information on it and to other systems it's allowed to connect to, such as e-mail. In a related issue, whenever a user accesses a secure site, such as a bank or an employer's internal system, the *device* — not the user — is often the only entity that has been verified as the trusted party. If the device is stolen, the thief might have full access to the user's secured sites — at least from the time the theft occurs to the time the user discovers and reports it.

✔ **Weak password protection:** If a login is required on a device, the password itself can be a security threat. Because of the difficulty to use keyboards on mobile devices, it is a real inconvenience for users to type all the characters needed for long, strong passwords. For this reason, users tend to use shorter, simpler passwords, which makes the device easier to break into. Building complex layers of security into mobile devices and applications is also difficult because mobile users are especially sensitive to the user experience of the devices. Mobile users have been known to reject devices whose user interface is inconvenient to use; worse, users might be inclined to circumvent security features and thereby leave themselves completely vulnerable.

✔ **Limited screen size that impedes readability:** Because of the small screen sizes of mobile devices, URLs that a device might access often aren't completely visible. If a "dangerous" URL is a small variation of a "safe" URL (as commonly happens in phishing attacks), the user is likely not to notice the variation and may provide private information to the malicious site.

✔ **Environmental distractions:** Because users often use mobile devices in crowded spaces, such as buses, or while engaged in other activities, such as walking or driving (a *bad* idea), they become distracted and give less than optimum attention to security warnings.

For example, some financial portals show users special, personalized images to verify that they're on legitimate websites. Someone using a desktop in an office setting is likely to notice that this image is missing after being directed to a site that's spoofing the legitimate site. A user on a mobile device, on the other hand, is likely to be distracted and *not* notice the missing image because of simultaneously having to navigate the interior of a shopping mall or attempt to maintain balance on a speeding train.

When your application is *demonstrably* safe, secure, and useful, it becomes an application that people trust and hence want to buy, download, and install. While the reliable, high-performing usefulness of an application is certainly a significant factor in establishing trust (trust happens as a side-effect of the app demonstrating it can "get the job done well"), security plays the largest role in establishing trust.

Looking at Security Holistically

An application developer wondering how to provide application security typically starts by considering specific (but random) topics such as types of encryption and password-based login.

However, as an app developer, you must first define the app's *threat model,* which defines the kinds of attacks the app must expect to handle, the assets that must be protected, and the likely degree of loss if those assets are violated or stolen. (See the later section "Defining the Threat Model for an Android Application.")

After you have defined the threat model, you need to identify the specific techniques to handle threats. Security techniques can be grouped in the following functional categories:

✓ **Authentication:** This includes techniques for validating and identifying who or what is using the system. Authentication may be done through a username/password scheme (like in Tic-Tac-Toe), or you can get very sophisticated and even use biometrics — such as fingerprint or retinal scans! Authentication is a key need in secure systems. If you can't validate and identify the user, then access control, audit trail, and non-repudiation become impossible.

✓ **Access control:** Manage who has access to which capabilities or data. Now that you know (through authentication) who the user is, you should only allow him to do what he is permitted to do.

✓ **Audit trail:** This is the concept of keeping track of who did what in the system. This is typically achieved by logging.

✓ **Data integrity:** This is ensuring that data doesn't become corrupted or harmed. An audit trail will help here, and so will access control. Also in this category are techniques that use checksums that can be used to test whether a piece of data has been inconsistently modified.

✓ **Non-repudiation:** This is ensuring that no user or agent can deny doing something after he (or it) has done it.

Another (related) classification of security techniques is defined by the *roles* that the above security techniques can play in implementing a secure system. There are four roles, as follows:

✓ **Resistance:** This is making the loss more difficult to occur. Authentication, access control, and data integrity certainly help make the system resistant to attack.

✔ **Detection:** This is determining that a loss or breach has taken place, so that the system can start to protect itself against further breaches or limit the extent of the breach.

✔ **Mitigation:** This is limiting the degree of loss or breach that takes place.

✔ **Recovery:** This is helping the user to recover from a loss, such as by recovering the data from a backup.

Use both the lists to guide you in finding out how to address the attacks the system is likely to face. This systematic approach can lead to much better protection of your app than does simply adding a few ad hoc security techniques. Incidentally, the set of threats the system is likely to face, the probabilities of the threats succeeding, and the losses that are likely to happen if the threats succeed are collectively known as the "threat model" for a system. We explain the threat model, and how to define it, in the next section.

Defining the Threat Model for an Android Application

To define the threat model, this section describes what types of Android vulnerabilities you have to (and don't have to) deal with.

On the good side, because Android is a *privilege-separated* operating system. This means that — because it runs on Linux — every application runs under its own user ID and group ID. In other words, applications run separately from each other and the system. Finally, whenever an application is uninstalled, all its private data (including preferences and SQLite databases) is removed. Many risks are therefore eliminated and do not need to be included in the threat model.

On the bad side (it's not the fault of Android, however), after your app has been downloaded to a device, virtually every one of its characteristics can be looked up by an attacker, because the `.apk` file can be parsed and all its separate components extracted, including the manifest file, executable code, resources, and images. The source code can then be *decompiled* (reconstructed) from the executable code and examined for useful information such as which algorithms are used and which strings represent user IDs and passwords. As you might imagine, implementing "security by obscurity" — that is, relying on the system being safe because no one knows anything about it — simply isn't possible. You have to assume that an attacker knows every detail about your app and then try to protect it.

Your application can become a security risk in six ways, for example, if you

✔ **Leave private data in files on the device and its SD card:** Other, unauthorized and malicious, software may be able to read the files.

✔ **Use SQLite databases in a manner vulnerable to database hacking techniques:** An example is a SQL injection — which we explain later.

✔ **Allow other, unauthorized, apps to gain access to private data by using *your* app:** Remember that your app can be launched from another app. If your app is a security risk, it can be exploited by other malicious apps. Even built-in Android apps — such as the browser — can be a security risk. A malicious app may access a malicious website via either the built-in browser or the underlying `WebView` class (Chapter 10) and download a virus or other malware without the user realizing it.

✔ **Leave private information in a human-readable form in your source code:** Examples are hard-wired or "special" user IDs (that provide a system-level, or higher, degree of access to certain data) and passwords or encryption keys.

✔ **Rely on security by obscurity, such as using simple algorithms for generating keys or encrypting data:** You must assume that your app code isn't private and that, after your code is read, any security measure you've applied can be broken.

The following sections look systematically at how to address these threats.

Understanding the Android Security Model

The security threat in your app lies in malicious code — or a malicious user — taking advantage of the capabilities granted to your application.

Let's start by looking at how your app gains those capabilities. Android's privilege model (the rules by which capabilities are granted to applications) is designed so that no application can, *by default,* give permission to do anything that can adversely affect other apps or the operating system. Essentially, every app runs in its own *sandbox* (for example, its own address space in memory, or its own processes, threads, and space on the file system). If your app needs to operate outside this sandbox, such as by launching another app, by using some system functionality, or by sharing resources with another app, it must explicitly ask for permission from the Android framework.

All Android applications (specifically the `.apk` files that are installed on the device) must be signed using a certificate that identifies the author of the application. Self-signing certificates are perfectly legal — certificates don't have to be signed by a signing authority that verifies your identity. Android just wants to be able to uniquely differentiate you from everyone else.

For this reason, you can ask for a couple different kinds of permissions:

✔ First, you can request that two applications share the same user ID, thereby sharing access to each other's files and SQLite databases. Note that only two applications requesting to share user IDs have to be signed with the same signature in order for their request to be granted. To see how it's done, visit `http://developer.android.com/guide/topics/manifest/manifest-element.html#uid`.

✔ Second, your Android app must (in its manifest file) explicitly ask for permission for every protected service it needs on the device. These protected services range from straightforward, such as accessing locations, to esoteric, such as "using `SurfaceFlinger` low-level features" (which gives your app fine-grained control of how objects are placed on the frame buffer — a data structure that mirrors the device display). At the time the application is installed, the installer presents the list of permissions that the app is requesting and asks the user to approve or reject them, as shown in Figure 9-1. If the user rejects any permission, the installer on the device will not install the app. Also, if the app does not request these permissions it will not be able to use these services (although the parts of the app that do not use these services will still work).

A particular permission can be enforced at a number of places during your app's operation:

✔ **When a call is made to a system function:** To prevent an unauthorized invocation

✔ **When starting an activity:** To prevent an unauthorized application from launching the activity of other applications

✔ **When sending or receiving broadcasts:** To determine who can receive a broadcast or send one to you

✔ **When accessing, and operating on, a content provider:** To prevent an unauthorized app from accessing the data in the content provider

✔ **When binding to, or starting, a service:** To prevent an unauthorized application from using the service

Figure 9-1:
Approving requested permissions for the popular game *Angry Birds.*

The following XML snippet shows examples (from the Tic-Tac-Toe application) of requesting permission to use the Internet, access the network state, find both coarse and fine locations, and read contacts from the built-in Contacts application. You can see the complete list of permissions at `http://developer.android.com/reference/android/Manifest.permission.html`. Note that this list isn't static but, rather, grows in each Android release. Neither does it contain the list of custom permissions defined by you (see the entry containing LAUNCHACTIVITY shown in the XML block below).

```
<uses-permission android:name="android.permission.READ_CONTACTS"/>
<uses-permission android:name="android.permission.INTERNET"/>
<uses-permission android:name="android.permission.ACCESS_NETWORK_STATE"/>
<uses-permission android:name="android.permission.ACCESS_COARSE_LOCATION" />
<uses-permission android:name="android.permission.ACCESS_FINE_LOCATION" />
<uses-permission
    android:name="com.wiley.fordummies.androidsdk.tictactoe.LAUNCHACTIVITY"/>
```

Note carefully where the `<uses-permission>` . . . `</uses-permission>` element is placed in the `AndroidManifest.xml file` (it must be outside the `application` block and inside the `manifest` block)!

In the preceding chunk of code, you can see that the last permission appears to be specific to the Tic-Tac-Toe application — and it is. In addition to requesting predefined system permissions, apps can define their own permissions. To define and use custom permissions, these three steps must take place:

1. These permissions must be defined by the app developer by using `<permissions>` . . . `</permissions>` elements in the manifest file. Here's an example from the Tic-Tac-Toe activity:

```
<permission
    android:name="com.wiley.fordummies.androidsdk.tictactoe.LAUNCHACTIVITY"
    android:label="Launch Tic-Tac-Toe Activity"
    android:description="@string/permission_launch_activity"
    android:protectionLevel="normal"
/>
```

Note carefully where this element is also placed in the `AndroidManifest.xml` file (outside the `application` block and inside the `manifest` block). Also, the complete list of attributes in the `permission` element is shown at http://developer.android.com/guide/topics/manifest/permission-element.html.

2. The component (an activity or a service) that wants to declare the need for the permission must do so in its `android:permission` attribute. Here's an example from the `Login` activity in Tic-Tac-Toe:

```
<activity
    android:name=".Login"
    android:label="@string/app_name"
    android:launchMode="standard"
    android:screenOrientation="portrait"
    android:permission=
        "com.wiley.fordummies.androidsdk.tictactoe.LAUNCHACTIVITY"
>
```

3. The using package must request this permission (we showed you how to request permissions a few paragraphs earlier):

```
<uses-permission
    android:name="com.wiley.fordummies.androidsdk.tictactoe.LAUNCHACTIVITY"/>
```

This request is needed by the package in which the activity itself is located. Any separate package that has applications that will invoke the `Login` activity must (obviously) also request this permission.

The Android framework also uses a permissions-based scheme to protect content providers. Note that the Tic-Tac-Toe application must declare the need for the following permission to be able to read information about your contacts (and send them your scores):

```
<uses-permission android:name="android.permission.READ_CONTACTS"/>
```

Finally, we give you some techniques in the remainder of this section to help you debug permission errors.

If an application fails because of a permission error, you see an entry like the following in the `logcat` window (it's one long line, but we indented it here to improve readability):

```
02-28 12:48:00.864: ERROR/AndroidRuntime(378):
    java.lang.SecurityException: Permission Denial: starting Intent {
        act=com.wiley.fordummies.androidsdk.tictactoe.Login
        cmp=com.wiley.fordummies.androidsdk.tictactoe/.Login }
    from ProcessRecord{407740c0
        378:com.wiley.fordummies.androidsdk.tictactoe/10033} (pid=378,
            uid=10033)
    requires
        com.wiley.fordummies.androidsdk.tictactoe.permission.LAUNCHACTIVITY
```

The key string in this example is, of course, `java.lang.Security Exception`. The following lines (also from `logcat`) indicate that the exception is being thrown from the `SplashScreen` activity when it is trying to start the `Login` activity:

```
02-28 21:04:39.758: ERROR/AndroidRuntime(914): at
    com.wiley.fordummies.androidsdk.tictactoe.SplashScreen$1.run
        (SplashScreen.java:36)
```

You use the next technique to install the `.apk` on either an emulator or a device, find the directory by using the `adb` executable supplied with your Android distribution, and open a `shell`, `cmd`, or `terminal` window in that directory. Type this line:

```
./adb shell pm list permissions
```

You will see the text shown below, with your custom permission (`LAUNCHACTIVITY`) nestling in it:

```
permission:android.permission.INTERNAL_SYSTEM_WINDOW
permission:android.permission.MOVE_PACKAGE
permission:android.permission.READ_INPUT_STATE
permission:com.google.android.providers.settings.permission.READ_GSETTINGS
permission:android.permission.REBOOT
permission:android.permission.STATUS_BAR
permission:android.permission.ACCESS_DOWNLOAD_MANAGER_ADVANCED
permission:android.permission.STOP_APP_SWITCHES
```

```
permission:android.permission.MANAGE_APP_TOKENS
. . .
permission:com.wiley.fordummies.androidsdk.tictactoe.LAUNCHACTIVITY
. . .
permission:android.permission.SET_ACTIVITY_WATCHER
permission:android.permission.BACKUP
permission:android.permission.SET_TIME
permission:android.permission.STATUS_BAR_SERVICE
permission:android.permission.PERFORM_CDMA_PROVISIONING
permission:android.permission.INSTALL_PACKAGES
permission:com.google.android.apps.maps.permission.C2D_MESSAGE
permission:android.permission.CALL_PRIVILEGED
permission:android.permission.CHANGE_COMPONENT_ENABLED_STATE
permission:android.permission.WRITE_GSERVICES
permission:android.permission.BIND_WALLPAPER
```

Finally, we show you what happens if you put your permission entry in the wrong place. The following lines are shown in `logcat` if the `LAUNCHACTIVITY` permission declaration is at the wrong level (for example, inside the `activity` element):

```
02-28 16:53:09.838: DEBUG/PackageManager(77):   Permissions: com.wiley.
           fordummies.androidsdk.tictactoe.LAUNCHACTIVITY

02-28 17:04:18.888: WARN/PackageParser(77): Unknown element under <application>:
           permission at /data/app/vmdl1654102309.tmp Binary XML file line
           #11

02-28 17:04:20.438: WARN/PackageManager(77): Unknown permission com.wiley.
           fordummies.androidsdk.tictactoe.LAUNCHACTIVITY in package
           com.wiley.fordummies.androidsdk.tictactoe
```

Protecting SQLite Databases

The primary security concern created by using SQLite databases is the *SQL injection* attack, in which the attacker is able to force the system to execute his own query and return data that he does not have authorization to access. Suppose that in response to a prompt for a person's name, you enter *Bob* on the form and the application returns Bob's e-mail address by looking up a table using this query:

```
Select e-mail from user_information where name = Bob
```

Before software developers understood SQL injection attacks, they (the software developers) would use string concatenation to create queries. Thus, for the example shown above, a string was programmatically created that looked exactly like the query shown in the preceding example. This string was then sent to the database to execute.

But note what happens if you enter `Bob; select table_names from user_tables` in the entry field of the user interface: The query string becomes

```
Select e-mail from user_information where name = Bob;
          select table_names from user_tables
```

Most SQL databases would execute both queries, returning not only Bob's e-mail but also the names of the programmer-defined tables in the system. (The `user_tables` view is standard in most databases that contain the names of all user-defined tables.) Armed with this information, an attacker can inject all kinds of queries into a database to read all the other tables — even the system tables.

Defending against this type of attack is a straightforward process. The trick is to use what are known as "bind" variables. We do this in the Tic-Tac-Toe application. Look at the following lines that were extracted from the file `DatabaseHelper.java`:

```
private static final String TABLE_NAME = "Accounts";
. . .
private static final String INSERT = "insert into " +
    TABLE_NAME + "(name, password) values (?, ?)" ;
. . .
public DatabaseHelper(Context context) {
. . .
    this.insertStmt = this.db.compileStatement(INSERT);
. . .
}
. . .
public long insert(String name, String password) {
    this.insertStmt.bindString(1, name);
    this.insertStmt.bindString(2, password);
    return this.insertStmt.executeInsert();
}
```

The constant `INSERT` defines a *template* for the database query, where the two question marks (?) define locations where data can be inserted. The `this.insertStmt = this.db.compileStatement(INSERT)` statement is compiling the query into an internal data structure, and the `insert(. . .)` method assembles the query from the parameters that are sent to it. If someone attempted the SQL injection attack from the preceding example (and added a query to the Password field), the query would look like the following line, which creates an odd password but does nothing harmful:

```
insert into Accounts (name, password) values ('Bob', '<password>; select table_
          names from user_tables')
```

Minimizing the Security Footprint of Your App

After you know how the Android security model works, we have to tell how to leverage it for security purposes. To begin with, follow the principle of *least privilege* and give your app the *least* possible level of capability so that if someone uses it in an unauthorized manner, the least amount of damage will be done. If your app needs only a coarse location (at the city level), for example, don't give it fine location capability. If your app doesn't need to save external files, don't write it so that it can save them. If your app doesn't need complete access to a content provider, give it access only to the Universal Resource Identifiers (URI) it needs.

You should also limit your app's accessibility with respect to other applications (those not developed by you). If certain activities in your app are security risks and are not to be started by other activities, declare custom permissions for these activities. Then if a malicious app wants to use your app, it must declare its true intentions by requesting these custom permissions. The user then has a chance to realize this malicious intent and refuse to accept the request.

Before we end this section, and so as to connect it with the security categories we covered in the earlier section, note that the above are *mitigation* tactics — they help you *minimize* the damage caused by a breach.

Going Beyond Permissions

The appropriate use of permissions can go a long way toward helping to make your apps secure. The following list describes some additional steps you can take to make your applications more secure (the categories the strategy belongs to are shown in parentheses):

- ✔ **Do not hard-wire secrets (such as special passwords) into your code.** Java code can be easily decompiled to reveal this type of constant in your code. (Resist)

- ✔ **Encrypt any files that hold sensitive information.** This advice isn't specific to Android — a good book on Java security (such as *Java Security Solutions,* by Rich Helton and Johennie Helton (John Wiley & Sons, Inc.)) should show you how. Note that you must keep hidden (from anyone who might hack your app's source code) the key you use to encrypt the file itself. (Resist, Data Integrity)

✔ **Back up your data so that you can restore it if your device ever gets hacked and its data corrupted.** The Android SDK provides an API to a service that can back up your app's data on Google's servers. We don't include a description of this service in this book because of certain Google limitations (no guarantee that the service will remain free and no guarantee of future support, for example). (Recover)

✔ **Log what your app does (such as the methods it calls) to a log file (and don't put sensitive, user-supplied information in the file or forget to encrypt it).** In particular, be sure to log all permission exceptions. The log file can also be used to determine whether an attack was made, and by whom. (Audit Trail, Non-Repudiation, Detect)

✔ **For especially sensitive operations or requests for data, don't rely only on permissions.** Add code that alerts the user to the sensitive access being requested and asks for user confirmation. (Resist, Access Control)

✔ **Keep intent filters to sensitive activities specific so that attackers cannot launch this type of activity by sending out high-level intents.** Validate intent parameters when they're received by activities, and don't put sensitive data (such as passwords) into an intent that's being used to start an activity. Malware can register higher-priority intent filters and have a user's sensitive data sent to it instead. (Resist, Access Control)

✔ **Of course, set up your user interface so that when sensitive data (such as a password) is entered, it's masked.** You probably can tell where in the Tic-Tac-Toe application we *didn't* do this (for a hint, look at the `Login` activity) and where we *did* mask the data entry (look at the `Account` activity). (Resist, Authentication)

Part IV
Enhancing the Capabilities of Your Android Application

The 5th Wave   By Rich Tennant

"Why, of course. I'd be very interested in seeing this new milestone in the project."

In this part . . .

This part of the book describes the SDK components needed to incorporate into your app the advanced capabilities of your mobile device. To that end, Chapter 10 addresses integrating the web and location services, and Chapter 11 covers the use of audio, video, and, most importantly, sensors.

Chapter 10

Channeling the Outside World through Your Android Device

....

....

Your Android device is your portal to the world. You can use it to interact with other people, see what else is going on in the rest of the world, and find out what's around you — shopping, dining, and local points of interest, for example.

Your Android device can do all this because of apps that can use the web, location-based services provided by a variety of providers (in particular, Google), and the device's own, built-in, location-finding capability.

We cover many topics in this chapter, from simply launching a browser from a URL, to embedding a browser in your application, to embedding and controlling a map based on device location. It's exciting stuff! This chapter first shows you how to write apps that can, for example, browse the web, call web services that provide you with specific services and information, present maps of places that might interest you, and indicate where *you* are on a map. The chapter also reveals the true potential of Android apps, by describing the capabilities that exist on your device and on the Internet to use external services — in particular, mapping and location-based services.

Launching a Browser from Your App

In our first (and simplest) example of channeling the outside world, the sample application launches the built-in browser on a specific web page identified by a Universal Record Locator (the familiar URL). We illustrate this concept within (what else?) the Tic-Tac-Toe application, by providing a means of opening the Wikipedia page that describes, from within the Help screen, the game of tic-tac-toe (`http://en.wikipedia.org/wiki/Tictactoe`). The Help screen itself is shown in Figure 10-1.

Figure 10-1: The Tic-Tac-Toe Help screen.

Pressing the Tic-Tac-Toe on Wikipedia button opens a browser on the Wikipedia website that describes the game of tic-tac-toe, as shown in Figure 10-2.

Figure 10-2: Tic-tac-toe on Wikipedia in the Android browser.

Networking basics

Any collection of interconnected computers is a *network*. The network can consist of computers in your house or workplace that are connected in *a local-area network* (LAN) or across the Internet in a *wide-area network* (WAN).

For different kinds of communications, computers also "speak" a communication language that follows a specific set of rules, or *protocol*. It's a formal description of the digital formats of the messages that are exchanged and the rules (signaling and acknowledgements, for example) for exchanging those messages.

We blur some technical distinctions here, but an Android device is supplied with the capability to speak, essentially, three kinds of protocols: Bluetooth, TCP/IP, and Hypertext Transfer Protocol (or HTTP), a higher-level protocol. Bluetooth is used for device-to-device communication in close range. TCP/IP is the most widely used protocol for computer-to-computer communication on the Internet. Layered on TCP/IP is the HTTP protocol, on which most web-based applications are built. Layered on top of HTTP are some capabilities that the Android framework itself provides. These capabilities (such as launching a web browser) hide even HTTP from you, making things even simpler.

This book describes only applications that you can build by using the HTTP protocol. Unless you're building a performance-critical application (such as a multiplayer game) that requires large numbers of messages to be exchanged in real-time, the HTTP protocol is the only one you need. Also, we've left out developing Bluetooth-based applications, as being too complicated for a *For Dummies* book.

The code for this task is straightforward. As we recommend in earlier chapters, open the code in Eclipse and follow along as you read this section. We begin by showing you the relevant code segments from `Help.java`. First, the following `onClick( . . .)` method is called whenever a button on the Help screen is pressed:

```
public void onClick(View v) {
    switch(v.getId())
    . . .
    case R.id.button_lookup_wikipedia:
        if (hasNetworkConnection()){
            LaunchBrowser("http://en.wikipedia.org/wiki/Tictactoe");
        }else{
            noNetworkConnectionNotify();
        }
        break;
    . . .
}
```

URLs and URIs

A *Uniform Resource Identifier,* or *URI,* is a string that identifies a resource on the web. You can think of a URI as the International Standard Book Number (ISBN) of a book in the library. A *Uniform Resource Locator,* or *URL,* is a URI plus a means of gaining access to the resource, and potentially acting on it. You can think of this term as an ISBN number plus a library location plus, potentially, a means (such as snail mail) of delivering the book to you. In most cases, you can consider the terms *URL* and *URI* to be interchangeable.

Now take a look at the `LaunchBrowser(.  .  .)` method:

```
private void LaunchBrowser(String URL){
    Uri theUri = Uri.parse(URL);
    Intent LaunchBrowserIntent = new Intent(Intent.ACTION_VIEW, theUri);
    startActivity(LaunchBrowserIntent);
}
```

Yes, it's that simple! The built-in browser on your Android device has declared an intent filter stating that it will accept the action `ACTION_VIEW` on data consisting of a web resource identified by a uniform resource identifier (or URI) and accessible using the HTTP protocol. Thus, when the intent containing this action-data pair is broadcast using `startActivity(.  .  .)`, the browser picks it up and launches itself on the specified `www.wikipedia.org` URL.

The URL `http://en.wikipedia.org/wiki/Tictactoe` is being automatically redirected to `http://en.m.wikipedia.org/wiki/Tictactoe`, which is the Tic-Tac-Toe web page for mobile devices (a page that doesn't use frames and has fewer embedded graphics, for example). Note also that the Back button on your device must be pressed twice to return to the Help activity in Tic-Tac-Toe. Because the browser application is being relaunched on the page for mobile devices, two browser activities are on the top of the activity stack. Also, all you can do is launch the browser so that it takes over the entire screen and then exits. For finer-grained control, you must embed the browser as a view in your application, which we describe in the next section.

Embedding a Browser in Your Android Application

The Android framework provides you with a `View` subclass named `WebView` that you can embed in your application's user interface. We show you this concept by implementing a new activity named `HelpWithWebView` that will have `WebView` as part of its view. This activity is launched from the `onClick` method of the `Help` activity. Its code is shown here:

```
public void onClick(View v) {
    switch(v.getId())
    . . .
    case R.id.button_lookup_wikipedia_in_web_view:
        if (hasNetworkConnection()){
            LaunchWebView("http://en.wikipedia.org/wiki/Tictactoe");
        }else{
            noNetworkConnectionNotify();
        }
        break;

    . . .
}
```

`LaunchWebView(. . .)` uses the same Wikipedia URL to launch the `HelpWithWebView(. . .)` activity, by using the following code snippet:

```
private void LaunchWebView(String URL){
    Intent launchWebViewIntent = new Intent(this, HelpWithWebView.class);
    launchWebViewIntent.putExtra("URL", URL);
    startActivity(launchWebViewIntent);
}
```

We're showing you something new in this example: how data can be passed from the launching activity to the launched activity via the Intent. You can use the `putExtra(. . .)` method to insert extra data in the form of name-value pairs. In the example, the Wikipedia URL is being embedded with the key `"URL"`. Now take a look at the `onCreate(. . .)` method of the following `HelpWithWebView` activity:

```
protected void onCreate(Bundle savedInstanceState) {
    String URL=null;
    super.onCreate(savedInstanceState);
    setContentView(R.layout.helpwithwebview);
    WebView helpInWebView=null;
    helpInWebView = (WebView) findViewById(R.id.helpwithwebview);

    View buttonExit = findViewById(R.id.button_exit);
    buttonExit.setonClickListener(this);
    Bundle extras = getIntent().getExtras();
    if(extras !=null)URL = extras.getString("URL");
    helpInWebView.loadUrl(URL);
}
```

Finally, we show you the layout for the user interface of the `HelpWith WebView` activity in which the `WebView` is embedded:

```xml
<?xml version="1.0" encoding="utf-8"?>
<ScrollView
    xmlns:android="http://schemas.android.com/apk/res/android"
    android:layout_width="match_parent"
    android:layout_height="match_parent"
    android:padding="10dip" >
    <LinearLayout xmlns:android="http://schemas.android.com/apk/res/android"
        android:orientation="vertical"
        android:layout_width="match_parent"
        android:layout_height="match_parent">
    <WebView
        android:id="@+id/helpwithwebview"
        android:layout_width="match_parent"
        android:layout_height="200dip"
        android:layout_weight="1.0"/>
            <Button
        android:id="@+id/button_exit"
        android:layout_width="match_parent"
        android:layout_height="wrap_content"
        android:text="Exit"/>
    </LinearLayout>
</ScrollView>
```

This example shows that we have simply embedded `WebView` along with an
`Exit` button inside `LinearLayout`, as shown in Figure 10-3.

Figure 10-3:
Showing a
web page in
an embed-
ded web
view.

Providing Maps and Location-Based Services

A smartphone is usually an integral part of its owner's life, and one that's used for many tasks — personal conversations, location-based activities, and buying decisions, for example. Because this mobile device is also a computer that can record and remember details, it retains intimate knowledge about the person — names of friends (from the address book and calling patterns) and common haunts, for example — that can be used to provide personalized, circumstance-specific, and highly targeted *context-based* services that appear to have been created just for the device owner.

A vital component of context is location, one that a smart Android device is especially capable of providing because it has the capability to be located, either via a built-in GPS device or a cellular phone tower or Wi-Fi hotspot. Because the device generally goes everywhere the user does, its location is also the user's location.

By using the Android framework's location-finding services, you can write apps that provide location-based services. These services have many uses, such as giving directions to places a user has never visited or providing information about points of interest (such as dining or popular sights) near the user's location.

All these location-based services have four fundamental components:

✔ Open a map.

✔ Invoke the service (a restaurant or point of interest, for example).

✔ Navigate the map to various positions or make a calculation related to the two positions (such as directions).

✔ Find out (from the device) the user's coordinates.

(We describe these four fundamental components in greater detail in the next few sections.)

We have implemented an activity in Tic-Tac-Toe, named `WhereAmI` (why not?), that makes use of the functionality we just described. This activity starts by displaying a map within the Android `MapClass` (a subclass of the `View` class). This map has zoom controls, so that the user can pan to different locations by dragging the map in any direction. Also, the user can enter a location name and ask the map to navigate to the location. Finally, the user can ask the map to navigate to his current location. The application determines where the device is by invoking the location services on the device and then positioning the map on that location.

Isn't it cool to watch the map orient itself to a location?!

Installing the necessary development components for writing map apps

The standard Android libraries don't contain the Google Map libraries you need in order to write map applications. Thus, if you build using only the standard Android SDK libraries (the ones named SDK Platform such and such — for example, SDK Platform 3.2 API 13, revision 1, in the SDK and AVD Manager), you will see build errors. Even if you build against the right libraries (see the next paragraph), but run your map-based application on an emulator that has only the Android SDK as a target, you will see a runtime error whenever you try to use the map-based functionality.

This problem isn't a big deal, though — you simply have to install the *Google* API library and build the app and the emulator with this library as the target instead. This library contains both the Android libraries and the Google Maps API.

Incidentally, the `AndroidManifest.xml` file then has to be modified with an entry for the Google Maps library. To do this, place the following line *inside* the `<application>` . . . `</application>` element in the manifest file:

```
<uses-library android:name="com.google.android.maps" />
```

Do *not* place this line outside the `<application>` element by mistake, or you will spend hours trying to debug your map functionality!

Next, request these permissions:

```
<uses-permission android:name="android.permission.ACCESS_NETWORK_STATE"/>
<uses-permission android:name="android.permission.ACCESS_COARSE_LOCATION" />
<uses-permission android:name="android.permission.ACCESS_FINE_LOCATION" />
```

Finally, if you're embedding maps in your application using `MapView`, you need a Google Maps API key. For information on how to obtain a map key, see `http://code.google.com/android/add-ons/google-apis/mapkey.html`. To briefly reiterate the instructions on this page, you must first create a certificate for your application by using Eclipse (see Chapter 13 or `http://developer.android.com/guide/publishing/app-signing.html#ExportWizard` on how to do this) and then use the MD5 fingerprint of your certificate to generate the map key online. Then you put the map key in the layout file specifically for the activity that seeks to use an embedded map view. (We show you where in the following section.)

Displaying a map by using MapView

We now illustrate how to display the map by walking you through part of the WhereAmI activity. (Again, feel free to follow along in Eclipse.) To start with, take a look at its layout file:

```
<Rajiv: Clarified>
<?xml version="1.0" encoding="utf-8"?>
<LinearLayout xmlns:android="http://schemas.android.com/apk/res/android"
    android:id="@+id/whereamiframe"
    android:orientation="vertical"
    android:layout_width="match_parent"
    android:layout_height="match_parent">
    <com.google.android.maps.MapView
        android:id="@+id/whereamiview"
        android:apiKey="0gnB1it3gGRvFkdhjqBahvgiSsVwUKuuNTXuUeA"
        android:layout_width="match_parent"
        android:layout_height="200dip"
        android:clickable="true"/>
    <TableLayout
        xmlns:android="http://schemas.android.com/apk/res/android"
        android:layout_width="match_parent"
        android:layout_height="100dip"
        android:stretchColumns="1">
        <TableRow>
            <Button
                android:id="@+id/button_locate"
                android:layout_width="match_parent"
                android:layout_height="wrap_content"
                android:text="Find"/>
            <EditText
                android:id="@+id/location"
                android:layout_column="1"
                android:text="Enter address ..."
                android:layout_width="match_parent"
                android:padding="3dip" />
        </TableRow>
        <TableRow>
            <Button
                android:id="@+id/button_locate_me"
                android:layout_width="match_parent"
                android:layout_height="wrap_content"
                android:text="Locate Me"/>
            <TextView
                android:id="@+id/my_location"
                android:layout_column="1"
                android:text="Where am I ..."
                android:layout_width="match_parent"
                android:padding="3dip"/>
        </TableRow>
```

```
    </TableLayout>
    <Button
        android:id="@+id/button_exit"
        android:layout_width="match_parent"
        android:layout_height="wrap_content"
        android:text="Exit"
    />
</LinearLayout>
```

Note the line android:apiKey=<long unintelligible set of char-
acters> inside the MapView element — that's where you would insert the
generated map key. (By the way, this is a made-up key, so don't try to use it!)

This layout file generates the user interface for the WhereAmI activity, as
shown in Figure 10-4.

Figure 10-4:
Using an
embedded
MapView.

Finally, look at the WhereAmI class (including the imports and the class
header) and the onCreate(. . .) method for this activity:

```
package com.wiley.fordummies.androidsdk.tictactoe;

import com.google.android.maps.GeoPoint;
import com.google.android.maps.MapController;
import com.google.android.maps.MapView;
import com.google.android.maps.MapActivity;

import android.location.Location;

import android.os.Bundle;
import android.view.View;
import android.view.View.onClickListener;
import android.widget.EditText;
```

```
import android.widget.TextView;

import com.wiley.fordummies.androidsdk.tictactoe.R;

public class WhereAmI extends MapActivity implements onClickListener {
    private MapController whereAmIController=null;
    private EditText locationEditableField=null;
    private TextView myLocationField=null;
    private GeoLocation myGeoLocator = null;
    private int locationQueryCount=0;

    protected void onCreate(Bundle savedInstanceState) {
        super.onCreate(savedInstanceState);
        setContentView(R.layout.whereami);

        MapView whereamiView=null;
        whereamiView = (MapView) findViewById(R.id.whereamiview);
        whereamiView.setSatellite(true);
        whereamiView.setBuiltInZoomControls(true);
        whereAmIController = whereamiView.getController();

        locationEditableField= (EditText)findViewById(R.id.location);

        View buttonLocate = findViewById(R.id.button_locate);
        buttonLocate.setonClickListener(this);

        View buttonExit = findViewById(R.id.button_exit);
        buttonExit.setonClickListener(this);

        myLocationField= (TextView)findViewById(R.id.my_location);
        View buttonLocateMe = findViewById(R.id.button_locate_me);
        buttonLocateMe.setonClickListener(this);

        myGeoLocator = new GeoLocation(this);
    }
    . . .
}
```

In this example, you see a bunch of imports that start with com.google.
android.maps as well as android.location.location. You need this
special set of imports in order to use location finding and maps.

Next, you see that WhereAmI extends MapActivity rather than Activity.
Make a note of this because the Android framework handles MapActivity differently. For example, it starts up background threads to display the MapView
so that the rest of the app doesn't get stuck waiting for the map to display.
Also, look at the code for the onCreate method. The first part is pretty normal
activity stuff. But then you will see that the code gets a handle to the MapView
control and sets various parameters, such as setting it to Satellite View mode
(other view modes are Street View mode and Traffic View mode) and turning

on zoom controls. The code also gets a handle to a `MapController` object, which is used to navigate the map to different locations.

Finally, it gets a handle to an instance of the `GeoLocation` class. We discuss the `GeoLocation` class in the section "Determining the location of your device."

That's it! When you launch the `WhereAmI` activity (by clicking the Where Am I button on the `GameOptions` screen), a map opens in `MapView`. We describe what you can do with this `MapView` in the next section.

Calling a geocoding web service and navigating the map

In this section, we show you how to call a web service to translate a location name to a map coordinate and how to navigate the map to the coordinate.

We start by demonstrating the application feature and then drilling into how it's implemented. Run the Tic-Tac-Toe application and launch the `WhereAmI` activity (refer to Figure 10-4). Enter an address — or the name of any reasonably well-known location, such as *Central Park New York City* or *London England*. Then tap the Find button to see the map navigate to the location.

To see how the map is made to navigate to the location, begin by looking at the `onClick` method of the `WhereAmI` activity. We list the relevant segment here:

```
public void onClick(View v) {
    switch(v.getId()){
        case R.id.button_locate:
        try{
            String locationName = this.locationEditableField.getText().
                toString();
            GeoPoint point = myGeoLocator.getGeoPointFromName(locationName);
            whereAmIController.setZoom(16);
            whereAmIController.animateTo(point);
        } catch (Exception e){
            e.printStackTrace();
        }
    ...
    }
...
}
```

The method `myGeoLocator.getGeoPointFromName(locationName)` returns the geocoding of the location (in a `GeoPoint` data structure, which contains the latitude and longitude of the location in *microdegrees.* (Using these millionths of degrees helps avoid the use of inaccurate floating-point arithmetic in map calculations, such as distance calculations.) Then `whereAmIController.animateTo(point)` navigates the map to that location, and `whereAmIController.setZoom(16)` sets a reasonable zoom level. The zoom value ranges from 1 to 21. Not all zoom levels apply in a given geographic area. This is because each zoom level navigates to a layer of the map. If a layer corresponding to a level does not exist in the map database, zooming to that level will fail and will keep the map at the current level.

The following snippet of code shows `myGeoLocator.getGeoPointFrom-Name`, which we describe next:

```
public GeoPoint getGeoPointFromName(String locationName) {
    GeoPoint tempGeoPoint=null;
    String cleanLocationName = locationName.replaceAll(" ","%20");
    HttpGet httpGet = new HttpGet(
                        http://maps.google.com/maps/api/geocode/json?address=
                        + cleanLocationName
                        + "&sensor=false");
    HttpClient client = new DefaultHttpClient();
    HttpResponse response;
    StringBuilder stringBuilder = new StringBuilder();
    try {
        response = client.execute(httpGet);
        HttpEntity entity = response.getEntity();
        InputStream stream = entity.getContent();
        int b;
        while ((b = stream.read()) != -1) {
            stringBuilder.append((char) b);
        }
        JSONObject jsonLocation= new JSONObject();
        jsonLocation= new JSONObject(stringBuilder.toString());
        tempGeoPoint = getGeoPointFromJSON(jsonLocation);
    } catch (Exception e) {
        e.printStackTrace();
    }
    return tempGeoPoint;
}
```

The `HttpGet` call is a call to a REST-based (or RESTful) web service. The *re*presentational *s*tate *t*ransfer (or *REST*) technique retrieves data from a website by providing a URL that's processed by the site to return data in either XML format or JavaScript Object Notation (JSON) format, as in this case. This particular service returns the geocoded coordinates of the location in JSON format, from which the latitude and longitude are extracted and then converted to a `GeoPoint`.

The code for extracting the geo coordinates is shown here (only for completeness because this code isn't Android-specific):

```
private static GeoPoint getGeoPointFromJSON(JSONObject jsonObject) {
    GeoPoint returnGeoPoint=null;
    try {
        Double longitude = new Double(0);
        Double latitude = new Double(0);
        longitude = ((JSONArray)jsonObject.get("results")).
                        getJSONObject(0).
                        getJSONObject("geometry").
                        getJSONObject("location").
                        getDouble("lng");
        latitude = ((JSONArray)jsonObject.get("results")).
                        getJSONObject(0).
                        getJSONObject("geometry").
                        getJSONObject("location").
                        getDouble("lat");
        returnGeoPoint = new GeoPoint((int)(latitude*1E6),(int)(longitude*1E6));
    } catch (Exception e) {
        e.printStackTrace();
    }
    return returnGeoPoint;
}
```

We also show you an example JSON string (containing the geocoded location of London, England) from which the latitude and longitude can be extracted using the preceding code snippet:

```
{ "results" : [ { "address_components" : [ { "long_name" : "London",
            "short_name" : "London",
            "types" : [ "locality",
                "political"
                ]
        },
        { "long_name" : "Westminster",
          "short_name" : "Westminster",
          "types" : [ "administrative_area_level_3",
              "political"
              ]
        },
        { "long_name" : "Greater London",
          "short_name" : "Greater London",
          "types" : [ "administrative_area_level_2",
              "political"
              ]
        },
        { "long_name" : "England",
          "short_name" : "England",
          "types" : [ "administrative_area_level_1",
              "political"
```

```
                ]
            },
            { "long_name" : "United Kingdom",
              "short_name" : "GB",
              "types" : [ "country",
                  "political"
                  ]
            }
          ],
      "formatted_address" : "Westminster, London, UK",
      "geometry" : { "bounds" : { "northeast" : { "lat" : 51.704064700000004,
                "lng" : 0.15022949999999999
              },
            "southwest" : { "lat" : 51.349352799999998,
                "lng" : -0.37835800000000003
                }
          },
        "location" : { "lat" : 51.500152399999997,
            "lng" : -0.12623619999999999
          },
        "location_type" : "APPROXIMATE",
        "viewport" : { "northeast" : { "lat" : 51.704064700000004,
                "lng" : 0.15022949999999999
              },
            "southwest" : { "lat" : 51.349352799999998,
                "lng" : -0.37835800000000003
                }
          }
        },
      "types" : [ "locality",
          "political"
          ]
    } ],
  "status" : "OK"
}
```

Determining the location of your device (or, wherever you go, there you are)

Android provides three types of location-finding capabilities as part of the Android SDK:

- ✔ **GPS:** The most accurate type is GPS, which uses a permanent ring of satellites to locate devices containing GPS receivers. However, GPS doesn't work (well) indoors, consumes a hefty amount of battery power, and sometimes takes a while to determine the location of the device.

✔ **Cell towers:** Cell towers that the device (if it's a phone) is communicating with know the approximate location, via triangulation based on signal direction and strength.

✔ **Wi-Fi access points:** Similar to cell towers, Wi-Fi access points that the device is connected to serve as approximate proxies for the device.

Despite the emergence of powerful mobile devices with embedded GPS components, and the availability of satellite GPS service, challenges in device location remain. All three of the techniques we described above are still approximations. Plus, as a user moves around or moves from outdoors to indoors, or as the weather changes, the different types of location services could become available or unavailable. Also, these services vary in accuracy depending on where the device is located and on environmental conditions (such as cloudy weather for GPS services or the material composition of the walls between the device and an access point). Thus, what was the most accurate location provider at a given instance of time may no longer be so a few minutes later.

To illustrate this concept, we show you some of the methods inside the `GeoLocation` class we have written. We start with the imports, the class header, and the constructor:

```
. . .
import com.google.android.maps.GeoPoint;
import android.content.Context;
import android.location.*;
import android.os.Bundle;

public class GeoLocation implements LocationListener {
    private Context thisContext=null;
    private LocationManager manager=null;
    private String bestProvider=null;
    private Location thisLocation=null;
    thisContext = theContext;

    manager = (LocationManager)
            thisContext.getSystemService(Context.LOCATION_SERVICE);
    Criteria criteria = new Criteria();
    bestProvider = manager.getBestProvider(criteria, true);
    registerForLocationUpdates();
}
```

To begin with, note that the class imports three packages within the Android framework that provide location services. Next, the `GeoLocation` class implements the `LocationListener` interface, which specifies the notification methods needed in order to let the location service notify your application when the location or another element of the service changes (such as a provider becoming disabled). Finally, the constructor of the class gets a handle to a location manager (the current best provider) and registers for location updates. Here's the code for `registerForLocationUpdates`:

```
private void registerForLocationUpdates(){
    manager.requestLocationUpdates(bestProvider,
                                   15000,
                                   1,
                                   (LocationListener) this);
}
```

The method `getBestCurrentLocation`, shown in the following code snippet, gets the current location of the device from what is now the best location provider:

```
public Location getBestCurrentLocation(){
    Location myLocation=null;
    myLocation = manager.getLastKnownLocation(bestProvider);
    if (myLocation == null){
        myLocation =
            manager.getLastKnownLocation(LocationManager.NETWORK_PROVIDER);
    }
    if (myLocation != null){
        System.out.println("GeoLocation is >"+myLocation.toString()+"<");
        thisLocation = myLocation;
    }
    return thisLocation;
}
```

After an app has registered for location updates, the location service on the Android device calls one or more of the following methods as characteristics of the service change:

```
public void onLocationChanged(Location location) {
    thisLocation = location;
}
public void onProviderDisabled(String provider) {
    // TODO Auto-generated method stub
}
public void onProviderEnabled(String provider) {
    // TODO Auto-generated method stub
}
public void onStatusChanged(String provider, int status, Bundle extras) {
    // TODO Auto-generated method stub
}
```

The most important method in this example is `onLocationChanged` because here's where the new location is set.

Building Them Right — Design Considerations for Web and Location-Based Apps

When you reach out to the web from your device to invoke a service or read data, you're essentially traveling into the wide blue yonder. Keep in mind the many things that can go wrong, such as losing connectivity or (worse, usually) suffering through a data connection with an extremely low bandwidth (because it neither fails so the app can report an error and move on, nor does a good job of transferring data). Your application must handle these situations and still provide a good user experience. The following two sections show you how.

Checking for connectivity

Obviously, the first thing you have to do in order to deal with connectivity issues is to check whether connectivity exists in the first place. If you take a look at the code for the `onClick` method in the `Help` activity, you see a section like this one:

```
. . .
case R.id.button_lookup_wikipedia:
    if (hasNetworkConnection()){
        LaunchBrowser("http://en.wikipedia.org/wiki/Tictactoe");
    }else{
        noNetworkConnectionNotify();
    }
. . .
```

The application is using `hasNetworkConnection()` to check to see whether an Internet connection is available before launching the browser. `hasNetworkConnection()` consists of the following chunk of code:

```
private boolean hasNetworkConnection(){
    ConnectivityManager connectivityManager = (ConnectivityManager)
        getSystemService(Context.CONNECTIVITY_SERVICE);
    NetworkInfo networkInfo =
        connectivityManager.getNetworkInfo(ConnectivityManager.TYPE_WIFI);
    boolean isConnected = true;
    boolean isWifiAvailable = networkInfo.isAvailable();
    boolean isWifiConnected = networkInfo.isConnected();

    networkInfo =
        connectivityManager.getNetworkInfo(ConnectivityManager.TYPE_MOBILE);
    boolean isMobileAvailable = networkInfo.isAvailable();
```

```
    boolean isMobileConnnected = networkInfo.isConnected();
    isConnected = (isMobileAvailable&&isMobileConnected)||(isWifiAvailable
            &&isWifiConnected);
    return(isConnected);
}
```

Note how the Android framework provides a simple way to check connectivity. The key call in this example is the one to get `ConnectivityManager` by calling an Android system service.

Using threading

The earlier section "Checking for connectivity" describes how to check for connectivity. If no connectivity exists, then the app can simply let the user know to try the operation again later.

However, the `hasNetworkConnection()` method we described in the previous section returns true if *any* connectivity exists, even if the connection is poor and has low bandwidth. So how do you deal with this situation? Essentially, you have to launch every call that involves data transfer over the Internet in its own thread. Then, despite the slow connection, your app won't appear to "hang" while the call is in progress.

We explain threading in Chapter 8, so head over to that chapter if you have to implement threads. Do note that, in many cases, you don't have to manage threads directly for apps that require communication with the outside world, such as apps that explore the web or location-based apps, because the Android framework takes care of this task for you. For example, when you launch `WebView` inside the `HelpWithWebView` activity — or when you open `MapView` in the `WhereAmI` activity — the Android framework creates threads in the background to complete this task so that the rest of the app remains responsive. (You can test it by clicking the Exit button on either activity screen — the activity exits immediately.) However, if the Android framework does not handle threading for the specific task you have to implement, you have to manage your own threads.

Understanding the SDK Components Used in This Chapter

After you follow our examples of how to work with browsers, maps, and web and location services, we give you a little more detail about the components (packages and classes) of the Android framework and its add-ons that provide the functionality we cover in this chapter. We don't go into great detail because Google provides web pages that are more comprehensive than we are, but we at least give you an idea of what the component can do and provide any insights we have.

SDK components for incorporating web pages into your application

The `WebView` subclass of `View` is used to display web pages or, more correctly, HTML-formatted text. `WebView` is built on the WebKit rendering engine. (It's part of the `android.webkit` package; see `http://developer.android.com/reference/android/webkit/package-summary.html`.) `WebView` includes methods to handle hyperlinks (so that the new page opens in `WebView` rather than launches a browser), navigate forward and backward in a history list, and zoom in and out, for example. Visit `http://developer.android.com/reference/android/webkit/WebView.html` to find complete `WebView` details (and more examples).

The `AndroidManifest.xml` file must contain the following two lines for any app that accesses the Internet:

```
<uses-permission android:name="android.permission.INTERNET"/>
<uses-permission android:name="android.permission.ACCESS_NETWORK_STATE"/>
```

SDK components for maps

The page at `http://code.google.com/android/add-ons/google-apis/reference/index.html` provides details of the Google add-on API that provides mapping functionality (the page at `http://code.google.com/android/add-ons/google-apis/maps-overview.html` provides an overview).

A core class in the map API is the `GeoPoint` support class that represents a geographical location, with latitude and longitude stored as integers representing micro-degrees (or millionths of a degree). The methods for `GeoPoint` include the constructor `GeoPoint(int latitudeE6, int longitudeE6)`, which — given the latitude and longitude — constructs a `GeoPoint`. Also included are the accessor methods `getLatitudeE6()` and `getLongitudeE6()` to extract latitude and longitude values from an instance of `GeoPoint`. Visit `http://code.google.com/android/add-ons/google-apis/reference/com/google/android/maps/GeoPoint.html` to find details about this class.

The `MapView` subclass of the Android `View` is specifically intended to display and manage maps. (See `http://code.google.com/android/add-ons/google-apis/reference/com/google/android/maps/MapView.html`.) `MapView` is supplied with methods to set it in one of three modes — Satellite, Traffic, and Street — namely, `setSatellite(boolean)`, `setTraffic(boolean)`, and `setStreetView(boolean)`, respectively (note that, although they are presented in the API as separate modes, the traffic and street views are simply overlays on the map or satellite view). You can add built-in zoom controls by using `setBuiltInZoomControls(boolean)`. You also get a handle to its controller — by using `getController()` — in order to manage the map through code (for example, to position, pan, and zoom it).

`MapView` must be used *only* within a class that extends `MapActivity`. This is because the `MapActivity` base class manages the threads and the state for `MapView` as part of its own life cycle. (When `MapActivity` is paused, for example, it saves the `MapView` state and shuts down the threads, and then it restores the state and resumes the threads when it starts up again.)

Don't forget to put a Map API key (see `http://code.google.com/android/add-ons/google-apis/mapkey.html`) in the layout file for `MapView` as the value for the attribute `android:apiKey`. Using `MapView` requires it.

The `MapController` class (at `http://code.google.com/android/add-ons/google-apis/reference/com/google/android/maps/MapController.html`) handles all control aspects of `MapView`. You first have to get a handle to the `MapView` controller by using `getController()`. Then you can

- ✔ Call `animateTo(GeoPoint geoPoint)` to navigate the map to a particular location.

- ✔ Set the center of the map to a specified location using `setCenter(GeoPoint point)`.

- ✔ Zoom to a level (a number between 1 and 21) using `setZoom(int zoomLevel)`, for example.

Maps consist of sections known as *tiles* at each of several levels. When you zoom to a level (using `setZoom()`), the map is actually zoomed to a tile within it. Not all tiles are necessarily available at all levels. When a tile isn't available, the closest tile is either enlarged or shrunk, sometimes causing distortion of the map image.

The `MapActivity` base class has the code needed to manage any activity that displays `MapView`, such as the setup and teardown of the threads and other elements and linking the `MapView` management to its own life cycle. As with other subclasses of `Activity`, the `onCreate(. . .)` method is where the activity is initialized — with any state — and its view is created. You may need to provide implementations for two methods that are special to this activity: `isRouteDisplayed()` and `isLocationDisplayed()`. They report to the Google server whether you are (respectively) displaying any routes or using the sensors (GPS, for example) to discover the device's current location. These methods simply return true or false. `isRoute Displayed()` is an abstract method in the `MapActivity` class, so you *must* provide an implementation. `isLocationDisplayed()` has a default implementation that you can override, if necessary.

Once again, do *not* forget to insert `<uses-library android:name="com. google.android.maps"/>` *inside* the `<application>` . . . `</application>` element in the `AndroidManifest.xml` file or else you receive a `classnotfound` exception when you try to use any map-related class. (Been there, done that.)

One somewhat complex capability we don't illustrate in this book is the creating and drawing of map markers and overlays. Refer to the second section in `http://developer.android.com/resources/tutorials/views/ hello-mapview.html` for a tutorial on overlays.

SDK components for finding locations

The Android framework provides a complete set of classes for using your device's location within your app in `android.location package`. (Details are at `http://developer.android.com/reference/android/ location/package-summary.html`.) This package contains two primary classes (`Location` and `LocationManager`) and two useful support classes (`Address` and `Criteria`). The `GeoCoder` class is intended to convert location names to coordinates, and vice versa, but you would experience intermittent failures using these methods, especially on an emulator. You can instead "roll your own" lookup and reverse-lookup methods, which work consistently. They make web-service calls directly to the Google map services and therefore serve to illustrate the use of REST-based web services.

The `Location` class (see details at `http://developer.android.com/ reference/android/location/Location.html`) represents a geographical *fix* — the geographical location returned by a location provider at a particular time and consisting of these attributes:

- ✔ Latitude
- ✔ Longitude
- ✔ Timestamp
- ✔ (Optional) Information about altitude, speed, and bearing

These attributes can be retrieved from a location using the accessor methods `getLatitude()`, `getLongitude()`, `getBearing()`, and so on. Latitude and longitude are provided as double-precision values accurate to five decimal places. (We don't know why micro-degrees weren't used here.) This class also provides two methods that can compute distance:

✔ `distanceTo(Location newLocation)`

✔ `distanceBetween(double startLatitude, double start-Longitude, double endLatitude, double endLongitude, float[] results)`

Additional information relevant to a particular provider or class of providers can be retrieved by the application by using `getExtras`, which returns a `Bundle` of key/value pairs.

An instance of the `LocationManager` class (see details at `http://developer.android.com/reference/android/location/LocationManager.html`) is retrieved by using `Context.getSystemService(Context.LOCATION_SERVICE)`. This class provides access to location providers via `getAllProviders()` and `getBestProvider(Criteria criteria, boolean enabledOnly)` and provides information about them — for example, via `isProviderEnabled(String provider)`. The `LocationManager` also provides a controller that objects implementing the `LocationListener` interface can register with — using one of the `requestLocationUpdates(. . .)` methods that are provided — in order to automatically receive location updates from a specific provider or by using specific criteria.

The `Address` class is essentially a data structure used to completely represent all aspects of an address, ranging from its latitude and longitude all the way to its locality, region, and country, for example. The methods of this class consist of get and set accessor methods for all fields.

The `Criteria` class is also a data structure that can be used to specify (at a fine grain) which criteria must be met in order to satisfy a location request to `LocationManager` — in other words, the accuracy of the latitude, longitude, bearing, speed, and altitude, for example, or the amount of power it might expend in providing the location. Whenever a location manager is asked for a fix, the location or locations it returns must live up to the specified criteria.

Chapter 11

Harnessing the Capabilities of Your Android Device

*M*obile devices have become powerful computing platforms and can therefore accommodate a wide range of hardware capabilities. New Android devices often have not only high-performance cameras but also built-in GPS and one or more sensors. Furthermore, Google wanted to make the Android platform as developer-friendly as possible so that developers would quickly create apps for it (and drive up Android's market share). Android also liberalized the policies around Android development — making them more open than the policies that governed older mobile devices and their platforms.

Thus, the Android SDK makes all capabilities available on the device accessible from a program. You can write apps that control the camera to take photographs, communicate via the device's phone to make calls and send text messages, and record and play audio and video. (Though we don't cover it in this book, you can also write programs that communicate in custom ways over Bluetooth and Wi-Fi.) Finally, not only can you incorporate all this functionality in your app, but the Android SDK makes programming apps that use these capabilities much easier than other platforms.

This chapter shows you two broad methods to incorporate these capabilities into your apps. In many cases, you can use Android intents and reuse functionality from the built-in apps on your system; or you can directly use Android SDK classes to create finer-grained control. Additionally, you can use a hybrid approach and use both intents and custom classes. We show you examples of all these strategies in this chapter.

As we show you these examples, we will, along the way, point out quirks in the Android framework, such as differences in the ways in which to handle different types of media (audio, video, and images). We will describe how we had to work around at least one "bug" in the framework in order to make the app work, as an example of issues you too could run into and have to find a way around. Also, dealing with sensors is more complicated than the framework lets on. Because not all devices have all sensors, sensors can generate a fire hose of data that you have to find a way to handle, and every sensor is different.

Finally, you will find it really difficult to properly develop and test programs that use the capabilities described in this chapter on an emulator. You really need an actual Android device. So buy, beg, or borrow a device if at all possible.

Let's get started!

Integrating E-Mail, SMS, and Telephony into Your App

All Android devices come with a built-in e-mail application that, like all Android applications, is composed of activities. In this case, the activities collaborate to send and receive e-mail. Furthermore, this e-mail application can be called from another application by constructing an intent and broadcasting it.

This example is somewhat hokey, but suppose that a user who's excited about a high score after playing the machine in the Tic-Tac-Toe application wants to send the score to a friend. To begin with, he configures an e-mail account on his device to send the e-mail from (you can — and must — do this in the emulator as well, for this example to work properly). Then, from the Tic-Tac-Toe app, the user brings up the Menu and then the Email Score button, as shown in Figure 11-1.

Tapping the Email Score button causes the e-mail client on the device to open. The subject and the message are already inserted, as shown in Figure 11-2, so the user only has to type the e-mail address of the intended recipient.

Figure 11-1:
Choosing
to e-mail a
tic-tac-toe
score.

After the user enters an e-mail address in the To field, the following code snippet (from GameSession.java) constructs an intent, inserts the subject and the message, and then invokes the e-mail app on your machine (or the emulator) to send the message:

```
public void sendScoresViaEmail() {
    Intent emailIntent = new Intent(android.content.Intent.ACTION_SEND);
    emailIntent.putExtra(android.content.Intent.EXTRA_SUBJECT,
                        "Look at my AWESOME TicTacToe Score!");
    emailIntent.setType("plain/text");
    emailIntent.putExtra(android.content.Intent.EXTRA_TEXT,
                        firstPlayerName + " score is  " + scorePlayerOne +
                        " and " +
                        secondPlayerName + " score is  " + scorePlayerTwo);
    startActivity(emailIntent);
}
```

Figure 11-2:
The Android
e-mail cli-
ent, invoked
from Tic-
Tac-Toe.

That's it. Note that you can pre-fill the address in the To field as well, and insert it into the appropriate entry field of the e-mail client by assigning the sender's e-mail address to android.content.Intent.EXTRA_EMAIL with another call to putExtra before you broadcast the intent. The user still must be the one who finally sends the message, but he now has less work to do outside of Tic-Tac-Toe.

To send scores by text message (SMS), you simply implement the following function and invoke it from the menu:

```
public void sendScoresViaSMS() {
    Intent SMSIntent = new Intent(Intent.ACTION_VIEW);
    SMSIntent.putExtra("sms_body",
                "Look at my AWESOME TicTacToe Score!" +
                firstPlayerName + " score is  " + scorePlayerOne +
                " and " +
```

```
                        secondPlayerName + " score is  " + scorePlayerTwo);
    SMSIntent.setType("vnd.android-dir/mms-sms");
    startActivity(SMSIntent);
}
```

The built-in SMS application launches, as shown in Figure 11-3. In this app also, the user must complete the process.

Figure 11-3: Sending an SMS by using the built-in SMS application.

Using intents isn't the only way to send SMS messages: You can also directly use the `SMS Manager` class within the SDK. (We provide links to the documentation on this class in the later section "Understanding the SDK Components Used in This Chapter.") If you plan to use this class directly in your code rather than let the built-in apps do the work for you, remember that you must request the appropriate permissions in the `AndroidManifest.xml` file. The permission for sending SMS is

```
<uses-permission android:name="android.permission.SEND_SMS"/>
```

Last, we show you how to make a telephone call for Tic-Tac-Toe help. This time, the intent is ACTION.CALL and you have to specify the phone number to launch the activity properly, as shown in Figure 11-4. The code is similar, however:

```
public void callTicTacToeHelp() {
    Intent phoneIntent = new Intent(Intent.ACTION_CALL);
    String phoneNumber = "842-822-4357"; // TIC TAC HELP
    String uri = "tel:" + phoneNumber.trim();
    phoneIntent.setData(Uri.parse(uri));
    startActivity(phoneIntent);
}
```

Figure 11-4:
Placing a
phone call.

We want to mention one more difference between making phone calls and sending e-mail and SMS messages: Your application must explicitly ask, in AndroidManifest.xml, for permission to use the phone, because the activity that responds to the intent doesn't have it. (You'll realize why when you see that the dialer immediately starts dialing after it's launched — other apps require the user to confirm the operation.) Here's the permission you need:

```
<uses-permission android:name="android.permission.CALL_PHONE"/>
```

All uses-permission entries go *inside* the <manifest> ... </manifest> elements and *outside* the <application> ... </application> elements.

Playing Audio and Video and Capturing Images

In this section, we illustrate the Android SDK's capabilities for playing and capturing audio, video, and images in multiple ways — sometimes by using intents to launch built-in applications and sometimes by using calls to the framework classes. Then, for audio playback, we create a hybrid of these two methods. As a result, you see a range of methods and can choose the appropriate one for your particular needs.

We have provided three sample files (SampleAudio.mp3, SampleVideo.3gp, and SampleImage.jpg) as part of the CD and on the website for you to use in the following sections. To make the sample code work correctly on an emulator or a device, all three files must be installed on the SD card, in the directory /mnt/sdcard.

To load the audio and video files into the locations specified in the code (we're using the DDMS perspective in Eclipse, as shown in Figure 11-5), simply click and highlight the directory into which you want to upload the file, and then select the little icon at the top of the window whose tooltip says, "Push a file onto the device." In the file browser window that opens, you can select the file you want to upload. Refer to Figure 11-5 to see where the examples used in the book (SampleAudio.mp3, SampleImage.jpg, and SampleVideo.3gp) have been uploaded.

Capturing and playing audio

In this section, we show you how to work with music and audio in Android. We demonstrate audio recording by using an intent to launch the built-in voice recorder, exhibit the playback of audio by creating a playback service that plays audio in the background, and then launch this service from within the Tic-Tac-Toe app by using an intent.

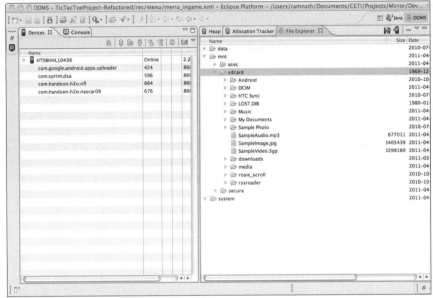

Figure 11-5:
Using the
DDMS per-
spective to
copy files to
the device.

To begin, we show you the layout of the Audio activity. It has four buttons as listed below (the activity itself is shown in Figure 11-6):

✔ Start Audio (playback)

✔ Stop Audio (playback)

✔ Start Audio (recording)

✔ Exit (the activity)

Here's the XML code for the layout:

```xml
<?xml version="1.0" encoding="utf-8"?>
<LinearLayout xmlns:android="http://schemas.android.com/apk/res/android"
        android:background="@color/background"
        android:layout_height="match_parent"
        android:layout_width="match_parent"
        android:padding="30dip"
        android:orientation="vertical">
    <Button android:layout_width="match_parent"
        android:layout_height="wrap_content"
        android:id="@+id/buttonAudioStart"
        android:text="Start Audio"/>
    <Button android:layout_width="match_parent"
        android:layout_height="wrap_content"
        android:text="Stop Audio"
        android:id="@+id/buttonAudioStop"/>
    <Button android:layout_width="match_parent"
        android:layout_height="wrap_content"
```

```
            android:id="@+id/buttonAudioRecord"
            android:text="Record Audio"/>
     <Button android:id="@+id/buttonAudioExit"
            android:layout_width="match_parent"
            android:layout_height="wrap_content"
            android:text="Exit" />
  </LinearLayout>
```

Figure 11-6:
The audio
activity.

Now let's show you the code, starting with the onCreate(...) method (see below). After setting up the buttons, the onCreate(...) method initializes audioFileURI from the path to the sample audio file (/mnt/sdcard/ SampleAudio.mp3):

```
protected void onCreate(Bundle savedInstanceState) {
    super.onCreate(savedInstanceState);
    setContentView(R.layout.audio);

    Button buttonStart = (Button) findViewById(R.id.buttonAudioStart);
    buttonStart.setOnClickListener(this);
    Button buttonStop = (Button) findViewById(R.id.buttonAudioStop);
    buttonStop.setOnClickListener(this);
    Button buttonRecord = (Button) findViewById(R.id.buttonAudioRecord);
    buttonRecord.setOnClickListener(this);

    Button btnExit = (Button) findViewById(R.id.buttonAudioExit);
    btnExit.setOnClickListener(this);
    audioFileURI = Uri.fromFile(new File(audioFilePath));
}
```

Next, we show you the onClick(...) method for audio recording (we want to save the playback part for last):

```
public void onClick(View v) {
    switch(v.getId()){
    case R.id.buttonAudioStart:
        if(!started){
            Intent musicIntent = new Intent(this, MyPlaybackService.class);
            musicIntent.putExtra("URIString", audioFileURI.toString());
            startService(musicIntent);
            started=true;
        }
        break;
    case R.id.buttonAudioStop:
        stopService(new Intent(this, MyPlaybackService.class));
        started=false;
        break;
    case R.id.buttonAudioRecord:
        Intent audioRecordIntent =  new Intent(MediaStore.Audio.Media.RECORD_
            SOUND_ACTION);
        startActivityForResult(audioRecordIntent,AUDIO_CAPTURED);
        break;
    case R.id.buttonAudioExit:
        finish();
        break;
    }
}
```

This activity uses the built-in audio recorder application on the Android device for recording audio. The couple of lines that start the recording are in the case R.id.buttonAudioRecord block of the onClick(...) method. An intent for android.provider.MediaStore.ACTION_AUDIO_CAPTURE is created and broadcast using the startActivityForResult(...) method.

Because the built-in audio recorder application has declared its intent filter to handle this event, the app is launched by Android. Note that the user starts and stops the recording, and then the path to the file in which the audio has been captured is returned as the Universal Resource Identifier (URI) to the activity via the following `onActivityResult(...)` callback method:

```
protected void onActivityResult (int requestCode, int resultCode, Intent data) {
    if (resultCode == RESULT_OK && requestCode == AUDIO_CAPTURED) {
        audioFileURI = data.getData();
        Log.v(TAGACTIVITYAUDIO, "Audio File URI: >" + audioFileURI + "<");
    }
}
```

In this example, you simply set the URI as the new value of the member variable `audioFileURI` so that when the user presses Start Audio again, the recently recorded audio is played.

Now you can work through the implementation of the audio playback service. To begin, you declare it as a service to the Android runtime via an entry in the `AndroidManifest.xml` file:

```
<service android:enabled="true"
        android:name=".MyPlaybackService"
/>
```

The code for this service is shown next. As you can see, a *service* is a class that extends the base class `Service`. (Ignore the `onBind(...)` method because you aren't implementing a "bound" service that can interact with multiple clients while it's running (for more information see `http://developer.android.com/guide/topics/fundamentals/services.html`):

```
public class MyPlaybackService extends Service {
    MediaPlayer player;

    @Override
    public IBinder onBind(Intent intent) {
        return null;
    }

    @Override
    public void onCreate() {
        player = MediaPlayer.create(this, R.raw.sampleaudio);
        player.setLooping(true);
    }

    @Override
    public void onStart(Intent intent, int startid) {
```

```
        Bundle extras = intent.getExtras();
        if(extras !=null){
            String audioFileURIString = extras.getString("URIString");
            Uri audioFileURI=Uri.parse(audioFileURIString);
            try {
                player.reset();
                player.setDataSource(this.getApplicationContext(),
                                    audioFileURI);
                player.prepare();
            } catch (Exception e) {
                // TODO Auto-generated catch block
                e.printStackTrace();
            }
        }
        player.start();
    }


    @Override
    public void onDestroy() {
        player.stop();
    }
}
```

This particular service encapsulates an object of the `MediaPlayer` class. It is this object that handles the audio playback. Note how this object is created in the `onCreate(...)` method of the service — by passing it a "raw" resource that serves as the default audio file for this player. (In other words, if the media player is started without giving it an audio file, this is what it plays.) If you look at the `res->raw` directory of the Tic-Tac-Toe application, you see a file named `sampleaudio.mp3`, which we placed there. It's a copy of the `/mnt/sdcard/SampleAudio.mp3` file, used as the default audio file in the `Audio` activity.

The intent that's created in the audio activity is received by the `onStart(...)` method. This method pulls out the URI of the audio filename that the calling activity wants it to play and sets it as the data source for the media player, after which it more or less calls the `start(...)` method of the player to start playing. We say *more or less* because the code has to jump through some hoops first because the media player is a subsystem that transitions through well-defined execution states, with only certain functionality being available in each of these states). These states are shown in Figure 11-7. Because we create the media player using the static method `MediaPlayer.create(...)` with a default resource, it's already in the Prepared state and ready to be started. Incidentally, to *change* the data source of the media player, you have to reset it, set the data source, and prepare it. Only then can you start it.

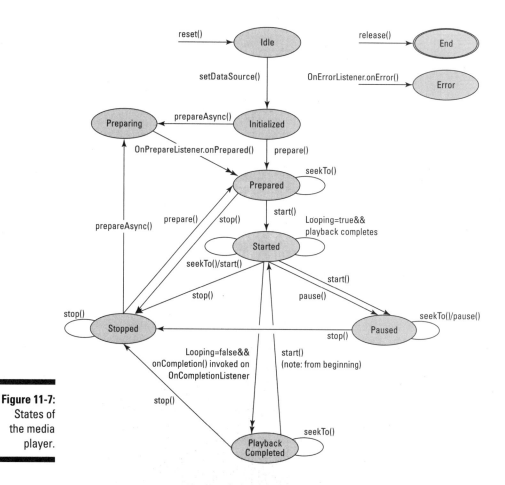

Figure 11-7:
States of
the media
player.

Finally, the onDestroy(...) method of the service stops the media player if this service is destroyed.

Recording and playing video

We describe video in a somewhat different manner than we describe audio. (See the earlier section "Capturing and playing audio.") The user obviously wouldn't want to play video in the background, so you don't create a video playing service. Instead, we demonstrate how to record and play video using the VideoView visual component, which is part of the Video activity's layout:

```xml
<?xml version="1.0" encoding="utf-8"?>
<LinearLayout xmlns:android="http://schemas.android.com/apk/res/android"
        android:background="@color/background"
        android:layout_height="match_parent"
        android:layout_width="match_parent"
        android:padding="30dip"
        android:orientation="vertical" >
    <VideoView android:id="@+id/videoView"
        android:layout_height="175dip"
        android:layout_width="match_parent"
        android:layout_gravity="center" />
    <Button android:layout_width="match_parent"
        android:layout_height="wrap_content"
        android:id="@+id/buttonVideoStart"
        android:text="Start Video"/>
    <Button android:layout_width="match_parent"
        android:layout_height="wrap_content"
        android:text="Stop Video"
        android:id="@+id/buttonVideoStop"/>
    <Button android:layout_width="match_parent"
        android:layout_height="wrap_content"
        android:text="Record Video"
        android:id="@+id/buttonVideoRecord"/>
    <Button android:id="@+id/buttonVideoExit"
        android:layout_width="match_parent"
        android:layout_height="wrap_content"
        android:text="Exit" />
</LinearLayout>
```

The Video activity that results from this layout is shown in Figure 11-8.

Here's the Video activity:

```java
package com.wiley.fordummies.androidsdk.tictactoe;
…
public class Video extends Activity implements OnClickListener{
    Button buttonStart, buttonStop, buttonRecord;
    VideoView videoView=null;
    static Uri videoFileURI=null;
    public static int VIDEO_CAPTURED = 1;

    @Override
    protected void onCreate(Bundle savedInstanceState) {
        super.onCreate(savedInstanceState);
        setContentView(R.layout.video);
        videoView = (VideoView) findViewById(R.id.videoView);
        buttonStart = (Button) findViewById(R.id.buttonVideoStart);
        buttonStart.setOnClickListener(this);
        buttonStop = (Button) findViewById(R.id.buttonVideoStop);
        buttonStop.setOnClickListener(this);
```

Figure 11-8:
The Video
activity.

```
        buttonRecord = (Button) findViewById(R.id.buttonVideoRecord);
        buttonRecord.setOnClickListener(this);
        Button btnExit = (Button) findViewById(R.id.buttonVideoExit);
        btnExit.setOnClickListener(this);
        File videoFile = new File("/mnt/sdcard/samplevideo.3gp");
        videoFileURI = Uri.fromFile(videoFile);
    }

    public void onClick(View v) {
        switch(v.getId()){
        case R.id.buttonVideoStart:
            // Load and start the movie
            videoView.setVideoURI(videoFileURI);
            videoView.start();
            break;
        case R.id.buttonVideoRecord:
            Intent intent =
                new Intent(android.provider.MediaStore.ACTION_VIDEO_CAPTURE);
            startActivityForResult(intent, VIDEO_CAPTURED);
```

```
            break;
        case R.id.buttonVideoStop:
            videoView.stopPlayback();
            break;
        case R.id.buttonVideoExit:
            finish();
            break;
    }

    protected void onActivityResult(int requestCode,int resultCode,Intent data){
        if (resultCode == RESULT_OK && requestCode == VIDEO_CAPTURED) {
            videoFileURI = data.getData();
        }
    }
}
```

As you can see in this method, `VideoView` has methods to set the video source and to start and stop the video player. Note that `VideoView` internally encapsulates an Android media player object. The `stopPlayback(…)` and `start(…)` methods on `VideoView` simply delegate their responsibilities to the media player object.

Although this `Video` activity uses the `VideoView` visual component for starting and stopping video play, it uses the built-in video recorder application on the Android device for recording video. The couple of lines that start the recording are in the `case R.id.buttonVideoRecord` block of the `onClick(…)` method. An intent for `android.provider.MediaStore.ACTION_VIDEO_CAPTURE` is created and broadcast using the `startActivityForResult(…)` method. Because the built-in camcorder application declares its intent filter to permit this event, it's launched by Android. Note that the user has to start and stop the actual recording. When the user finishes, the path to the file in which the video has been captured is returned as a URI as the result of the activity. In the code sample, you simply set this URI as the new value of the member variable `videoFileURI` so that when the user presses Start Video again, the recently recorded video is shown.

Displaying and capturing images

We describe images in a manner similar to describing video. The differences in the coding patterns arise from the Android SDK not working with images exactly how it works with video. For example, video is played directly from a file containing the video, but an image is converted into a bitmap that's completely pulled into memory before being displayed.

The Android framework offers the `ImageView` visual component, which you use to display images in various formats. We use this component to demonstrate how captured images are handled. We demonstrate how to capture an image in the first place, by launching the built-in camera application by using an Intent. All the example image-handling functionality in Tic-Tac-Toe has been encapsulated within the `Images` activity. So let's go through that activity, starting with its layout, shown below:

```xml
<?xml version="1.0" encoding="utf-8"?>
<LinearLayout xmlns:android="http://schemas.android.com/apk/res/android"
        android:background="@color/background"
        android:layout_height="match_parent"
        android:layout_width="match_parent"
        android:padding="30dip"
        android:orientation="vertical" >
    <ImageView android:id="@+id/imageView"
        android:layout_height="175dip"
        android:layout_width="match_parent"
        android:layout_gravity="center" />
    <Button android:layout_width="match_parent"
        android:layout_height="wrap_content"
        android:id="@+id/buttonImageShow"
        android:text="Show Image"/>
    <Button android:layout_width="match_parent"
        android:layout_height="wrap_content"
        android:id="@+id/buttonImageCapture"
        android:text="Take Picture"/>
    <Button android:id="@+id/buttonImageExit"
        android:layout_width="match_parent"
        android:layout_height="wrap_content"
        android:text="Exit" />
</LinearLayout>
```

If you've followed along throughout this chapter, you should see nothing new here. Although you may not have used `ImageView` already, this component is described in the layout file in much the same way as any other component.

Here's the code for the `Images` activity:

```java
public class Images extends Activity implements OnClickListener{
    public int flag=0;
    ImageView imageView=null;
    public static int IMAGE_CAPTURED = 1;
    static Uri imageFileURI=null;
    String imageFilePath="/mnt/sdcard/SampleImage.jpg";
    Bitmap imageBitmap=null;
    static final String TAGIMAGE="ActivityShowImage";


    @Override
    protected void onCreate(Bundle savedInstanceState) {
        super.onCreate(savedInstanceState);
        setContentView(R.layout.images);
        imageView = (ImageView) findViewById(R.id.imageView);
        Button buttonShow = (Button) findViewById(R.id.buttonImageShow);
        buttonShow.setOnClickListener(this);
        Button buttonCapture = (Button) findViewById(R.id.buttonImageCapture);
```

```
        buttonCapture.setOnClickListener(this);
        Button buttonExit = (Button) findViewById(R.id.buttonImageExit);
        buttonExit.setOnClickListener(this);
        imageBitmap = BitmapFactory.decodeFile(imageFilePath);
    }

    public void onClick(View v) {
        switch(v.getId()){
        case R.id.buttonImageShow:
            // Use BitmapFactory to create a bitmap
            imageView.setImageBitmap(imageBitmap);
            break;
        case R.id.buttonImageCapture:
            Intent cameraIntent =
                new Intent(android.provider.MediaStore.ACTION_IMAGE_CAPTURE);
                    startActivityForResult(cameraIntent, IMAGE_CAPTURED);
            break;
        case R.id.buttonImageExit:
            finish();
            break;
        }
    }

    protected void onActivityResult (int requestCode,
                                int resultCode,
                                Intent cameraIntent) {
        if (resultCode == RESULT_OK && requestCode == IMAGE_CAPTURED) {
            Bundle extras = cameraIntent.getExtras() ;
            imageBitmap = (Bitmap) extras.get("data");
            imageView.setImageBitmap(imageBitmap);
        }
    }
    @Override
    protected void onPause() {
        Log.d(TAGIMAGE, "Entering onPause");
        super.onPause();
        System.gc();
    }
}
```

The `Images` activity uses the `ImageView` visual component for showing the picture and uses the built-in camera for taking the picture. The couple of lines that start the picture-taking are in the `case R.id.buttonImage Capture` block of the `onClick(…)` method. An intent for `android. provider.MediaStore.ACTION_IMAGE_CAPTURE` is created and broadcast using the `startActivityForResult(…)` method. Because the built-in camera application declares its intent filter to permit this event, it's launched by Android. The user has to initiate the picture-taking. The picture is then returned as a bitmap, as the result of the activity. In the code sample, you simply set this bitmap in the `ImageView` component, which causes this new picture to be displayed.

TIP

Note the use of the `BitMapFactory` in the `onCreate(…)` method to create a bitmap from the default image in the file. This is one difference between images and videos in the Android SDK. The SDK has no way to directly render an image from a file, as it does for videos. Instead, the contents of the file have to be pulled into memory as a bitmap and then shown.

One issue with this technique is that your app can run out of memory and crash if the bitmaps it handles exceed the allocated space. Related to this topic is a known bug in Android (see `http://code.google.com/p/android/issues/detail?id=8488` for details) that requires the app (as a work-around) to force the system garbage collector to run so that any unreferenced bitmaps are "garbage-collected" in time. We show you this work-around in the `onPause(…)` method of this activity (you'll see the `onPause(…)` method with the call to `System.gc(…)`, the garbage collector in the code above).

Finally, Figure 11-9 shows the `Images` activity executing.

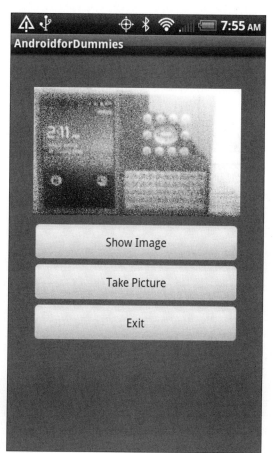

Figure 11-9:
The Images
activity.

Bringing In the Outside World by Using Sensors

To follow the unwritten rule of always saving the best for last, in this section we describe one more set of capabilities on your device: its sensors. Like the GPS and network components (wireless, cellular, and BlueTooth) covered in Chapter 10, sensors sense phenomena taking place in the outside world — such as the temperature, the pull of gravity, orientation, magnetic fields, ambient light, and sound, and they feed these sensed values to your app. Your app can then use these values to provide cool functionality. For example, given a communication interface to your heating or A/C unit, the app can act as a thermostat, the app can talk to the user more loudly if it senses greater ambient sound levels, and so on.

Listing, understanding, and monitoring the sensors on your Android device

Sensors vary among devices, so although we show examples of several sensors in this chapter, we leave others for you to uncover. After you've seen a few sensors, however, you've seen them all — in the sense that the way you incorporate them in your app is similar.

To get started, we created the Sensors activity within Tic-Tac-Toe. This activity first finds out which sensors exist on your device and lists them. Then it monitors the sensors and logs the data it receives from each of them.

 As we suggest in other examples in this book, open Eclipse on the Tic-Tac-Toe project, open the files we refer to in this section — the Sensors.java file and the Sensors.xml file — and follow along.

Here's the layout file for the Sensors activity:

```xml
<?xml version="1.0" encoding="utf-8"?>
<LinearLayout xmlns:android="http://schemas.android.com/apk/res/android"
    android:background="@color/background"
    android:orientation="vertical"
    android:layout_width="match_parent"
    android:layout_height="match_parent"
    android:padding="20dip">
    <TextView android:text="Sensors"
        android:layout_height="wrap_content"
        android:layout_width="wrap_content"
        android:layout_gravity="center"
        android:layout_marginBottom="15dip"
        android:textSize="20.5sp"/>
```

```
        <ScrollView android:orientation="vertical"
            android:layout_height="250dip"
            android:layout_width="match_parent"
            android:layout_gravity="top">
            <TextView android:layout_width="match_parent"
                android:layout_height="match_parent"
                android:id="@+id/sensorsListTextView"/>
        </ScrollView>
        <Button android:id="@+id/buttonSensorsExit"
            android:layout_width="match_parent"
            android:layout_height="wrap_content"
            android:text="Exit" />
</LinearLayout>
```

The `Sensors` activity is declared this way:

```
public class Sensors extends Activity implements SensorEventListener,
            OnClickListener {
    …
}
```

As you can see, the `Sensors` activity has the standard `Activity` methods, and, because it has a user interface, it also implements the `OnClickListener` interface. To handle sensor events, though, the `Sensors` activity must also implement the `SensorEventListener` interface — the two methods `onSensorChanged(…)` and `onAccuracyChanged(…)`.

The `onCreate(…)` method of the activity is shown next. This method gets a handle to an instance of the `SensorManager` class by calling `getSystemService(SENSOR_SERVICE)` and receiving in return a list of sensors that it then displays in the `TextView` component of the user interface, as shown in Figure 11-10:

```
public void onCreate(Bundle savedInstanceState) {
    super.onCreate(savedInstanceState);
    setContentView(R.layout.sensors);
    listSensorsView = (TextView) findViewById(R.id.sensorsListTextView);
    Button buttonExit = (Button) findViewById(R.id.buttonSensorsExit);
    buttonExit.setOnClickListener(this);
    sensorManager= (SensorManager) getSystemService(SENSOR_SERVICE);
    sensorList = sensorManager.getSensorList(Sensor.TYPE_ALL);
    StringBuilder sensorDescriptions = new StringBuilder();
    int count=0;
    for (Sensor sensor : sensorList) {
        String sensorName = sensor.getName();
        sensorDescriptions.append(count+ ". " + sensorName + "\n" + " " +
                            " Ver:" + sensor.getVersion() +
                            " Range: " + sensor.getMaximumRange() +
                            „ Power: „ + sensor.getPower() +
                            „ Res: „ + sensor.getResolution());
        sensorDescriptions.append(„\n");
        count++;
```

```
        }
    listSensorsView.setText(sensorDescriptions);
}
```

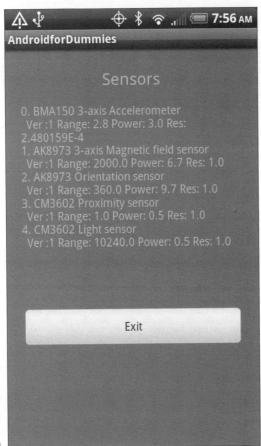

Figure 11-10:
A list of
sensors on
a device.

Using sensors on the emulator

You really need an actual Android device to develop and test a program that uses sensors. Certain software lets you "fake" sensors on the emulator; however, you must first make a small change in your code. For more on this topic, see http://code.google.com/p/openintents/wiki/SensorSimulator.

Registering with the sensor manager and receiving sensed values

In order to receive updates on sensor values, the activity must register itself with the sensor manager. The best place to do the registering is in the activity's onResume method:

```
@Override
protected void onResume() {
    super.onResume();
    for (Sensor sensor : sensorList) {
        sensorManager.registerListener(this,
                                       sensor,
                                       SensorManager.SENSOR_DELAY_NORMAL);
    }
}
```

Incidentally, the activity must unregister itself from the sensor manager, ideally in the activity's onPause(...) method:

```
@Override
protected void onPause() {
    ...
    super.onPause();
    // Stop updates
    sensorManager.unregisterListener(this);
    ...
}
```

The most important method of this activity is the onSensorChanged(...) method. It has lots of code, so we show it to you twice. The first time, we show it to you with most of the code removed so that you can see how it receives changed sensor values and then writes their details to the debug log by using Log.d(...):

```
public void onSensorChanged(SensorEvent event) {
    ...
    String sensorEventString = sensorEventToString(event);
    ...
    Log.d(LOGTAG, "--- EVENT Raw Values ---\n" + sensorName + "<\n" +
                  "Distance  Last= >" + distanceOfLastValue + "<\n" +
                  "Distance  This= >" + distanceOfThisValue + "<\n" +
                  "Change = >" + change + "<\n" +
                  "Percent = >" + percentageChange + "%\n" +
                  "Last value = " + lastValueString + "<\n" +
                  sensorEventString);
    ...
}
```

While we're at it, here's `sensorEventToString(…)`:

```
private String sensorEventToString(SensorEvent event){
    StringBuilder builder = new StringBuilder();
    builder.append("Sensor: ");
    builder.append(event.sensor.getName());
    builder.append("\nAccuracy: ");
    builder.append(event.accuracy);
    builder.append("\nTimestamp: ");
    builder.append(event.timestamp);
    builder.append("\nValues:\n");
    for (int i = 0; i < event.values.length; i++) {
        builder.append("   [");
        builder.append(i);
        builder.append("] = ");
        builder.append(event.values[i]);
    }
    builder.append("\n");
    return builder.toString();
}
```

Most of the code in `onSensorChanged(…)` is there to deal with sensor "noise" — which is sensors returning sensed values at a high frequency. You have to filter out most of these values in order to detect the real change you're looking for (such as changing the orientation or darkening the room). However, different sensors have different ranges and resolutions, so you need to filter out values differently. For example, the accelerometer returns values in meters per second squared, with a baseline value of 9.8 m/s^2 on one of three axes when the device is laid flat; the orientation sensor returns azimuth values between 0 and 359 degrees around one axis, pitch between 0 and 180 degrees around a second axis, and roll from between –90 and 90 degrees on a third.

We want to give you at least an idea of how to filter values, so we include some code in `onSensorChanged(…)`. In the interest of full disclosure, this code is somewhat crude, but it should give you an idea of what to do and how to do it:

```
...
private static final float TOLERANCE = (float) 10.0;

...
public void onSensorChanged(SensorEvent event) {
    String sensorName = event.sensor.getName();
    String lastValueString = "No previous value";
    String sensorEventString = sensorEventToString(event);
    float percentageChange = (float)1000.0 + TOLERANCE;// Greater than tolerance
    float distanceOfLastValue = (float)0.0;
    float distanceOfThisValue = (float)0.0;
    float change = (float)0.0;
    float[] lastValue = lastSensorValues.get(sensorName);
    lastSensorValues.remove(sensorName); // Hash table is "open" and can store
            multiple entries for the same key
```

```
    lastSensorValues.put(sensorName, event.values.clone()); // update the value
    if (lastValue != null){
        // Compute distance of new value, change and percentage change
        StringBuilder builder= new StringBuilder ();
        distanceOfLastValue = (float)0.0;
        for (int i = 0; i < event.values.length; i++){
            distanceOfLastValue = distanceOfLastValue + (float) Math.pow
                (lastValue[i], 2);
            distanceOfThisValue =
                distanceOfThisValue + (float) Math.pow (event.values[i], 2);
            change = change + (float) Math.pow ((event.values[i]-lastValue[i]),
                2);
            builder.append("   [");
            builder.append(i);
            builder.append("] = ");
            builder.append(lastValue[i]);
        }
        lastValueString = builder.toString();
        change = (float) Math.sqrt(change);
        distanceOfLastValue = (float) Math.sqrt(distanceOfLastValue);
        distanceOfThisValue = (float) Math.sqrt(distanceOfThisValue);

        percentageChange = (float)1000.0 + TOLERANCE; // large value > tolerance
        if (distanceOfLastValue != 0.0)
            percentageChange = change*(float)100.0/distanceOfLastValue;
        else if (distanceOfThisValue != 0.0)
            percentageChange = change*(float)100.0/distanceOfThisValue;
        else percentageChange = (float) 0.0; // both distances are zero
    }
    Log.d(LOGTAG, "--- EVENT Raw Values ---\n" + sensorName + "\n" +
        "Distance  Last= >" + distanceOfLastValue + "<\n" +
        "Distance  This= >" + distanceOfThisValue + "<\n" +
        "Change = >" + change + "<\n" +
        "Percent = >" + percentageChange + "%\n" +
        "Last value = " + lastValueString + "<\n" +
        sensorEventString);
    if (lastValue == null || percentageChange > TOLERANCE){
        Log.d(LOGTAG+sensorName,
            "--- Event Changed --- \n" +
            "Change = >" + change + "<\n" +
            "Percent = >" + percentageChange + "%\n" +
            sensorEventString);
    }
}
```

This code sample is intended to detect a *significant* change in the element
being sensed and to then report a value. Essentially, it saves (in a hash table)
the previously sensed value for every sensor modality, and when a new
value arrives that's more than a certain tolerance percentage (defined in the
constant TOLERANCE) away from the old value, it writes it with a special tag
(in the form Sensors<Sensor Name>; for example, TestSensorsCM3602
Light sensor) to the log file. The code sample computes the percentage

change as the vector distance between the previous and new values divided by the distance of the previous value from the origin (or the distance of the new value from the origin, if the previous value is <0, 0, 0>).

You can observe this filtering in the `logcat` window, shown in Figure 11-11 (check out Chapter 12 for more on the `logcat` window), by defining a filter on the log tag for every type of sensor and one using the tag. For example, for the light sensor, the filter is for the log tag `TestSensorsCM3602 Light sensor`. When you run the app and enter the `Sensors` activity, you see the main sensor filter showing a rapidly growing number of lines, whereas the others show changes only when you move the sensor around, change its orientation, or dim the room, for example.

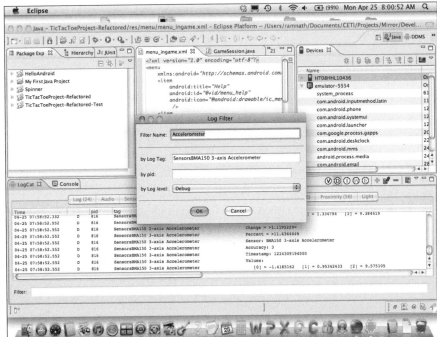

Figure 11-11:
The `logcat` window, showing filtered sensor values.

A sample log entry (for the light sensor) is shown here, for good measure:

```
Light Sensor:

04-23 16:17:42.784: DEBUG/SensorsCM3602 Light sensor(2389): --- Event Changed
04-23 16:17:42.784: DEBUG/SensorsCM3602 Light sensor(2389): Change = >0.0<
04-23 16:17:42.784: DEBUG/SensorsCM3602 Light sensor(2389): Percent = >1010.0%
04-23 16:17:42.784: DEBUG/SensorsCM3602 Light sensor(2389): Sensor: CM3602 Light
        sensor
04-23 16:17:42.784: DEBUG/SensorsCM3602 Light sensor(2389): Accuracy: 3
```

```
04-23 16:17:42.784: DEBUG/SensorsCM3602 Light sensor(2389): Timestamp:
        13348252950000
04-23 16:17:42.784: DEBUG/SensorsCM3602 Light sensor(2389): Values:
04-23 16:17:42.784: DEBUG/SensorsCM3602 Light sensor(2389):    [0] = 320.0    [1]
        = 0.0    [2] = 0.0
04-23 16:17:50.514: DEBUG/SensorsCM3602 Light sensor(2389): --- Event Changed
        ---
04-23 16:17:50.514: DEBUG/SensorsCM3602 Light sensor(2389): Change = >160.0<
04-23 16:17:50.514: DEBUG/SensorsCM3602 Light sensor(2389): Percent = >50.0%
04-23 16:17:50.514: DEBUG/SensorsCM3602 Light sensor(2389): Sensor: CM3602 Light
        sensor
04-23 16:17:50.514: DEBUG/SensorsCM3602 Light sensor(2389): Accuracy: 3
04-23 16:17:50.514: DEBUG/SensorsCM3602 Light sensor(2389): Timestamp:
        13355983358000
04-23 16:17:50.514: DEBUG/SensorsCM3602 Light sensor(2389): Values:
04-23 16:17:50.514: DEBUG/SensorsCM3602 Light sensor(2389): [0] = 160.0    [1] =
        0.0    [2] = 0.0
```

Understanding the SDK Components Used in This Chapter

After you read the examples in this chapter of how to work with SMS, e-mail, telephony, audio, video, images, and sensors, you're ready for a little more detail about the components (packages and classes) of the Android framework and its add-ons that provide the functionality covered in this chapter. We don't go into much detail because Google already provides comprehensive web pages, but we want to give you at least an idea of what a component can do and our insights on it.

SDK communication components: SMS, e-mail, and telephony

In this chapter, we show you only how to send text (SMS) messages and e-mail and make calls via built-in applications. However, these applications are built on classes in the Android SDK that are also available to your application (at least for SMS and telephony). The Android SDK does not appear to have any classes for sending and receiving e-mail (there is an interesting discussion thread on this issue here: http://groups.google.com/group/android-developers/browse_thread/thread/c58d75c1ccfe598b/3bb7cf1ad6fd3a4f). However, open source resources, that work just fine for Android, are available on the web for this task.

For sending SMS messages, the only class needed is SmsManager (see http://developer.android.com/reference/android/telephony/SmsManager.html for details). You can get a handle on the (singleton) object via the class method SmsManager.getDefault(), after which this class has methods to send single and multipart messages.

Currently the Phone app on a device is the only way (that we know of) to programmatically make a call from an app. However, starting in version 2.3, Android provides the Session Initiation Protocol (SIP) package for VOIP-based calling (see http://developer.android.com/reference/android/net/sip/package-summary.html for details). Anyone you call must have a SIP account from a provider, and many providers provide free accounts. Because this package is new and we're still experimenting with it, we don't include an example of its use. Look for it at this book's URL at www.dummies.com/go/androidsdkprogramming, or feel free to e-mail one of us.

SDK components for handling media

The main classes for playing and recording both audio and video media are MediaPlayer (see http://developer.android.com/reference/android/media/MediaPlayer.html) and MediaRecorder (see http://developer.android.com/reference/android/media/MediaRecorder.html). The MediaStore class (see http://developer.android.com/reference/android/provider/MediaStore.html) contains the resources necessary to operate on media — to extract metadata and the constants you need in order to form intents, for example. In case you're wondering, the MediaRecorder class uses the built-in audio recorder app as the input source. The Camera class (see http://developer.android.com/reference/android/hardware/Camera.html) serves as an interface to the Camera service.

Finally, BitmapFactory (see http://developer.android.com/reference/android/graphics/BitmapFactory.html) creates bitmap objects from various streams. You may have seen how it's used to create a bitmap from an image stored in a file. The Bitmap class (see http://developer.android.com/reference/android/graphics/Bitmap.html) is used for manipulating bitmaps, such as returning image dimensions for scaling.

SDK components for handling sensors

In the sensor examples earlier in this chapter, we cover four classes. The first, SensorManager (see http://developer.android.com/reference/android/hardware/SensorManager.html), gives you access to the sensors on the device. In other words, you can use it to get back objects of the Sensor class (see `http://developer.android.com/reference/android/hardware/Sensor.html`), which you can use to find details about the sensors on the device, such as their names, types, and range. Finally, you register activities with `SensorManager` to get sensed data, which is returned as objects of type `SensorEvent` (see `http://developer.android.com/reference/android/hardware/SensorEvent.html`). These objects have methods that return sensed values, with the range and meaning of the values dependent on the type of sensor.

The last component relevant to sensors is the `SensorEventListener` interface (see `http://developer.android.com/reference/android/hardware/SensorEventListener.html`), with two methods:

- `onSensorChanged(SensorEvent event)`, which is the callback for receiving sensor events
- `onAccuracyChanged (Sensor sensor, int accuracy)`, which should be used to change how you handle (for example, smooth and filter) these events.

Other SDK components for handling media

To complete this section, we need to mention the SDK components for one of the support components in this chapter: services. The page at `http://developer.android.com/guide/topics/fundamentals/services.html` and the pages it links to provide information in detail. The main class here is `Service` (see `http://developer.android.com/reference/android/app/Service.html`), and the main methods are the *life cycle* methods of the service (`onStart(…)`, `onBind(…)`, and `onDestroy(…)`, for example).

Part V

Effectively Developing, Testing, and Publishing Apps

The 5th Wave   By Rich Tennant

"Of course your current cell phone takes pictures, functions as a walkie-talkie, and browses the internet. But does it shoot silly string?"

In this part . . .

In this part, we visit (or revisit) Eclipse, in Chapter 12, to cover in more detail the Android add-ons to Eclipse. In particular, we describe the unit testing and performance optimization capabilities that Eclipse on Android gives you. We also provide an example of a couple of unit tests used to test the sample Tic-Tac-Toe application. Chapter 13 focuses on the endgame; after you develop your app, you probably want to make it commercially available.

Chapter 12

Effectively Using Your Integrated Development Environment

In This Chapter

▶ Maximizing the capabilities of Eclipse in developing Android applications

▶ Finding and fixing bugs in Android applications by using the debugger

▶ Tracking the progress of your app by using the logcat window

▶ Writing specialized unit tests for Android apps

*M*ost of us who were (or will admit to) programming in Java back when it was originally released used Java command line tools such as `javac` to compile Java programs, `java` to run them, and `jdb` to debug them. These tools were simple to use and did the job well. When Java was made open by Sun Microsystems, the size of the Java software development community exploded and companies making Java products just couldn't leave well enough alone. Sun itself, and then IBM and Oracle, created open (and open source) integrated development environments (IDE) aimed at making large-scale Java development easier.

What we mean by *open* that is that the Java IDE had an extensible "plug-in" architecture in which new functionality could be added to a foundation (that was essentially a framework, like the Android framework — except for building development and development support tools), such as language-specific editors, integration with version controls systems such as CVS (`http://www.nongnu.org/cvs/`) and SVN (`http://subversion.apache.org/`), and extensions for specific frameworks such as the Android SDK. Of these IDEs, Eclipse has become the most widely used. It was pushed by IBM (which, in addition to providing a high-quality initial code base, invested a considerable amount of money to spur Eclipse development via Eclipse innovation grants).

The Eclipse integrated development environment (IDE) with the Android extensions is a powerful tool for app development. This chapter builds on Chapter 2 to discuss specifically the specialized support that Eclipse provides for Android development — how to use Eclipse *effectively* for making Android apps. First, we give you a brief overview of Eclipse (because we want to quickly get to the Android-specific information). We then talk about how to use Eclipse tools to develop and debug Android apps and trace their progress. Finally, we cover the cool topic of the unit test framework that's provided within Eclipse to test Android apps. Our goal is to give you the knowledge necessary to effectively leverage your IDE's capabilities to build enterprise-class and commercial-quality Android apps.

Eclipse and Android: A Beautiful Friendship

Eclipse provides a complete suite of tools to develop, debug, test, and deploy Android programs. The tools are really well integrated, and will mostly seem to you like they are one seamless tool. With that, let's get into Eclipse functionality.

Let's start by quickly going over Eclipse's standard capabilities. Every Eclipse instance is associated with a *workspace* in which multiple projects can exist. *Projects* serve as conceptual repositories for the software developed in Eclipse. The software resides in folders and files in your computer's file system. Workspaces, projects, folders, and files are collectively known as *resources*. Figure 12-1 illustrates the relationships among these resources.

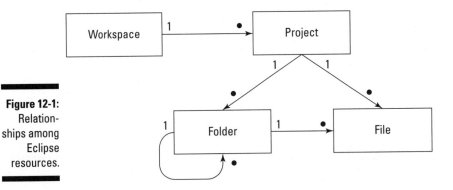

Figure 12-1:
Relationships among Eclipse resources.

Projects are specific to the kind of software you're developing (such as a pure Java project, an Enterprise Java (J2EE) project, or an Android project). The kind of project is known as its *nature.* (You can determine the nature of a project by looking at its project icon in the Eclipse Package Explorer window: A Java project has the letter *J* in its icon, and an Android project has a tiny, barely distinguishable "Android squiggle.") The nature of a project determines how it's configured and built, for example.

Gaining perspective in Eclipse

A *perspective* is a collection of views in which you can perform specific actions. Eclipse usually comes with eight standard perspectives (although this depends on the version of Eclipse that you install). Three (source code control, team synchronization, and plug-in development) are for development teams and for extending Eclipse, so we don't discuss them in detail in this book. The remaining five types of perspectives — the most useful ones — are described in this list:

- ✔ **Resource:** From this default perspective, shown in Figure 12-2, you can browse projects and their contents and run programs, for example.

- ✔ **Java:** This perspective, shown in Figure 12-3, shows you the classes in a project and lets you view one class at a time. It also has (by default) a console window in which you can track running programs.

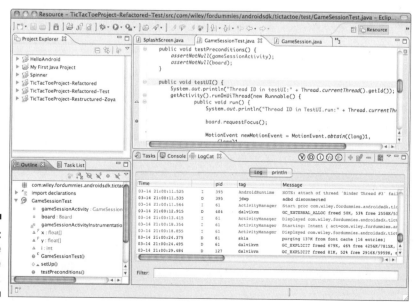

Figure 12-2:
The Eclipse
Resource
perspective.

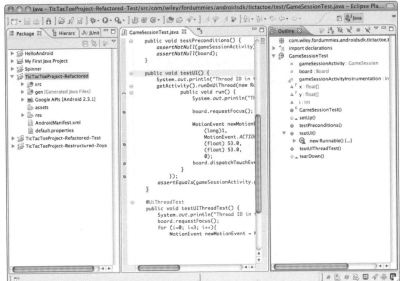

Figure 12-3:
The Eclipse
Java
perspective.

✔ **Java Browsing:** This perspective, shown in Figure 12-4, is useful for exploring large projects because it's a single perspective that shows you all resources in a project.

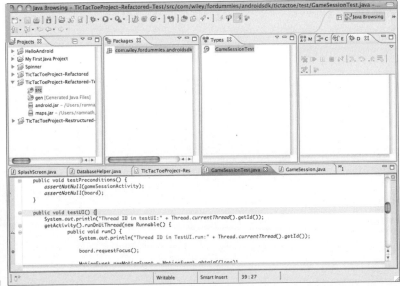

Figure 12-4:
The Eclipse
Java
Browsing
perspective.

✔ **Java Type Hierarchy:** To see the source code, members, and type hierarchy of a single class at a time, use this perspective, shown in Figure 12-5.

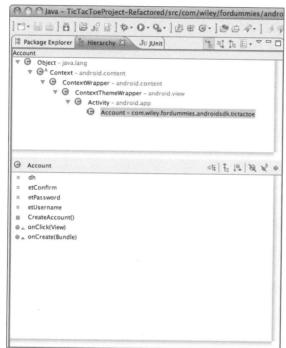

Figure 12-5:
The Eclipse
Java Type
Hierarchy
perspective.

✔ **Debugging:** See the state of your running code in the debugger by using the Debugging perspective, shown in Figure 12-6. Note that certain debugging actions (such as setting breakpoints) can be done in the other perspectives but that any action related to the runtime state of the program (such as inspecting variables) must be done in the Debugging perspective.

If you haven't already done so, create a Java project (choose File⇨New Java Project) using a couple of files, and browse the perspectives we describe in the previous list. Also, browse the menus and actions in these perspectives and notice that they have no Android-specific information. The default Eclipse installation only has tools for you to develop Java programs and enterprise Java applications.

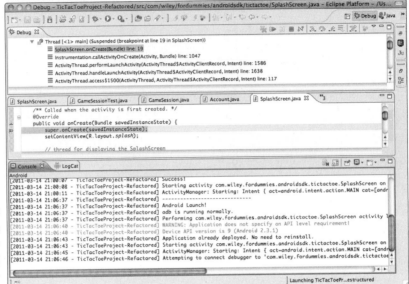

Figure 12-6:
The Eclipse
Debugging
perspective.

Customizing Eclipse for Android

After you install the Android SDK Starter Package, the Android SDK Components, and the Eclipse Plug-In for Android (as explained in Chapter 2), you bring Android-specific components into Eclipse and it becomes a powerful tool for developing Android apps, with Android-specific actions and menus. For example:

✔ In the Resource perspective, choose File⊏>Project. You see that the New Project Wizard now has a group for Android (see Figure 12-7) that contains Android Project and Android Test Project.

✔ If you right-click an Android project, you see the menu selection Run As⊏>Android Application, as shown in Figure 12-8.

✔ From under the main Window menu in Eclipse, you can bring up the Android SDK and AVD Manager, which lets you download updates to the SDK and create and manage Android emulators (Figure 12-9 shows the Android SDK and AVD Manager).

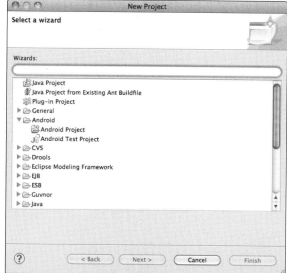

Figure 12-7:
The New
Project
Wizard
selection,
showing
the Android
group.

Figure 12-8:
Running
an Android
application.

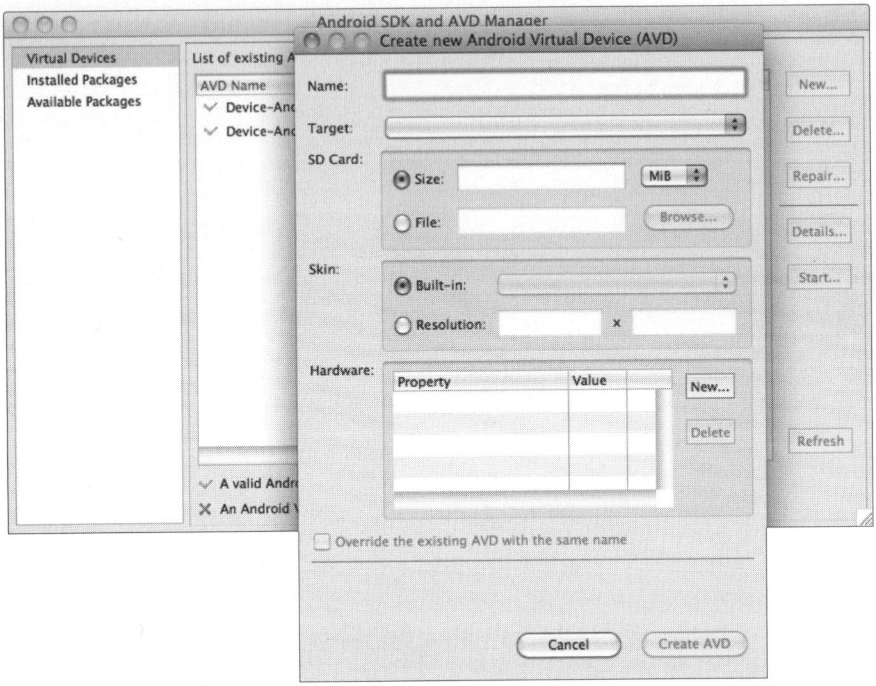

Figure 12-9:
Android
SDK and
AVD
Manager.

Observing, Debugging, and Tracking an Android App Using Eclipse Perspectives

You will need to use a set of key Eclipse components in order to do Android development. To familiarize yourself with these components, start in either the Resource or Java perspective and see whether a window at the bottom of the perspective is labeled Console. If it isn't, choose Window⇨Show View⇨Console and add this view to the perspective. When you run an Android app in the IDE, you will see this window explode into action and show the progress of the start-up sequence of the app, as shown in Figure 12-10. If a problem occurs during start-up (such as having no virtual devices with the correct API level), you see them here. After the app is properly installed and the main activity is started (in the case of Tic-Tac-Toe, it's the SplashScreen activity), this window comes back to normal.

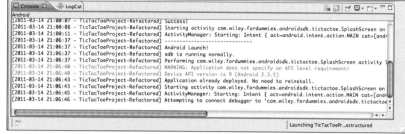

Figure 12-10:
The Console
window in
Eclipse.

A second (and even more useful) window is the LogCat window (see Figure 12-11). You add this view by choosing Window⇨Show View⇨Other, going into the Android folder, and selecting logcat. This view shows you everything the Android runtime can tell you about the app as it's running, such as

✔ When activities are launched

✔ When the debugger is attached and detached from your application

✔ How much memory is allocated or freed from the heap, and when

✔ Which error messages are generated when the app is loaded

✔ When the AndroidManifest.xml file is read and parsed

Finally, and by default, all app output sent to System.out (for example, by using System.out.println) or to System.err is redirected to the logcat window.

Figure 12-11:
The
logcat
window,
shown in
Eclipse.

Familiarize yourself thoroughly with the logcat window. It is extremely useful in helping determine why something went wrong with your program. It has helped us many times and has even been useful in finding errors we've made in the manifest file, such as putting an element in the wrong place in the file. If you are trying to figure out why your app isn't working, start by looking inside the logcat window to see if there are any error messages.

Notice that every message has associated with it a priority and a tag, which indicates the component that's generating the message. Just look at the two columns of the message (following the timestamp and separated by the process ID). In the following example, the priority is D (for debug) and the tag is AndroidRuntime:

```
03-12 23:14:32.200: D 7480 AndroidRuntime Shutting down VM
```

The priority is one of these character values, in order from least to highest priority:

- ✔ V: Verbose
- ✔ D: Debug
- ✔ I: Info
- ✔ W: Warning
- ✔ E: Error
- ✔ F: Fatal
- ✔ S: Silent

In addition to being message parameters, these values can be set as filter parameters in logcat. The filters are *ordered;* thus, if a priority is set as a filter, messages with that priority and higher are shown. In other words, if you set I as the filter, messages with I, W, E, and F priorities are shown. If the S priority value is set as the filter parameter in the logcat window, nothing is printed.

In the logcat window, you can click on a priority (see the top bar of that window to find where to click) and apply it as a filter. You can also create a filter by clicking on the Plus (+) icon and entering filter parameters in the dialog box that opens. The example shown in Figure 12-12 is filtering out everything except the println messages.

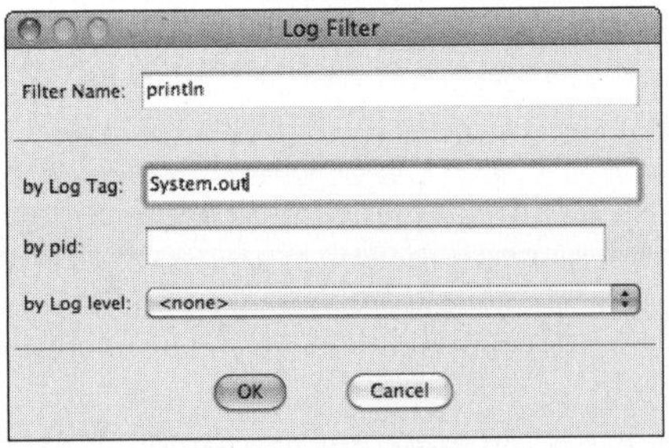

Figure 12-12:
Setting up
a logcat
filter.

	Log Filter
Filter Name:	println
by Log Tag:	System.out
by pid:	
by Log level:	<none>
	OK Cancel

Following the execution of an Android app is straightforward — and much the same as for a Java application. From the Resource perspective or the Java Browsing perspective, right-click on the project and choose Debug As⇨Android Application. The Debug perspective, shown in Figure 12-13, displays. Note that the Console and the logcat window aren't shown, by default. In Figure 12-13, we added them by choosing Window⇨Show View⇨Console and Window⇨Show View⇨logcat, respectively.

In the Debug perspective, you can set break points in the source file, step through the program in a variety of ways, and inspect variables, for example.

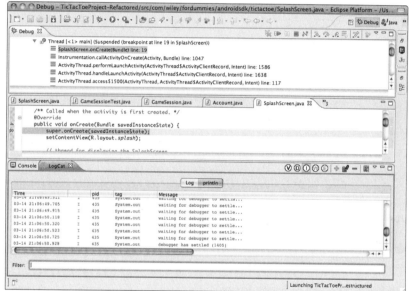

Figure 12-13: Debugging Android apps in Eclipse.

A useful, Android-specific Eclipse perspective is the Dalvik Debug Monitor Server (DDMS) perspective, shown in Figure 12-14. From there, you can see what resources have been allocated to every virtual device. Navigate to data⇨data⇨com.wiley.androidsdk.tictactoe⇨shared_prefs or data⇨data⇨com.wiley.androidsdk.tictactoe⇨databases. For example, you can see that the Tic-Tac-Toe application has (among other things) a database named TicTacToe.db (which is what we name the database in DatabaseHelper.java). Note that if you uninstall Tic-Tac-Toe from the virtual device, the database is also deleted, along with the preferences file and any data files created by the app.

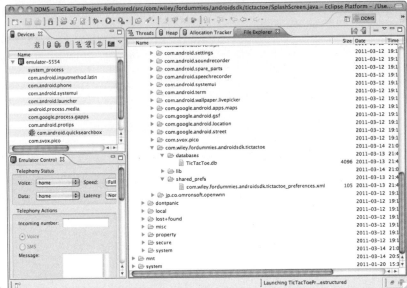

Figure 12-14:
The Android
DDMS
perspective
in Eclipse.

You can inspect files from the device by selecting the file (the `shared_prefs` file or the `tictactoe.db` file, for example) and clicking the Pull a File from Device button in the upper-right corner of the device's file browser in DDMS. (The button looks like a small floppy disk with an arrow piercing it.) You can also interact with the program from this perspective by sending it (fake) GPS locations from the Emulator Control pane.

You can do other tasks from here as well: Determine how heap memory is being used or how objects are being allocated and inspect threads, for example. An in-depth discussion of these topics is beyond the scope of this book. We're sure that you'll want to explore these features, however, so visit the Android page on DDMS (`http://developer.android.com/guide/developing/debugging/ddms.html`) to see all the details.

Getting Serious about Testing — Using the Android Testing Framework

One slick piece of application development capability provided in the Android SDK is a unit test framework built on the Java JUnit framework. We illustrate the use of this framework by using a couple of simple tests, written to test the game-playing functionality of Tic-Tac-Toe.

The Java JUnit framework?

The Java JUnit framework (www.junit.org) is a simple framework for structuring, writing, running, automating, and managing *unit* tests — tests written by the developer (you) to individually test the components of a program — such as methods, functions, and classes.

In JUnit, a test class is written for every target class (a class you want to test). The methods of the test class are in two categories: *test methods* that call methods in the class and verify their results and *setup* and *tear-down methods* that act as "fixtures" that set up the initial conditions of the test and then clear at the end any permanent resources allocated (delete all objects created by the test).

To begin unit testing, you have to create a test project (to use with the development project). You do this in either the Resource or Java perspective by choosing File⇨New⇨Other⇨Android Test Project. We created the test project named `TicTacToeProject-Test` by using the dialog box shown in Figure 12-15, where we gave it its name and set the name of the Android *development* project that it's testing.

Figure 12-15: Creating an Android test project.

You see that the project, shown next, has its own `AndroidManifest.xml` file with its own settings. In this project, we requested permission to disable the key guard so that when the test starts, it can run immediately without waiting for you to swipe the key guard:

```xml
<?xml version="1.0" encoding="utf-8"?>
<manifest xmlns:android="http://schemas.android.com/apk/res/android"
        package="com.wiley.fordummies.androidsdk.tictactoe.test"
        android:versionCode="1"
        android:versionName="1.0">
    <application
        android:icon="@drawable/icon"
        android:label="@string/app_name">
        <uses-library android:name="android.test.runner" />
    </application>
    <uses-permission android:name="android.permission.DISABLE_KEYGUARD"/>
    <instrumentation
        android:targetPackage="com.wiley.fordummies.androidsdk.tictactoe"
        android:name="android.test.InstrumentationTestRunner" />
</manifest>
```

Inside this project, we created the test class named `GameSessionTest`
with three tests: `testPreconditions()`, `testUI()`, and `testUIThread`
`Test()`. Here's the skeleton of the class:

```java
public class GameSessionTest extends
            ActivityInstrumentationTestCase2 <GameSession>{
    private GameSession gameSessionActivity;
    private Board board;
    private Instrumentation gameSessionActivityInstrumentation=null;
    final float x[]={(float)56.0, (float) 143.0, (float) 227.0};
    final float y[]={(float)56.0, (float) 143.0, (float) 227.0};
    int i = 0;

    public GameSessionTest(){
        super("com.wiley.fordummies.androidsdk.tictactoe.GameSession",
            GameSession.class);
    }

    protected void setUp() throws Exception {
        super.setUp();
        setActivityInitialTouchMode(false);
        gameSessionActivityInstrumentation = getInstrumentation();
        gameSessionActivity = getActivity();
        board = (Board) gameSessionActivity.findViewById(R.id.board);
    }
    public void testPreconditions() {
        …
    }
    public void testUI() {
        …
    }
    @UiThreadTest
    public void testUIThreadTest(){
        …
    }
    protected void tearDown() throws Exception {
        gameSessionActivity.finish();
    }
}
```

This skeleton highlights the important elements of how this class is set up. To begin with, this class is created from a generic class `ActivityInstrumentationTestCase2`, which is passed the test target class (`GameSession`) as the class parameter for the generic. Its constructor simply calls the constructor on the generic and again passes the target of the test as a parameter to the constructor. Next, note the use of the `setUp()` method to get references to the necessary member variables from the `GameSession` class. Finally, note the use of the `tearDown()` method to clean up after the test is complete.

The three methods `testPreconditions()`, `testUI()`, and `testUI ThreadTest()` are the three tests in the class. If you simply run this class from Eclipse (by choosing Run As⇨Android JUnit Test after right-clicking on the test project), these three tests are run. Take a look at each one of them, beginning with `testPreconditions()`:

```
public void testPreconditions() {
    assertNotNull(gameSessionActivity);
    assertNotNull(board);
}
```

Note the use of the assert statements (`assertNotNull`) — it's standard JUnit material. Essentially, you're testing to ensure that the `GameSession` activity and the `Board` object have been properly created. The two methods `testUI` and `testUIThreadTest` make similar tests. The `testUI` method is creating a `MotionEvent` object and dispatching it to the board (and thereby simulating a Tic-Tac-Toe move by the human user). Then it tests to verify that two moves have been made — one by the human user and one by Android.

```
public void testUI() {
    System.out.println("Thread ID in testUI:" + Thread.currentThread().getId());
    getActivity().runOnUiThread(new Runnable() {
        public void run() {
            System.out.println("Thread ID in TestUI.run:" +
                               Thread.currentThread().getId());
            board.requestFocus();
            MotionEvent newMotionEvent =
                MotionEvent.obtain((long)1,(long)1,MotionEvent.ACTION_DOWN,
                                   (float) 53.0,(float) 53.0,0);
            board.dispatchTouchEvent(newMotionEvent);
        }
    });
    . uals(gameSessionActivity.getPlayCount(), 2);
}
```

`testUIThreadTest` is making a similar test, except that it's simulating a series of three moves. Then it verifies that six moves have been made — three by the human user and three by Android. `testUIThreadTest` does this (like `testUI`) by making use of the `assertEquals(…)` method that is part of the generic JUnit framework (incidentally, the `assertEquals(…)`

statements will sometimes fail and sometimes succeed. Can you see why? We explain why later on in this section.):

```
@UiThreadTest
public void testUIThreadTest() {
    System.out.println("Thread ID in testUI:" + Thread.currentThread().getId());
    board.requestFocus();
    for (i=0; i<3; i++){
        MotionEvent newMotionEvent = MotionEvent.obtain((long)1,
                                                        (long)1,
                                                        MotionEvent.ACTION_DOWN,
                                                        (float) x[i],
                                                        (float) y[i],
                                                        0);

        board.dispatchTouchEvent(newMotionEvent);
    }
    assertEquals(gameSessionActivity.getPlayCount(), 6);
}
```

We have much more to tell you about these tests. First, you might be wondering how to get the coordinates you're using for the test (–53.0, 53.0) in the first test (testUI) and the values in the two arrays x[…] and y[…] in the second test (testUIThreadTest)). You get these from actually playing Tic-Tac-Toe. All you do is insert a few println(…) statements in the onTouchEvent(MotionEvent event) method of the Board class in Tic-Tac-Toe to see the pixel values of the motion events sent to it. You then use these pixel values in the testing.

Incidentally, we figured out how to create motion events by rooting around in the *Android Developer Guide* on the web (specifically, at http://developer.android.com/reference/android/view/MotionEvent.html) and taking an educated guess at how obtain works. Similarly, we rooted around the View class (http://developer.android.com/reference/android/view/View.html) to find out how to send the Board an event (noting that Board is a subclass of View). Another alternative is to call the onTouchEvent(…) method of Board directly, but Board may delegate the handling of this event, and such a method may not exist in Board. The way we did it more or less simulates a human interacting with Board.

You most likely have noticed the elephant in the room, so to speak — the reference to threads in two of the methods. In testUI(…), you're creating an instance of a runnable class and running it in the gameSessionActivity of the user interface thread. In testUIThreadTest, you're annotating the entire method with the annotation @UIThreadTest. Before we explain why you do this, we need to briefly explain the Android thread model.

The Android framework runs all its user interface (UI) operations in a single thread. In fact, all user interface operations *must* run on this thread because the UI libraries on Android aren't thread-safe. In other words, because user interface operations in multiple threads cause strange behaviors, they're disallowed.

Therefore, any tests that involve the user interface (such as these two tests) must run on the UI thread. You can do this in two ways:

- ✔ Create a `runnable` object and assign it to the UI thread (as in the method `testUI(…)`).
- ✔ Designate that the entire method must run in the UI thread by using the `@UIThreadTest` annotation (as we did in `testUIThreadTest(…)`).

By the way, we added `println` statements in the test methods and also in some of the Tic-Tac-Toe methods that send the current thread ID to `System.out` — and hence to the `logcat` window. After you run the test, look at this window to identify the thread IDs. (For easy viewing, create a filter that shows you only the `println` statements.) You can clearly see the test running in a separate thread from the UI.

Incidentally, if the `logcat` window doesn't show anything, click on the Devices tab and select the device on which the test was deployed on and is running.

We need to add one more topic related to threads and testing: When an application runs normally, the UI thread starts whenever the application begins and remains active until the application ends — but that isn't the case when testing. The UI thread is subordinated to the thread that runs the JUnit test, and when *this* thread ends, the UI thread is also terminated. Programs that run normally, therefore, may not work when being unit tested. Tic-Tac-Toe has this issue because of the way machine play is implemented. Look at the method `scheduleAndroidsTurn(…)` in the `GameSession` activity (we reproduced this method here, for your convenience):

```
private void scheduleAndroidsTurn() {
    System.out.println("Thread ID in scheduleAndroidsTurn:" +
                        Thread.currentThread().getId());
    board.disableInput();
    if(!testMode){
        Random randomNumber = new Random();
        Handler handler = new Handler();
        handler.postDelayed(new Runnable(){
                        public void run(){

                                        androidTakesATurn();
                            }
                        },
                        500 + randomNumber.nextInt(2000)
                        );
        );
    }else{
        androidTakesATurn();
    }
}
```

You post the machine move as a delayed task in order to make the machine play more realistically — the delay is intended to be perceived as the machine "thinking" about which move to play. Note that the task is posted on the UI thread. However, in Test mode, the test thread (which spawned the UI thread, as you know) terminates before the posted task becomes active. In Test mode, therefore, the machine never gets a chance to make a move!

You can work around this problem and allow unit testing by implementing Test mode in Tic-Tac-Toe wherever machine play is directly executed (and not posted as a delayed task). Take another look at scheduleAndroids Turn(...) in the preceding example. For completeness, we show you the (simple) method setInTestMode() now:

```
private void setInTestMode(){
    testMode=true;
}
```

We call this method in the onCreate(...) method of the GameSession activity, in which we also turn off the key guard (recall that we requested the permission to do so in the manifest file) by using this bit of code:

```
public void onCreate(Bundle savedInstanceState) {
    super.onCreate(savedInstanceState);
    KeyguardManager mKeyGuardManager = (KeyguardManager)
    getSystemService(KEYGUARD_SERVICE);
    KeyguardLock mLock = mKeyGuardManager.newKeyguardLock("GameSession");
    mLock.disableKeyguard();
    this.setInTestMode();
    this.startSession();
}
```

Here's a final note about the assertEquals(...) statements at the end of the two user interface test methods: Because machine play has been implemented as a random selection from the empty squares in the Tic-Tac-Toe grid, determining whether the simulated human moves play an empty square or a square where the machine has already played is a hit-or-miss issue. Sometimes, assertEquals(...) turns out to be true, therefore, and sometimes it's false. We deliberately left this behavior in place so that you can see how the test framework behaves when the tests pass, as shown in Figure 12-16, and when a test fails because an error is found, as shown in Figure 12-17.

This *extremely* rich framework is neither fully developed nor, especially, fully documented. For example, the sample code you see on the Android SDK site shows only a test with keyboard events. We had to hack our way through the SDK to figure out how to test with MotionEvent and had difficulty getting the example to work within the Android thread model. Thus, we have only barely introduced the testing framework to you in this book. We expect this framework, and in particular, its documentation, to improve eventually. As we learn more, we will figure out and post more examples on this book's website. So check the website periodically, and feel free to contact us and ask us questions.

Figure 12-16:
The JUnit window, showing passed unit tests.

Figure 12-17:
The JUnit window, showing a failed test.

Understanding the SDK Components Used in This Chapter

In this section, we give you a little more detail about the package and class components of the Android framework and its add-ons, which provide the functionality we cover in this chapter. We don't go into great detail because Google provides comprehensive web pages, but we want to give you an idea of what the component can do and any insights we have.

The Android logging framework

The standard methods provided in the logging framework consist of `Log.v(…)`, `Log.d(…)`, `Log.i(…)`, `Log.w(…)`, and `Log.e(…)`, where the suffixes (v, d, i, w, and e) stand for *v*erbose, *d*ebug, *i*nformation, *w*arning, and *e*rror, respectively. When you're deciding which method to use, follow these guidelines:

- `Log.v(…)`: Provides every detail about your program's execution. You use this method to provide a detailed execution trace of the program.

- `Log.d(…)`: Allows observers to debug key aspects of the program.

- `Log.i(…)`: Allows observers to verify that key states in the application have been reached. For example, you can use it to report on the start of an activity or when a certain key service (such as Google Maps) is invoked.

- `Log.w(…)`, `Log.e(…)`: Used, obviously, when you want to report a non-fatal warning and a nonfatal or fatal error in processing, respectively.

You will find the variants of these methods with the signature (`String tag, String message`) to be most useful. Every method also has a variant with a three-parameter signature. The first two parameters are as just described; however, the third parameter is an exception that may have been thrown and that the app will report.

You can find more details on the logging API at `http://developer.android.com/reference/android/util/Log.html`.

The testing framework API in Android

The Android testing classes essentially extend the Java unit-testing framework JUnit (`www.junit.org`) to provide testing services specific to Android components. The base class in the Android SDK is `AndroidTestCase`, which extends the base `TestCase` class from JUnit. This base class has added `assert(…)` methods to test whether an activity requires permission to launch a service or gain access to a Universal Resource Identifier (URI). Note that this test class is used for testing characteristics about an activity (such as permissions) that doesn't require it to be running. For tests on running activities, you need a test class that returns a handle to an `Instrumentation` object that allows you to monitor and control a running instance. In the example, we use the `ActivityInstrumentationTestCase2` generic class.

Finally, you should understand how to create events of various sorts and then dispatch them to views. The `MotionEvent` class that we use in the example is described at

```
http://developer.android.com/reference/android/view/MotionEvent.html
```

Key events are described at

```
http://developer.android.com/reference/android/view/KeyEvent.html
```

To help build your knowledge beyond the introduction to the testing framework that we just presented, we list some links that we find useful (and we hope that you do, too):

✏ Find an overview on the Android testing framework at

```
http://developer.android.com/guide/topics/testing/testing_android.html
```

✏ Find a link to the unit testing framework fundamentals at

```
http://developer.android.com/guide/topics/testing/testing_android.html#JUnit
```

✏ Find the details of the base testing class at

```
http://developer.android.com/reference/android/test/AndroidTestCase.html
```

Note that we show a sample use of the `ActivityInstrumentation TestCase2` generic class.

✏ Special considerations for testing Android activities are presented at

```
http://developer.android.com/guide/topics/testing/activity_testing.html
```

Chapter 13

Selling Your Application on the Market

. . . .

. . . .

A ndroid is by itself a platform on which mobile phone applications run. Android needs apps in order to be useful, because the platform is only as successful as the apps that are created for it. As a relative latecomer to the mobile phone market, Google realized that in order to compete with Apple and others in this area, it had a lot of catching up to do. Rather than try to become an app developer and app seller, Google, like Apple, decided to let its users become its app developers, and they completed the deal by making it easy for users to sell (or at least give away) apps to other users.

Because Google wants to establish market share as quickly as possible, it has tried to make publishing and selling apps as easy as possible: Though it has set up its own, well-known electronic marketplace, known as the *Android Market,* it also allows almost anyone else to set up a marketplace for Android apps. A major player, Amazon.com, has recently taken advantage of this policy to set up a portal for selling (and buying) Android apps. Two other major marketplaces for Android apps are AppBrain (at www.appbrain.com) and GetJar (at www.getjar.com), which serves up free apps for more plat-forms than just Android. Consistent with Google's open approach to Android so far (and, unlike with iPhone apps), you can distribute your applications directly to your users, by allowing them to download your apps from your website — you don't have to use the Android Market. However, if you want to make your applications available to the masses, publishing to a market is the best route to take.

Another way Google makes selling apps easier is that, unlike iPhone apps sold at the Apple App Store, no long process for vetting apps is required by Google. (Essentially, every marketplace can set its own policy; the Amazon Appstore has an approval process.) Google's own Android Market, in particular, doesn't vet apps: After you upload your app, it almost immediately becomes visible on the Market.

In this chapter, we first cover the tasks you need to complete to prepare your app for all markets. Then we detail how to publish your app at the main Google marketplace: Android Market. We also briefly cover other online marketplaces for Android: Amazon Appstore, AppBrain, and GetJar. Finally, we give you some guidance on how to help your application gain market acceptance.

Preparing Your App for the Market

In this section, we walk you through all the tasks you need to complete to prepare your application (and yourself) for the various app marketplaces.

Testing your application

We describe how to test Android apps in Chapter 12, and in this chapter, we reemphasize testing. We can't emphasize this point enough: Make your application as bug-free as possible, and ensure that it works well (see Chapter 8) and is safe and secure (see Chapter 9). The quality of an app is the primary determinant of its long-term success in the market.

Because Android devices come in many shapes and sizes, and with different screen resolutions and different versions of the operating system, you have to be sure to test your app on a wide range of devices. You don't have to *own* a bunch of devices in order to test them (although most software companies that build Android apps usually have extensive labs featuring all kinds of devices — old and new, small and large). You can simply use different emulators to ensure that your application runs reasonably well on the range of devices you want to target. However, make at least one complete test on a physical phone: Handling one in a real-life environment is a different experience from using an emulator and you have to make sure that your app is easy to use on a real device. Also, on a real device operating in the real world, your app may have to deal with several issues such as low network bandwidth, a complete loss of connectivity, loss of battery power, low-light situations, errors in GPS locations, difficulty in using the tiny buttons on the keypad, and so on. If you develop and test only on an emulator, you simply won't see these issues in order to be able to deal with them.

After you're satisfied with the quality (including the user experience of your app), you're ready to move on.

Naming and versioning your application

To finalize the package name of your application, pick a name that makes sense and that is general enough that it doesn't lose its applicability even as the app evolves, say by adding more features or by changing its look and feel. Most folks follow the format below for the package name:

```
com.businessname.applicationname
```

Note that every application must have a unique package name that is the primary identifier of the application in the Android Market.

After an app is on the market, the package name cannot be changed — not easily, anyway. To change the package name of an app, you would have to remove the app from the market and force all users to uninstall it (a proposition that isn't easy to enforce) and then put it on the market again as a new app.

The package name is entered into the `AndroidManifest.xml` file (for details on the `AndroidManifext.xml` file, see Chapter 2). Here's a snippet from this file that shows a package name entry and where it needs to be placed:

```
<manifest xmlns:android="http://schemas.android.com/apk/res/android"
    package="com.wiley.fordummies.androidsdk.tictactoe"
    android:versionCode="15"
    android:versionName="Uno.1.0.1">
. . .
</manifest>
```

Next, you have to take care of versioning your application for two reasons:

- **"Pest" control:** When users report a bug, they can report it against the correct version. Or, whenever a bug is fixed, you can tell potential and new users which version fixes the bug.

- **Marketing:** Every time you upload a new version, you can advertise it, thus keeping your app in the consciousness of your potential users.

Two version fields, both in the `AndroidManifest.XML` file, must be set for your application:

✔ android:versionCode: Think of this number (and it must be an integer) as the release count (known sometimes as the "minor" version). Increment this number *every time* you release the app *after any change,* be it a significant change such as the addition of a new feature or a bug fix for a customer, or even a minor change that does not change the behavior of the app at all, such as the removal of a few unused variables or package declarations. If you are putting out a new release of the app, change this number.

✔ android:Name: A string — think of this entry as a descriptive version string.

For android:Name, we recommend that you use a three-part string, with the parts separated by periods:

```
<major-version>.<minor version>.<maintenance release>
```

Here's what you do with this name. Periodically, you should review the code for all hastily fixed bugs and refactor the app to deal with all the things you fixed in a proper way (you might have also released different patches to different customers; this is the step in which you consolidate all these patches into a single release). After you have done so, increment the maintenance release number before releasing the app again. Next, if you add a few new features, increment the minor version. If you make a major design change to the application, change the major version. That's about it!

Some folks (Google, for example) often add a "marketing" name android:versionName. So, if you like, give your app a cool name and prepend it to the three-part string you created for android:versionName.

Android names its operating system versions after desserts, in alphabetical order: Cupcake (1.5), Donut (1.6), Eclair (2.0), Froyo (2.2), Gingerbread (2.3), Gingerbread maintenance release (2.3.3), and Honeycomb (3.0).

Globalizing your application

You're most likely building an application for one market, such as speakers of a certain language. However, if you want to provide an application for multiple markets — for people who speak different languages, for example — you must set up display strings in your application for all markets (in this case, languages) that your application must work with.

The res folder in your Android project becomes a factor now. (Read more about this folder in Chapter 2.) Assuming that you haven't hard-wired strings into your code, the values of all strings are in the file res/values/strings.xml. Follow these steps:

1. **Make a copy of the values directory.**

2. **Name the copy**

   ```
   values-<language suffix>
   ```

   where *<language suffix>* is the suffix for the language you want to target.

 For a list of allowed language suffixes, go to `http://developer.android.com/sdk/android-2.3.html#locs` to see the suffixes along with a region code (for example, `ar_EG` for Arabic, as written in Egypt).

The region code isn't required. If you omit it (when naming the `values` directory for a language), the default version of the language is used.

Dealing with devices that have limited capabilities

Suppose that you have built a useful app that's feature-rich and uses a wide range of capabilities, such as the camera, touchscreen, accelerometer, and light sensors. As a result, your application requires a full-featured Android device on which to run. You need to at least warn potential users about — if not prevent them from — installing your app on devices that lack all the capabilities necessary for all the features of your app to work properly. Android provides you with a way to specify the capabilities your app needs: the `AndroidManifest.xml` file. These specifications *may* (this is not a requirement) then be looked at by the installer of your app (such as the Android Market application), which may either require you to approve the installation or simply filter out the apps that require capabilities your device doesn't have.

You specify required capabilities by using two XML elements: `uses-configuration` and `uses-feature`. As you can likely guess, `uses-configuration` lets you state which input devices are needed, or preferred, for your app.

Suppose that your application requires a trackball. Add the following line to `AndroidManifest.xml`:

```
<uses-configuration android:reqNavigation="trackball"/>
```

You can find the full set of allowable configurations online at

```
http://developer.android.com/guide/topics/manifest/uses-configuration-element.html
```

For other capabilities you need — hardware devices such as the camera or software versions such as the OpenGL library version — you use `uses-feature`. For example, to state that your application needs Bluetooth and OpenGL (for embedded systems) version 2.1, add the following entries to the `AndroidManifest.xml` file:

```
<uses-feature android:name="android.hardware.bluetooth" />
<uses-feature android:glEsVersion="0x00020001" />
```

The full set of features that you can specify is listed at

```
http://developer.android.com/guide/topics/manifest/uses-feature-element.html
```

Setting permissions requests

The capability elements described in the preceding section are used to ensure compatibility, but they are guidelines that *may* be considered by applications that *install* apps — such as Android Market — yet are not automatically enforced by the Android framework.

However, those elements are different from permissions requests, such as requests to gain access to system functionality in order to prevent the device from sleeping when your app is playing. (We cover permissions requests in depth in Chapter 9.) To recap, these requests are specified using the `uses-permission` element:

```
<uses-permission android:name="android.permission.WAKE_LOCK"/>
```

When the app is being installed, the user is asked to grant these permissions. (Figure 13-1 shows you an example from the popular, and addictive, Angry Birds game.) These permissions are indeed enforced by the Android runtime. If the user doesn't grant permission, certain features of the application don't work.

Signing your application

Google requires that every application package (or *APK*) be signed with a certificate establishing that you're providing the application and certifying it. You must create a new certificate for every application. Every certificate is encrypted by a private key that you provide — and should keep private. All your certificates are stored in a keystore file on your development computer. This keystore file is password-protected.

Figure 13-1:
Granting
permissions
to an app.

You use the Java tools `keytool`, `jarsigner`, and `zipalign`, all of which are available in your development environment, to create the keystores and certificates. Because you're using Eclipse with the Android Development Toolkit (ADT) plug-in (see Chapter 3), we show you how to sign your app using Eclipse, by using the Export Android Application Wizard to export a signed APK (and even create a new keystore, if necessary). This wizard will perform all the necessary interactions with the Java tools.

To create a signed `.apk` in Eclipse, follow these steps:

1. **Right-click on the project and choose Android Tools⇨Export Signed Application Package (as shown in Figure 13-2).**
2. **After the wizard launches, click Next.**

   The wizard will walk you through the process of signing your package.

Using embedded maps

If (and *only* if) you're using the Android `MapView` class to embed maps in your application, you need to get a separate `MapView` API key. You do this from the command line because the ADT plug-in doesn't yet provide a wrapper for this task. Find all the details at

```
http://code.google.com/android/add-ons/google-apis/mapkey.html
```

Briefly, you must first generate the certificate for the app and then get the Map key by registering the certificate with the Google Maps service. Next, you have to modify the layout file for `MapView` to include the key and then export the program again.

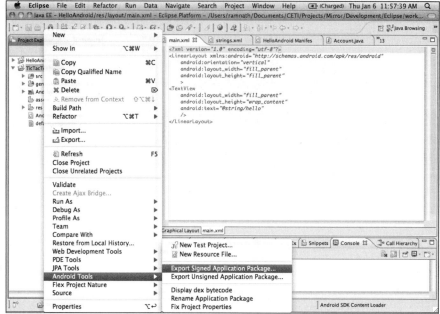

Figure 13-2:
Exporting
a signed
application
package
using
Eclipse.

Publishing on the Android Market

The Android Market, which is Google's own online store for buying and selling Android applications, is the most well-known marketplace for Android apps. According to Google bloggers (at `http://googleblog.blogspot.com/2011/05/android-momentum-mobile-and-more-at.html`), hundreds of thousands of applications are now available on the Android Market, more than half of them free.

The Android Market has two components: a website (`www.android.com/market`) and the Android Market application, installed on most Android phones. The website, shown in Figure 13-3, serves as a publicity site that showcases "featured" and highly ranked apps that are available on the Android Market. It also provides a link that walks developers through the process of putting apps on the store.

The Android Market app, shown in Figure 13-4, is how potential users of Android devices can browse the Marketplace and download Android apps for free or by purchasing them. The Market app is free and comes installed on all Android devices purchased from "accepted" vendors — such as service providers (Sprint, T-Mobile, and others) — and from Google.

Figure 13-3:
Home page of the Android Market website.

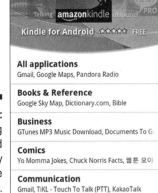

Figure 13-4:
Browsing the Android Market by using the Market app.

Let us just add in passing that if the Market app isn't installed on your device (because you bought your device from someplace other than a Google-accepted vendor), you have to find the install package for the Market app on the web. Just Google the term "vending.apk" to find sites that have this package for download and manually install it on your device. We can't vouch for the provenance of the package or the sites, so do this at your own risk. A less risky approach may be to extract `vending.apk` from a device on which it has been pre-installed and copy it to your device. Once again, in the interest of full disclosure, let us state that Google has not explicitly forbidden (or allowed) doing this! So once again, do this at your own risk.

In later sections, we give you a tour of the Android Market and show you how to prepare and then publish your application to it.

Before you can publish your apps to the Android Market, you have to complete a couple of steps, as described next.

Creating a developer account

The first step before publishing an app to the Android Market is to create a developer account: Navigate to `http://developer.android.com/` and click on `Learn more …` in the Publish section of the page (you may also directly use the `http://market.android.com/publish` link). This opens the page shown in Figure 13-5. Sign in to your Google account. (Or create a Google account and then sign in, if you don't already have an account.) The page is essentially a wizard that guides you through the account creation steps.

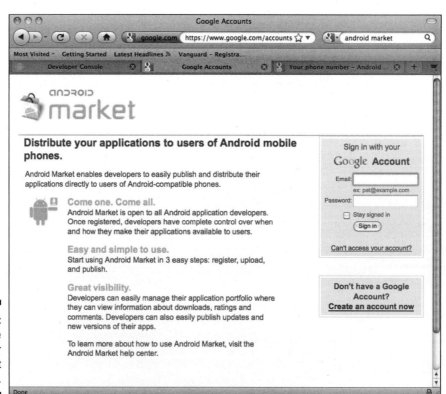

Figure 13-5:
The
Developer
account
login page.

On the Getting Started page, shown in Figure 13-6, set your developer profile. Completing certain fields is mandatory, such as your e-mail address and valid phone number. Google requires a telephone number only in case someone there needs to call you, but Google promises to not reveal your phone number to anyone else. A web page is also required. Of course, if you have a dedicated web page that applies to (and can promote) your application, enter its link. However, any valid URL is accepted. A final note: You have to pay a small one-time registration fee ($25, as of this writing, see `http://www.google.com/support/androidmarket/developer/bin/answer.py?hl=en&answer=113468`) to create a developer account.

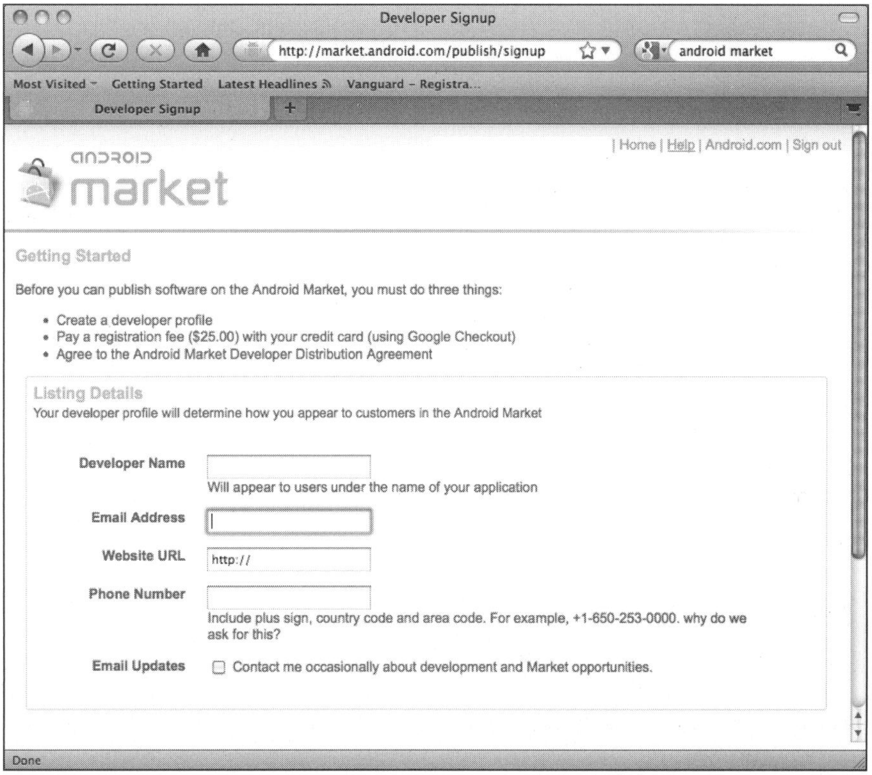

Figure 13-6:
Creating a developer profile.

Creating a merchant account

After you create a developer account, you must create a merchant account in Google Checkout, the payer site that all customers must complete. (Google has said that other payer sites, such as PayPal, will be allowed, but at the time this book was written, they weren't.) Figures 13-7 and 13-8 show the landing page and the account creation page, respectively, in Google Checkout.

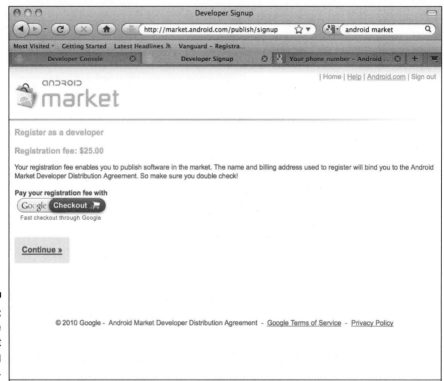

Figure 13-7: The Google Checkout landing page.

When you create an account, we suggest that you provide a support e-mail address — one that your customers can use to contact you for support — and that is *separate* from the e-mail address you normally use for regular communications with friends and family.

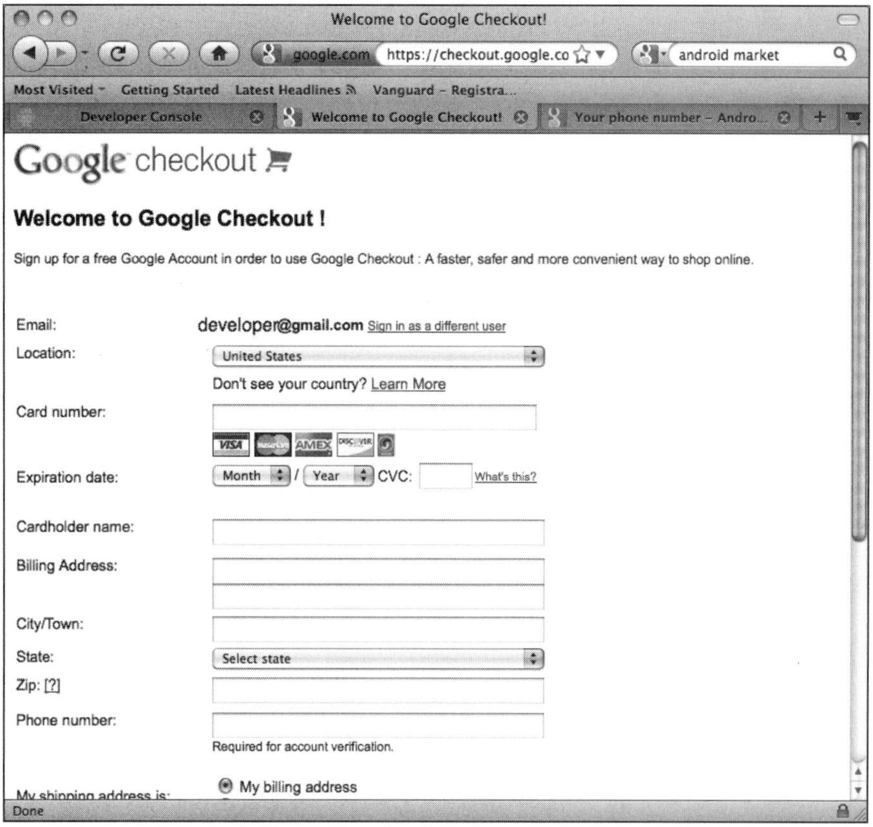

Figure 13-8:
The Google
Checkout
account
creation
page.

After you do all this, you see the page shown in Figure 13-9, which means that you're ready to upload your application to the market. This page is known as the Developer Console.

After you upload your app to the market, it almost *immediately* becomes visible. You don't have to endure a long validation period.

Now that you know what to do to sell your app, you can find out about other information — such as how to prepare your app and check out some legalities.

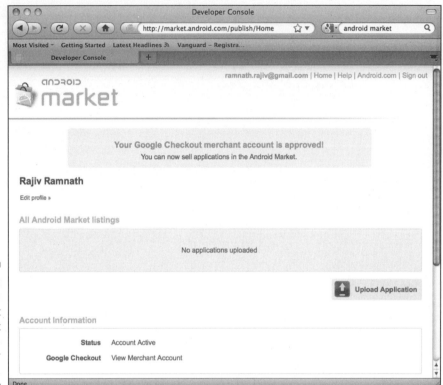

Figure 13-9:
The Android Market management page on the Developer Console.

Understanding the Android Market license agreements

Placing your app in the Android Market binds you to legal agreements with Google in order for it to continue to permit you to sell your app there. In this section, we summarize these agreements for you, but you should still look at the documents. In spite of the fair bit of legalese, the agreements are reasonable. We see nothing that would qualify as an impediment to your selling your app as long as you act in good faith. Incidentally, the developer account creation page (refer to Figure 13-6) guides you through the various legal agreements; you don't have to manually find and click through every agreement.

In addition to perusing some branding guidelines, you should consider three legal agreements, as discussed in the following sections.

The Google Terms of Service agreement

The first agreement you have to consider is the Google Terms of Service (ToS) agreement. You can find it in its entirety at `www.google.com/accounts/TOS`. It governs your "use of Google's products, software, services and web sites," — in other words, you consent to abide by this agreement whenever you use any Google service, such as Gmail or Google Groups, Sites, or Docs or whenever you access Google Maps from within your application. In a nutshell, the ToS agreement says that Google

- ✔ Makes no guarantees of how well the service will work

- ✔ Can update or change its products in any way it sees fit

- ✔ Is used at your own risk

Your content is your responsibility, and it is up to you to behave responsibly. You get an assurance that Google doesn't own your content; however, you give Google a license to host it and to show it to others to whom you give access. Finally, you may not disclose any Google trade secrets, in case you run across them as you use its services.

The Android Market Developer Distribution agreement

The most relevant agreement to you as an Android app developer is the Android Market Developer Distribution agreement, available at

`www.android.com/us/developer-distribution-agreement.html`

Wherever overlap occurs, the terms of this agreement override the ToS agreement (see the preceding section) or the Google Checkout Merchant agreement (see the following section). As the name of this agreement indicates, the Android Market Developer Distribution agreement is composed of the terms that govern you when you place an app on the Android Market, for sale or as a free app, including these terms:

- ✔ **You must have a developer account in good standing.** Google hasn't closed your account because you did something bad, and you're legally allowed to use and develop Android software.

- ✔ **If you charge for your app, you must also have an account with a "payment processor" affiliated with Android Market.** That way, payments, refunds, and similar transactions can take place, and a transaction fee (currently 30 percent), payable to Google, can be charged.

- ✔ **The Android Market Developer Distribution agreement overrides any agreement with the payment processor.**

✔ **If your application has a free version along with an upgraded version you charge for, you must process the charge through the aforementioned payment processor so that Google can take its cut when you get paid, in return for allowing you to market your free app on the Market.**

✔ **If you have an app advertised as free, you may not charge a subscription for it.** Essentially, *free* means free.

✔ **Buyers can download and install your app as many times as they want unless you remove your app from the Market.** They can also "return" your app for a full refund within 48 hours. Of course, they must also uninstall it from their devices, but, as far as we know, Android has no means of ensuring that they do so.

✔ **You (more accurately, your app) must protect the information of its users, and it must not use any user information without permission.**

✔ **Google may display product ratings given to your app by your customers.**

✔ **You must provide accurate information about your product, such as what it does, including the permissions it needs on your device.** You also may not spam the Market with repetitive information.

✔ **You may not (obviously) break any laws via your application; display sexually explicit material or hate speech; allow gambling; or engage in deceptive practices (such as impersonating the operating system) or in malicious activity (such as transmitting viruses).**

The Google Checkout Merchant agreement

Another agreement you have to consider is the one between you and the payment processor. At the time of this writing, Google Checkout is the only payment processor affiliated with the Android Market, so the Google Checkout Merchant agreement is the only payment processor agreement that governs you. It's posted here:

```
https://checkout.google.com/termsOfService?type=SELLER
```

The merchant agreement basically says that

✔ Google is only a payment processor. It neither warrantees your product nor guarantees the buyer a good product, nor does it endorse the buyer in any way.

✔ You must process payment only when the product has been shipped or otherwise transferred to the buyer.

✔ There is no minimum or maximum payment amount.

✔ Google Checkout transfers funds by the second business day. It can issue a chargeback if the credit card or bank requests one.

✔ Google states that collecting sales tax is not its responsibility, so you have to collect the sales tax appropriate to your state. A good resource for calculating sales tax is BizTaxLaw.com (specifically, `http://biztaxlaw.about.com/od/typesofbusinesstaxes/ht/state salestax.htm`).

✔ You may promote your association with Google Checkout, and it can promote you. However, see the next bullet.

✔ Every party retains the right to its brand and features.

✔ You're responsible for protecting buyer information, if you gather it.

Branding restrictions

Google has the following rules for branding your app, available online at

`http://www.android.com/branding.html`

✔ You may not use *Android* or *Droid* in any name.

✔ You may *describe* your app using *Android* or *Droid* — for example, `Tic-Tac-Toe for Android` — but *Android* must be in a smaller font than the name of your application so that it's clear that *Android* (or *Droid*) is only a descriptor.

✔ You may not use fonts from the Android custom typeface in your marketing material.

Uploading your application to the Android Market

After you process and deal with everything in this chapter (whew!), you're ready for the final step: literally uploading your app to the Market. This part is easy. Go to the Developer Console (refer to Figure 13-9) and upload your app. As we say elsewhere, there's no long waiting period where Google checks out your app (unlike the Apple Store, for example). Your app almost immediately shows up. Keep a couple of points in mind when you upload:

✔ **Set the Locations to All Current and Future Countries with Payment for paid apps and All Current and Future Locations for free apps.** You might as well sell your app everywhere.

✔ **Turn off copy protection.** This option is useless because it's just an inconvenience and a determined user can simply work around it.

Taking Advantage of Other Marketplaces for Android Apps

In this section, we describe other online marketplaces for Android apps, including a look at the Amazon Appstore and a couple of mostly niche sites.

The Amazon Appstore for Android

The Amazon Appstore for Android (navigate to `http://www.Amazon.com` and select `Appstore For Android` in the menu down the left side, or directly click on `http://www.amazon.com/mobile-apps/b/ref=sa_menu_adr_app4?ie=UTF8&node=2350149011` as of this writing) debuted in March 2011. Given Amazon's presence and reach, this online marketplace for Android apps is likely to become a serious, mainstream competitor to Google's Android Market.

The developer sign-up process is straightforward. To begin with, your developer account is also your Amazon customer account (the one you use to buy items from Amazon.com), so you don't have to set up a seller account, as you have to do with the Android Market. For every application, you have to provide a description of the application and a few other bits of information, such as its category, the form factor of the targeted device, the date you plan to release the app, its content rating, and your support contact information. You can also upload any promotional material you want to make available about the app — icons used in the app, screen shots, and any other images and videos. You pay a yearly registration charge of $99 to set up a developer account on the Appstore; however, it's waived for the first year.

Buyers from the Appstore also use an app as their way into the store. However, this app doesn't come preinstalled on any Android device. Instructions for installing the app have been provided by Amazon. Essentially, you have to request a link to the app to be sent to you from Amazon (`www.amazon.com/app-email`) and then install the app from that link. You can also enter the link from a browser on your device. You might have to change a setting on your device to allow the installation of applications from sources other than the Android Market: First, open Settings on your device, tap Applications, and then select Unknown Sources if it's deselected.

Your legal relationship with the Amazon Appstore

As with Google, placing your app on the Amazon Appstore binds you to a legal relationship with Amazon. The complete agreement may be found at `https://developer.amazon.com/settings/docs.html` after you click Get Started and sign in. You will see that the agreement is quite similar to the one you enter into with Android Market.

To begin with, Amazon pays you a royalty on the sale of every copy of your app, and it takes care of collecting and remitting sales taxes on the sale. You have to make sure that the app you place on the Amazon Appstore is the latest version for sale anywhere else and is priced no higher than anywhere else. Next, to continue to have the rights to your software, and Amazon to theirs, you must make sure that you have rights to use any digital material you use in your app (ranging from the code to any bitmaps, music, video, or other elements), and Amazon has the right to use this material to promote your app and its store. This is, of course, obvious, but you may not use your app as spyware, and you must adequately protect private user information that your app may have access to. Finally, you must adequately support your app. You must respond within 24 hours to any critical support request and within five business days for other requests.

Amazon Web Services — cloud services from Amazon

Just as Google has done with Google Maps, Amazon has tried to sweeten the pot for developers by providing cloud-based services — known as *Amazon Web Services,* or *AWS* — that developers can use within their apps. These services are provided via the AWS Android Library that hides, according to Amazon, "much of the lower-level plumbing, including authentication, request retries, and error handling." In addition, these services may be used to access Amazon's existing cloud services, such as Amazon Simple Storage Service (Amazon S3), SimpleDB, Simple Queue Service (Amazon SQS), and Amazon Simple Notifications Service (Amazon SNS). Included in the AWS SDK are code samples and documentation.

We have to tell you that because all this AWS information is new, we haven't had the opportunity to include examples of using the AWS in this book. However, check this book's website later, because we hope to have examples showcasing these services soon.

Other marketplaces for Android apps

Two other online Android app marketplaces worth mentioning are AppBrain (www.appbrain.com) and GetJar (www.getjar.com). AppBrain isn't a marketplace but, rather, an enhanced portal into the Android Market. As its marketing material says, "AppBrain is a website which makes sense out of the high number of Android apps available in the Google Android market!" Apps are easier to find. Also, using the downloadable AppBrain app means that any updates to apps you already have are automatically downloaded and installed, thus keeping your device in sync with the latest versions of your stuff. (Now you can see how the versioning information we cover earlier in this chapter can be useful in interesting ways!)

The GetJar site (at http://www.getjar.com) provides apps on a range of platforms — Android, of course, but also Blackberry and Windows Mobile. Apps on GetJar are free.

Becoming Successful in the Market

Here's our two cents' worth on how to be successful in the Android Market.

Fee or free?

We believe that the predominance of free apps will slowly change over the next few years as Android Market comes into the commercial mainstream (like the Apple Store) and as (or if) larger companies (with many more employees to pay) start putting their wares on the Android Market.

So what should you do? Offer a free app or ask people to pay for it? Make a free app paid after a time? People complain like crazy if you make an app paid that was once free, so our advice is to offer two versions from the start: a free version with limited functionality and a paid version with all the bells and whistles. You can certainly make a paid app free, but don't do it too often, either, lest people simply wait for your app to become free before buying it.

Your free app can help upsell your paid app by incorporating Android Market itself. As we talk about in Chapter 3 (where we cover intents), you can even invoke the Android Market app! So, from an appropriate activity in your free app, you can ask the user to upgrade to the Pro version, and if the answer is yes, you fire off the Market app with an intent with an embedded Search key that takes you directly to your paid app. Below are two code snippets for the intent creation. If you want to search for the app by giving part of its name (for example if you want to let the user select between multiple versions of paid apps), use:

```
Intent intent =
    new Intent(Intent.ACTION_VIEW,          Uri.parse("market://
            search?q=pname:MY_PAID_APP_NAME_SUBSTRING"));
            startActivity(intent);
```

If you want to use the exact name of the app, the intent creation code is shown below:

```
Intent intent =
    new Intent(Intent.ACTION_VIEW,          Uri.parse("market://
            search?q=pname:MY_PAID_APP_NAME")); startActivity(intent);
```

How to drive customers to your app

Most books we have read about apps say that if you do the fly-right things we mention in this book, your app has a good chance of doing well.

We think you have to do that, of course. But you have to do more to give your app commercial legs. Clayton Christensen, the guru of disruptive innovation theory, says that people buy stuff not because they're members of certain demographic groups (teenagers, seniors) but, rather, because they want to address certain *circumstances* (such as peer pressure). Geoffrey Moore, another guru with respect to how start-ups succeed, says you must create a "whole product" — something that addresses a need completely. He also says that after you're able to sell to the key players in a market

segment, the others will fall like bowling pins in a tornado. (Yes, we're paraphrasing heavily!) But their points are well taken. For your app to sell well, you have to do more than have a cool idea; you have to use that cool idea to target a circumstance that people want to address, such as tracking appointments, or even emotional circumstances such as boredom or peer pressure. If you plan to create a paid-for app, make sure it solves someone's circumstance in as complete a manner as you can make it, and then find a way to market it — outside the Android Market itself — to key people who want that need addressed and that others think of as players to be imitated.

Good citizenship: Providing good service

After you create a high-quality (stable, usable, high-performing) product that works as expected, be a good seller. In the information about the app you provide on the store, you obviously want to advertise your app's capabilities in order to sell it, but also be transparent about what your application does, which capabilities it needs, and why it needs them. That way, when customers install the app, they aren't surprised by what it wants to do.

Be responsive to customer requests and feedback. Fix bugs promptly. Be polite to your elders! And, of course, don't do anything illegal in your app.

A few more hints

Even if you haven't targeted your app for selling outside the United States, you might as well sell it in all countries and take advantage of any long tail, if one exists. We show you how to do this for the Android Market earlier in this chapter.

Always watch the ratings for your app and be sure to respond quickly with updates and fixes if you see them start to drop.

Part VI
The Part of Tens

The 5th Wave   By Rich Tennant

"Until we work the kinks out, David will be providing the audio portion of our game demonstration."

In this part . . .

No *For Dummies* book is complete without a Part of Tens. Chapter 14 covers the top ten developer resources on the Web, and Chapter 15 covers the best of the Android applications, not so much to advertise these apps as to give you examples of how these cool apps (and they *are* cool) leverage the Android SDK.

Chapter 14

The Ten Best Developer Resources for Android

*N*ot so long ago, folks began programming by reading books written by a small number of experts and gaining expertise from only the people they worked with. Now that the World Wide Web exists, the expertise pool is vastly larger. Virtually anyone can contribute their own ideas and learn from other contributors in forums where people with like interests communicate, interact, and learn.

This chapter covers forums related to the Android SDK and Android app development — places where you can visit freely, gain knowledge, and find help. We hope that as you gain expertise in Android development, that you will even contribute your knowledge to these forums.

Every site we mention in this chapter has been invaluable to us in understanding how to develop Android apps and how to find help and handle bugs, for example. Interestingly, one author (who shall remain nameless!) thought he had discovered a bug in his code but could find no mention of the bug in the Android developer forums. Eventually, he realized his mistake: There *was* no bug! The forums are so active and up-to-date that if you believe you have discovered a problem in the SDK and can find no mention of it in the forums, you should seriously consider reviewing your code again because *that's* likely where the bug is located.

Browse a site for a while to develop a feel for its content. The sites we describe in this chapter are in various stages of organization; some are monitored, managed, and generally organized much better than others.

Learning More About Android Development

Hopefully this book has whetted your appetite about Android development. Now you want to know more, more, MORE! These first two sites described below are perfect for quenching your thirst for Android knowledge.

Seeking out information at the Android Developers home page

```
http://developer.android.com
```

The place to look to find information about the Android SDK is the Android Developers home page, created by Google and shown in Figure 14-1.

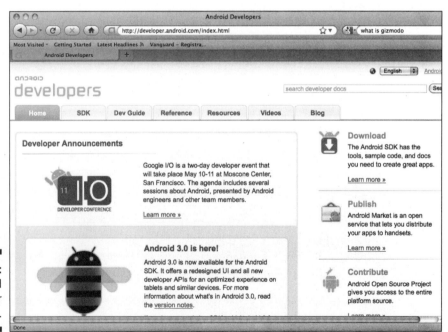

Figure 14-1:
The Android developer site.

At this site, clicking the SDK tab opens pages that describe the various SDK versions, from SDK level 1.5 to SDK version 3.2 (the version that was current when we wrote this book).

You can view SDK highlights, new features, and revisions within SDK levels, and, if you search for *Android API Differences Report,* read about changes made in the SDK since the previous API level (from 6 to 7 or from 8 to 9, for example). View every difference, or filter them by package, class, constructor, method, or field. Don't forget to click the Statistics link in the upper-right corner to view statistics — for example, the number of changed packages. If you're trying to decide which API level to target for an app, these statistics are especially useful when correlated against the market penetration of the various Android versions. You can also download SDK packages.

The Dev Guide tab is a hyperlinked programmers' guide that describes the various capabilities in the SDK and links you to the Java documentation of the SDK classes on the Reference tab — which holds a package-by-package documentation of the SDK. The rest of the site includes a grab bag of how-to articles (on the Resources tab), videos (Videos tab), and a blog.

We admit that we spend quite a bit of time on this treasure trove!

Getting advice from experts at the Google I/O sessions

Google I/O, held at the Moscone Center in San Francisco since 2008, is an annual two-day (so far, anyway) developer conference where the geeks meet to rub elbows with the Android developers at Google. You might think that the presentations here are esoteric and over everyone's head who has not been immersed in Android for years. And you would be wrong! Remember that Android is an emerging platform; Google is using this forum for sharing its vision with the world. Thus, the presentations here have *plenty* of introductory material for developers (although there's the really deep stuff too for dessert!). Visit these sites to find videos of talks and other material presented at the conferences:

- **Google I/O 2008:** http://sites.google.com/site/io
- **Google I/O 2009:** www.google.com/events/io/2009
- **Google I/O 2010:** www.google.com/events/io/2010; see Figure 14-2

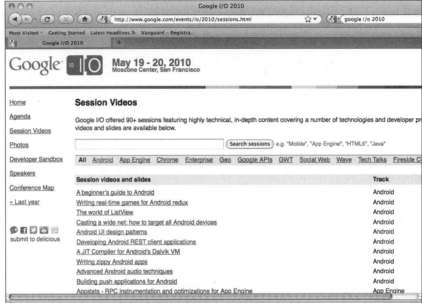

Figure 14-2:
Android informational resources at Google I/O 2010.

Taking Advantage of Android Resources On the Web

This section talks about where you can get tangible resources to speed your development of Android apps. You can get enhanced widgets, fonts, and skins to make your app look pretty, as well as sample code to accelerate your development.

Finding window dressing at Speckyboy.com

```
http://speckyboy.com/2010/05/10/android-app-developers-gui-kits-icons-fonts-and-
        tools
```

Speckyboy Design Magazine, shown in Figure 14-3, was launched in October 2007 and has now become a comprehensive design resource. Check out its collection of GUI kits, icons, fonts, and tools for Android.

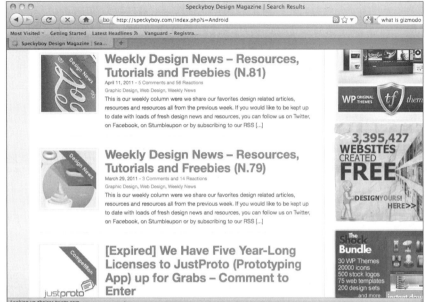

Figure 14-3:
Android
resources at
Speckyboy.

Finding sample code at the Google Code site directory

```
http://code.google.com/more
```

To paraphrase Hans and Franz from the infamous *Saturday Night Live* skit, hear us now, listen to us later, and believe us some other time: Before you try to write new code for any Google product, including Android, check out the offerings at the Google Code site directory, shown in Figure 14-4. For Android-specific code, simply enter *Android* in the Search field. In particular, look for Google Maps code and anything related to location services.

Figure 14-4:
Code repos-
itories at
the Google
Code site
directory.

Finding Android Development Help from Experts and Others Like You

There were so many times we wanted to see if the bugs we were seeing or the head-scratching issues we were encountering were legitimate issues, and if they were, had others run into them before us and found a way to solve them. Or if they were issues no one had seen before (which, as it turned out, is actually quite rare), was there a forum to post a question and have a like-minded crowd help us think our way through to an answer? We found two wonderful sites, which we describe in this section.

Android Developers Google Groups

```
http://groups.google.com/group/android-developers
```

As you might already know, Google has created a set of cloud services for collaboration and sharing documents, for example. (One well-known cloud service is Google Groups, at `http://groups.google.com`.) Google itself uses these services for its own collaborations, so be sure to check out the special Android Developers Google Groups page, shown in Figure 14-5. It's probably the most qualified resource for getting questions answered or problems solved because the responses to questions are (usually) from Google engineers, such as those working on Android.

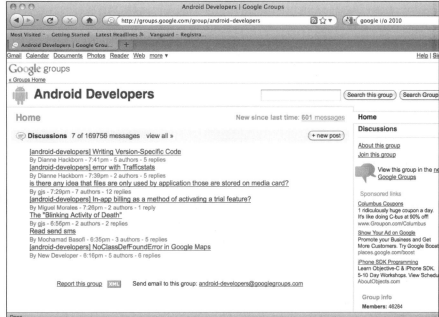

Figure 14-5: Navigating the Android Developers Google Groups page.

StackOverflow.com

`http://stackoverflow.com/tags`

The excellent Stack Overflow site lets you pose questions about programming — and find answers. The folks who run this site (apparently, about 75 percent are developers, and the rest are in sales and management) have tried to combine the best features of wikis, forums, blogs, and recommendation sites. The questions and their related answers are grouped and then tagged with keywords so that you can search for already posted Q&A combinations using specific tags and tag combinations. Figure 14-6 shows search results for the *Android* tag.

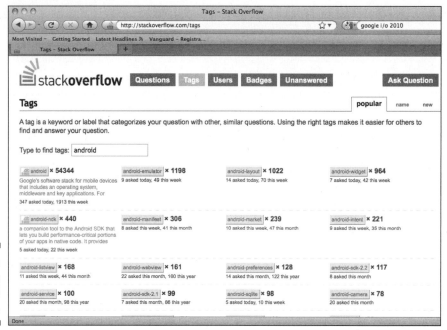

Figure 14-6:
Searching
for Android
answers.

The Android forums at Phandroid.com

http://androidforums.com/

AndroidForums.com, which by the way, redirects to http://phandroid.com/, advertises itself as "the FIRST independent website dedicated to delivering Android news." It does go back to 2007, so its claim might be mostly true. But regardless, we are not here to judge its pedigree but to proclaim its usefulness!

Pondering the Direction of Android Technology

Let's say that you're thinking of sticking with Android for a while, and you're wondering if this loyalty will be a wise decision. Or, you're a developer on another platform and are looking to see whether Android is a smart addition to your portfolio of expertise. The two sites in this section are good places to visit to stay ahead of the game.

Gizmodo.com

The Gizmodo blog, shown in Figure 14-7, generally blogs about technology, and specifically about consumer electronics. Rather than provide help to developers, this current — and somewhat controversial — site (you might recall the police search of the Gizmodo blogger who acquired an unreleased version of the iPhone 4) showcases hot new gadgets, including, of course, Android gadgets.

Figure 14-7:
Finding Android-related material at Gizmodo.

TalkAndroid.com

The TalkAndroid site serves as another resource database for Android. Although its focus appears to be on handsets, it also aggregates (and publishes articles containing) the latest news — and rumors. The site also features Android development resources related to the Open Handset Alliance and the Android platform.

Looking for Help When You Don't Know Where to Start

www.google.com

When we were frantically trying to figure out how to get an app to work with deadlines looming, and needed to find information quickly, we didn't waste our time with the other sites listed in this chapter — we visited the Google home page, shown in Figure 14-8. After typing a few keywords about our problem (you can even enter error messages or lines of code verbatim), we simply followed wherever the search results led us. (Thank you sincerely, Google Search page!)

Figure 14-8:
The classic Google Search page.

Chapter 15

The Ten Most Illustrative Applications for Android

In This Chapter

▶ Useful and engaging Android apps

▶ Applications that illustrate the various features of the Android SDK

*A*fter experimenting with approximately 300 apps in the Android Market, we have found what we think are the 10 outstanding Android apps to showcase in this chapter. We present these 10 apps in four popular categories: gaming and entertainment, productivity, health and wellness, and map-based. The idea is to give you a sense of how feature-rich and engaging an app must be in order to be successful in the Android Market. The apps we chose also nicely illustrate the use of the various Android capabilities we describe in earlier chapters, so we point out these uses in our descriptions.

Some apps in this chapter showcase the more complex capabilities of the Android SDK that we *don't* cover in this book. We point them out as well so that at least you know they exist and can find out more from the resources we list in Chapter 14.

The nice part about these apps is that you don't have to spend money for them — because they're all free.

Angry Birds (Rovio Mobile Ltd.)

Angry Birds is one of the most addictive games *ever,* and it's technically well done. In addition to its attractive, smooth, and silky graphics, it incorporates realistic physics and has a plethora of levels (440 of them) to keep you engaged.

Playing Angry Birds is simple (see Figure 15-1): In a nutshell, you catapult cute — and annoying — birds at the enemy pigs' fortresses, hoping to demolish them and, er, make irrelevant the pigs inside.

As you're playing the game, click the Menu button to see the pop-up Options menu, shown in Figure 15-2. It uses the Android SDK menu capabilities we discuss in Chapter 3. You can see that these menus have no text — only icons (albeit *cool* icons).

Figure 15-1:
Playing
Angry Birds.

Figure 15-2:
The Options
menu in
Angry Birds.

While you're at it, notice that you can click the Speaker icon on the Options menu to stop and start the background music. The app does this by making a call to a music service, in a manner similar in implementation to the service illustrated in the Tic-Tac-Toe application in Chapter 11.

Sudoku Free (Genina.com)

We freely admit that anything beyond the Easy level of Sudoku is beyond us, too! That said, Sudoku Free, shown in Figure 15-3, helps us while away the time while watching students struggle during our long, difficult, and boring exams.

Figure 15-3:
Playing
Sudoku.

We have found more than one Sudoku game on the market. Of these, we consider Sudoku Free the best. Understanding how to play the game is easy — winning a game is, of course, quite difficult.

This game provides good examples of multiple SDK capabilities:

✔ **The use of 2D graphics (refer to Figure 15-3)**

✔ **An animated and threaded splash screen on which you tap your way to a new game even while the animation is progressing**

   The animated image shown in Figure 15-3 also shows an example of live wallpaper — a topic we don't cover in this book but still a cool capability in the Android SDK.

✔ **The use of PreferenceActivity (see Figure 15-4)**

Figure 15-4:
Sudoku
prefer-
ences.

Change the orientation of the device to see the use of different layouts for different orientations.

Pandora (Pandora Internet Radio)

Move over, iTunes — here comes Pandora! Okay, we might be exaggerating, but even with a collection of a thousand or more songs in a library, all of us grow bored with our collection and want to listen to something new. Pandora, shown in Figure 15-5, is just the thing — an Internet radio-like application that streams music to an Android device, just like a radio station streams to a radio.

We want to point out a feature intended to make Pandora more usable. When you first open the app, notice that it presents a data usage warning, as shown in Figure 15-6. Pandora is looking out for users by sensibly pointing out that accessing numerous songs over the Internet, most likely via cellular networks, will cost some serious green. Note also that the app lets users choose not to see the warning so that it doesn't continually annoy them after they have been warned.

Figure 15-5:
Pandora
Internet
Radio for
Android.

Figure 15-6:
The
Pandora
data usage
warning.

Pandora uses threading, an Android SDK feature, within its splash screen activity, to implement the waiting period of the splash screen (like we do in the Tic-Tac-Toe app). Pandora then makes use of the Options menus (tap the Menu button on various Pandora screens to see these menus) and the

LinearLayout layout element, along with the ListView widget to list
users' radio stations. When you tap the name of a radio station, you see an
ImageView element that shows a picture of the band playing the current
song. Note that Pandora (most likely) uses an audio player service, similar
to the one used in our Tic-Tac-Toe example, because the music continues to
play even when you open another app on top of Pandora. However, unlike
the simple audio service in Tic-Tac-Toe, Pandora's service is streaming the
music over the network (using a web service; see Chapter 10).

Voice Recorder (Mamoru Tokashiki)

The simplicity of design in the Voice Recorder app has won it four stars and
more than 20,000 downloads. Someone using this app can record any type
of audio, such as a memo or a music performance. The audio is then saved
on the device, and the file is automatically titled by the date and time of the
recording (see Figure 15-7).

Figure 15-7:
The Voice
Recorder
Home
screen.

Users can, of course, replay files, send them via Gmail, or set them as ring-
tones. Other neat touches include being able to search by title and date and
schedule recordings to start at specific times and for specific durations (see
Figure 15-8).

Figure 15-8:
Additional
options
in Voice
Recorder.

A Voice Recorder walk-through shows these elements of the Android SDK in use:

- ✔ `PreferenceActivity`
- ✔ Options menu
- ✔ Intents (to launch other applications, such as Gmail)
- ✔ `ListView` layout (in its listing of the audio files that are created)
- ✔ A browser being launched and directed to the developer's website (`www.tokasiki.com`) when users make donations

Most of these topics are covered in Chapter 3, with additional details and examples in Chapter 11. Layouts are covered in Chapter 5, and launching a browser is covered in Chapter 10.

AppAlarm LITE (episode6)

The free version of AppAlarm LITE (as we were writing this book, AppAlarm Pro also became free) allows an Android device to be used as a reminder service, and even as a clock radio. You use AppAlarm to set alarms that are tied to other apps. You can see the alarm setup screen in Figure 15-9. When an alarm goes off, the app tied to the alarm is launched. When you hook up the app to Pandora, for example, you can have Pandora launch a specific radio station.

Figure 15-9: The alarm settings screen in AppAlarm LITE.

So how does AppAlarm fire off the apps the alarms are linked to? If you guessed "By using an intent" (see Chapter 3 and Chapter 11), you guessed correctly. In fact, the screen from which you select the app, shown in Figure 15-10, lets you define a custom intent. Go ahead — launch your e-mail from AppAlarm (see Chapter 11) — we don't care!

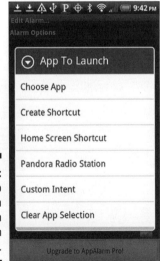

Figure 15-10: The App to Launch screen in AppAlarm LITE.

Evernote (Evernote Corporation)

In Evernote, shown in Figure 15-11, you create notes representing thoughts, plans, and reminders and then save them to the cloud. You can access these notes on your Android device, and also through the web.

Figure 15-11: The Evernote Welcome screen.

When you create an account, note that as you enter your username, you receive immediate feedback, via a web service (see Chapter 10), about whether the username already exists.

We imagine that the layout of the note creation screen, shown in Figure 15-12, was created using `GridView`.

Finally, try to create a Snapshot note. Note how the built-in camera app is launched using an intent and the `startActivityForResult(. . .)` method (see Chapter 11).

Figure 15-12:
The
Evernote
note
creation
screen.

Cardio Trainer (WorkSmart Labs, Inc.)

Yes, as the Cardio Trainer app description, shown in Figure 15-13, says, it *is* our app for walking, running, biking, and other activities.

Figure 15-13:
Cardio
Trainer has
lots of
features.

Cardio Trainer has a comprehensive set of features; you can create workouts, exercise by using your phone, and (as you become fitter by the day) track your progress!

From the Home screen, tap Settings to view the Settings menu, shown in Figure 15-14. We hope that you thought, "Aha! It's a `PreferenceActivity`!" (Refer to Chapter 3.)

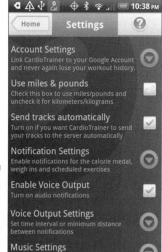

Figure 15-14: The Cardio Trainer Settings menu.

RunKeeper (FitnessKeeper Inc.)

The RunKeeper website says, "RunKeeper makes tracking your workouts fun, social, and easy to understand so that you can improve the quality of your fitness." We agree.

From an Android SDK point of view, RunKeeper is an outstanding location-based application. When you create an activity with the GPS input type, as shown in Figure 15-15, and tap the Start Activity button, the app tracks the total distance, as shown in Figure 15-16.

Figure 15-15:
Creating an
activity in
RunKeeper.

Figure 15-16:
Recording
activity
data in
RunKeeper.

Yelp (Yelp.com)

According to the Yelp.com website, "Yelp is the fun and easy way to find and talk about great (and not so great) local businesses." As you can see in Figure 15-17, the types of businesses are shown in GridView (see Chapter 5).

Figure 15-17:
The Yelp
Home
screen.

Based on the number of posted reviews, Yelp is most often (and best) used for finding restaurants and bars and similar locations. (If you're wondering whether *For Dummies* authors visit bars, the answer is "Heck, yeah!") Yelp is also helpful for finding *anything* local, ranging from auto repair to ATM machines.

After you select a category, such as Restaurants, Yelp shows you a sorted list using `ListView` (see Chapter 5). Though, by default, the list is sorted by Best Match, you can filter the sort order to sort by distance and rating, by distance and price, and whether the business is open at this moment. (By using these criteria, you can look for a nearby gas station or cheap restaurant that's open late, for example.)

Implicit in this functionality is that Yelp is using the user's location to identify locations close to him. We describe how to use location services in Chapter 10. Considering that Yelp is a location-based app, you can expect it to use `MapView` (described in Chapter 10), and it does, as shown in Figure 15-18.

Try turning off the network and then using the app. You will see an error message about the network. See Chapter 8 to find out how to test the network before accessing it so that the app does not appear to hang.

Figure 15-18: Using Map view in Yelp.

Places (Google Inc.)

A blurb on AndroidAndMe (a new Android-specific forum; also see `http://androidandme.com/2010/07/applications/google-maps-brings-places-to-android-with-4-4-update/`) says, "Google Maps brings Places to Android with 4.4 update." The Places Home screen is similar to Yelp (described in the preceding section), as you can see in Figure 15-19, though you can see some differences and subtle improvements on the Yelp interface, such as showing the filtering and sorting criteria on the list screen itself.

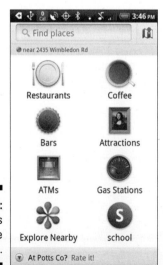

Figure 15-19: The Places Home screen.

The SDK capabilities that Places uses are also similar to the ones Yelp uses:

- ✔ `GridView`: Used on the Home screen (refer to Figure 15-19).

- ✔ `ListView`: Used on lists (see Chapter 5).

- ✔ `MapView`: Used when locations are shown on a map (see Chapter 10 for how to use `MapView`). Another small Places improvement over Yelp is in performance — see the speed with which the Map view is displayed. For hints on how to make your app perform well, see Chapter 8.

Of course, the various menus are shown using the Options menu capability of the Android SDK. You can see how to implement Options menus in Chapter 3.

The screen shown in Figure 15-20 illustrates how to ensure responsiveness and, consequently, usability in an app. When you tap a category name and the network is slow, you see the screen shown in the figure. This slight delay is by itself a good thing because it shows the user that the computer isn't frozen — just working away. You can see that the application is still responsive because the message is being displayed in a thread and the main application thread is still active. If you tap either the Back or Home button, Android navigates away from the application.

Figure 15-20:
Waiting for network response.

Index

• U •

• V •

Apple & Macs

iPad For Dummies
978-0-470-58027-1

iPhone For Dummies,
4th Edition
978-0-470-87870-5

MacBook For Dummies, 3rd
Edition
978-0-470-76918-8

Mac OS X Snow Leopard For
Dummies
978-0-470-43543-4

Business

Bookkeeping For Dummies
978-0-7645-9848-7

Job Interviews
For Dummies,
3rd Edition
978-0-470-17748-8

Resumes For Dummies,
5th Edition
978-0-470-08037-5

Starting an
Online Business
For Dummies,
6th Edition
978-0-470-60210-2

Stock Investing
For Dummies,
3rd Edition
978-0-470-40114-9

Successful
Time Management
For Dummies
978-0-470-29034-7

Computer Hardware

BlackBerry
For Dummies,
4th Edition
978-0-470-60700-8

Computers For Seniors
For Dummies,
2nd Edition
978-0-470-53483-0

PCs For Dummies,
Windows
7 Edition
978-0-470-46542-4

Laptops For Dummies,
4th Edition
978-0-470-57829-2

Cooking & Entertaining

Cooking Basics
For Dummies,
3rd Edition
978-0-7645-7206-7

Wine For Dummies,
4th Edition
978-0-470-04579-4

Diet & Nutrition

Dieting For Dummies,
2nd Edition
978-0-7645-4149-0

Nutrition For Dummies,
4th Edition
978-0-471-79868-2

Weight Training
For Dummies,
3rd Edition
978-0-471-76845-6

Digital Photography

Digital SLR Cameras &
Photography For Dummies,
3rd Edition
978-0-470-46606-3

Photoshop Elements 8
For Dummies
978-0-470-52967-6

Gardening

Gardening Basics
For Dummies
978-0-470-03749-2

Organic Gardening
For Dummies,
2nd Edition
978-0-470-43067-5

Green/Sustainable

Raising Chickens
For Dummies
978-0-470-46544-8

Green Cleaning
For Dummies
978-0-470-39106-8

Health

Diabetes For Dummies,
3rd Edition
978-0-470-27086-8

Food Allergies
For Dummies
978-0-470-09584-3

Living Gluten-Free
For Dummies,
2nd Edition
978-0-470-58589-4

Hobbies/General

Chess For Dummies,
2nd Edition
978-0-7645-8404-6

Drawing
Cartoons & Comics
For Dummies
978-0-470-42683-8

Knitting For Dummies,
2nd Edition
978-0-470-28747-7

Organizing
For Dummies
978-0-7645-5300-4

Su Doku For Dummies
978-0-470-01892-7

Home Improvement

Home Maintenance
For Dummies,
2nd Edition
978-0-470-43063-7

Home Theater
For Dummies,
3rd Edition
978-0-470-41189-6

Living the
Country Lifestyle
All-in-One
For Dummies
978-0-470-43061-3

Solar Power Your Home
For Dummies,
2nd Edition
978-0-470-59678-4

Internet

Blogging For Dummies,
3rd Edition
978-0-470-61996-4

eBay For Dummies,
6th Edition
978-0-470-49741-8

Facebook For Dummies,
3rd Edition
978-0-470-87804-0

Web Marketing
For Dummies,
2nd Edition
978-0-470-37181-7

WordPress
For Dummies,
3rd Edition
978-0-470-59274-8

Language & Foreign Language

French For Dummies
978-0-7645-5193-2

Italian Phrases
For Dummies
978-0-7645-7203-6

Spanish For Dummies,
2nd Edition
978-0-470-87855-2

Spanish
For Dummies,
Audio Set
978-0-470-09585-0

Math & Science

Algebra I
For Dummies,
2nd Edition
978-0-470-55964-2

Biology For Dummies,
2nd Edition
978-0-470-59875-7

Calculus For Dummies
978-0-7645-2498-1

Chemistry For Dummies
978-0-7645-5430-8

Microsoft Office

Excel 2010 For Dummies
978-0-470-48953-6

Office 2010 All-in-One
For Dummies
978-0-470-49748-7

Office 2010 For Dummies,
Book + DVD Bundle
978-0-470-62698-6

Word 2010 For Dummies
978-0-470-48772-3

Music

Guitar For Dummies,
2nd Edition
978-0-7645-9904-0

iPod & iTunes For
Dummies, 8th Edition
978-0-470-87871-2

Piano Exercises
For Dummies
978-0-470-38765-8

Parenting & Education

Parenting For Dummies,
2nd Edition
978-0-7645-5418-6

Type 1 Diabetes
For Dummies
978-0-470-17811-9

Pets

Cats For Dummies,
2nd Edition
978-0-7645-5275-5

Dog Training For Dummies,
3rd Edition
978-0-470-60029-0

Puppies For Dummies,
2nd Edition
978-0-470-03717-1

Religion & Inspiration

The Bible For Dummies
978-0-7645-5296-0

Catholicism For Dummies
978-0-7645-5391-2

Women in the Bible
For Dummies
978-0-7645-8475-6

Self-Help & Relationship

Anger Management
For Dummies
978-0-470-03715-7

Overcoming Anxiety
For Dummies,
2nd Edition
978-0-470-57441-6

Sports

Baseball
For Dummies,
3rd Edition
978-0-7645-7537-2

Basketball
For Dummies,
2nd Edition
978-0-7645-5248-9

Golf For Dummies,
3rd Edition
978-0-471-76871-5

Web Development

Web Design
All-in-One
For Dummies
978-0-470-41796-6

Web Sites
Do-It-Yourself
For Dummies,
2nd Edition
978-0-470-56520-9

Windows 7

Windows 7
For Dummies
978-0-470-49743-2

Windows 7
For Dummies,
Book + DVD Bundle
978-0-470-52398-8

Windows 7 All-in-One
For Dummies
978-0-470-48763-1

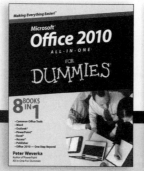

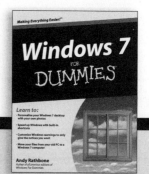